TROJAN HORSE

TROJAN HORSE

HOW THE LEFT IS DESTROYING AMERICA

BRAD ROBERTS

LIBERTY HILL PUBLISHING

Liberty Hill Publishing
2301 Lucien Way #415
Maitland, FL 32751
407.339.4217
www.libertyhillpublishing.com

© 2023 by Brad Roberts

[First Draft, October 2022]

All rights reserved solely by the author. The author guarantees all contents are original and do not infringe upon the legal rights of any other person or work. No part of this book may be reproduced in any form without the permission of the author.

Due to the changing nature of the Internet, if there are any web addresses, links, or URLs included in this manuscript, these may have been altered and may no longer be accessible. The views and opinions shared in this book belong solely to the author and do not necessarily reflect those of the publisher. The publisher therefore disclaims responsibility for the views or opinions expressed within the work.

Unless otherwise indicated, Scripture quotations taken from the Holy Bible, New International Version (NIV). Copyright © 1973, 1978, 1984, 2011 by Biblica, Inc.™. Used by permission. All rights reserved.

Scripture quotations are taken from the (NASB®) New American Standard Bible®, Copyright © 1960, 1062, 1063, 1968, 1971, 1972, 1973, 1975, 1977, 1995, 2020 by The Lockman Foundation. Used by permission. All rights reserved. www.lockman.org.

Paperback ISBN-13: 978-1-6628-6748-4
Ebook ISBN-13: 978-1-6628-6749-1

DEDICATED TO MY FATHER,
A TRUE AMERICAN PATRIOT

TABLE OF CONTENTS

Introduction ix

One.	Antifa.	1
Two.	Antifa's Friends in High Places	17
Three.	The Mainstream Media	25
Four.	The Spectre of Racism	49
Five.	America's Fight against Slavery	63
Six.	The Anti-Police Movement	89
Seven.	Debunking Police Racism	119
Eight.	Indoctrination	127
Nine.	Critical Race Theory: The Monster in Our Schools . . .	145
Ten.	Discrimination and Disparities	157
Eleven.	Abortion	177
Epilogue.	Time to Take a Stand against the Trojan Horse	193

Acknowledgments 197

Notes 199

Index 221

INTRODUCTION

I am convinced that there are leftists among us who are working to destroy the founding principles of the United States of America, the greatest country the world has ever known. When I look around at what's happening in our country today, I can't help but recall a story from Greek literature.

The story of the Trojan War is filled with legends, gods, goddesses, love, deception, and death. This is the tale of a wedding between a sea nymph, Thetis, and a hero of Thessaly, Peleus. This was an ostentatious celebration, given that all the great gods and goddesses—with the exception of Eris, the goddess of discord—were invited. Eris wasn't invited, but she decided to crash the party.

And she didn't show up empty-handed. She carried an apple with the inscription, *For the Fairest One*. Three goddesses came forward to claim this apple—Athena, Aphrodite, and Hera—but they knew it could only be given to one. While many wondered which of the beauties would receive the gift, and the title, the three goddesses asked Zeus to judge which one of them was truly the fairest of them all.

To their dismay, Zeus passed the job to Paris, someone he trusted to judge with fairness and honesty. Paris was a Trojan mortal, and each goddess tried to bribe and persuade him to select her. Athena, who was best known for her wisdom, offered skills that would enable Paris to defeat his enemies. Hera bribed him with the offer to make him king of the surrounding lands. Aphrodite, the goddess of love, offered Paris the most beautiful woman in the world, Helen of Sparta.

Paris had a difficult time judging between the three beautiful goddesses. After a long consideration, he chose Aphrodite, and was given Helen of Sparta in exchange for the inscribed apple. There was only one catch: Helen of Sparta was already married to the Spartan king Menelaus.

King Menelaus discussed the situation with his brother, Agamemnon, who was the overseer of all the Greeks. Agamemnon gathered all the Greek cities and kings to exact revenge for his brother. Arriving in Troy, the Greeks surrounded the city for ten years, laying siege after siege, day in and day out. Piles of men, fallen in battle, lay deceased against the outermost walls of the city. In the most famous strategic move of the Trojan war, the Greeks retreated, leaving only a giant wooden horse behind. The horse was so massive that the Trojans had to break down their own walls to get it into the city. They didn't know that the horse contained Greek soldiers, who were awaiting the opportune time to invade the city from within its walls. When the Trojans let down their guard to celebrate their victory, the Greeks stormed out of the wooden horse and set about destroying the city of Troy.

This tale has been told for thousands of years. But it is still as relevant as today's headlines, because it mirrors the perils of the struggles we are experiencing in America today. America is still a young nation with its own dark past—a past that was once filled with war, tragedy, and deception; but that past made way for a society based on the ideals of life, liberty, and the pursuit of happiness.

I believe that a modern-day Trojan horse has tragically entered our lives today. It poses a danger to our country, just as the ancient wooden horse threatened the lives of the oblivious people of Troy. The Trojan Horse within our walls today is not built of wood or metal but of leftist ideas and movements. The ones who hide inside will destroy this nation unless we stop celebrating and fight back. These are men and women who

INTRODUCTION

do not embrace free speech or capitalism, but who seek to destroy our country from the inside.

The primary difference between America today and the ancient Greeks is that we are not yet fighting with swords or spears but with words. In a nation of free speech, ideas and arguments from different viewpoints must be heard so that people have a chance to judge whose opinion and viewpoint is right and whose is wrong. The America we all love can only win when, as a country, we judge between what is good and what is evil. Unless we choose what is good, our values, our national identity, and the life we enjoy could be destroyed. We must question the validity of the arguments and opinions we hear, and decide whether they are trustworthy, logical, and have merit. If the Trojans had inspected the horse to see if it was trustworthy—and if it made sense to bring it into their city—then they may have saved themselves from the danger that lay within it. Their unquestioning embrace of its novelty put the great city at risk. We must learn from the error of the Trojans, and we must allow free speech to thrive so we can hear arguments, inspect them, analyze them, and decide if they have merit.

Unfortunately, today's Trojan horse has already been brought within the walls of America. Leftists are already working to destroy the principles that have built the United States, and our own complacency has let them in.

THE STAKES ARE HIGH

Troy was destroyed after a long-fought battle over a woman. The Trojans ignored logic and reason, and they did not question why the Greeks would present them with a giant wooden horse even as they seemed to withdraw from the city. In twenty-first-century America, the battle is being fought between "conservatives" and "progressives." The conservatives fight for Lady Liberty, while the progressives among us seek to destroy her. It is my hope that the ideas and discussions presented in the chapters ahead will equip conservative readers, not with physical weapons, but with weapons of knowledge, discernment, and understanding so we can defeat the Left on the basis of morals, facts, and history.

We will start by looking at some of the forces that are seeking to destroy our country from within.

One
ANTIFA

Antifa, which stands for "anti-fascist," is one of the many groups/movements that has infiltrated society from the left. On the surface one might find it counterintuitive to oppose anyone who stands against fascism. Who in their right mind would agree with fascism? Fascism, by all accounts, has been responsible for the deaths of millions of people. Surely, any rational person would despise this ideology. The problem with Antifa as a group and as an ideological movement is that those who participate in Antifa have proved themselves to be, ironically, fascists in disguise.

As a Christian, I am reminded of the letters Paul wrote to the church in Corinth. In the eleventh chapter of his second epistle to the Corinthians, Paul warns his readers to beware of those who preach a false gospel but use elegant words so it sounds believable. In contrast to this, Paul says, in essence, "I may not be a trained speaker, but I do have knowledge" (2 Cor. 11:6 author's paraphrase).

The immense value of knowledge is that it allows one to decide who is telling the truth and who is lying. Paul goes on to write in the same chapter:

> For such men are false apostles, deceitful workers, disguising themselves as apostles of Christ. No wonder, for even Satan disguises himself as an angel of light. Therefore, it is not surprising if his servants also disguise themselves as servants of

righteousness, whose end will be according to their deeds. (2 Corinthians 11:13–15)

These are powerful words. There may always be people speaking and teaching "false truths"—ideas that sound good and are easy to accept but in reality, are harmful or altogether incorrect.

One of the most important lessons passed down through centuries of Christianity is the necessity of discerning fact from fiction or truth from lies. Just as people during the time of Christ masqueraded as teachers of righteousness and justice, there are activists today who wear the title of "anti-fascist" only on the surface.

Surely, there are individuals in Antifa who genuinely believe they are going against fascism; in the same way that the misguided false teachers of Paul's time genuinely believed they were spreading the truth. In this instance, those within Antifa fall short because they lack understanding of what fascism truly is. By equipping ourselves with an understanding of the history of fascism, we can ensure that this group and its false ideology does not destroy our country.

When we look at Antifa's professed values, and their actions as a movement, we can see that they have no intention of making this country a better place. Antifa adherents describe themselves as being against the free market, capitalism, and our system of government. They express their contempt for everything this country stands for and for the values it was built on. It is not uncommon for Antifa members to write and chant "Death to Capitalism" and "Capitalism Is the Pandemic." They also intermingle with communists, socialists, and anarchists. Although they differ in ideologies, these groups have a common agenda, which is to destroy capitalism, the police system, and America itself.

I believe, as President Trump does, that because of their beliefs and actions, Antifa should be considered a domestic terror group.

THE HISTORY OF FASCISM

The first iteration of fascism came about in the early 1900s. The original fascists were the followers of the *Fasci Rivoluzionari d'Azione Internazionalista*. The word *fascism* comes from the Italian word *fascio*, meaning bundle. While the original word referred to a bundle of sticks, it was also used to refer to a bundle of people, commonly a political group or organization. In Ancient Rome, *fasces* or *fascio littorio* was a bundle of wood with a projecting axe blade, which became a symbol of the authority to judge, held by a civic magistrate. *Fasces* would later be extrapolated by Benito Mussolini into the creation of fascism, suggesting strength through unity.

Benito Mussolini was born on July 29, 1883. in Verano di Costa, Italy. His father, Alessandro Mussolini, was a blacksmith and a proclaimed socialist. He wrote articles for the local socialist newspapers. When he was not writing, he could be found on the streets taking part in political activism. He believed the government should control the mode of production and the working class should run society. Alessandro was well known for his ill-temper. He made several violent threats toward his opponents and caused destruction to their property. His behavior resulted in frequent encounters with police and time spent in jail. When he wasn't locked up in a cell, you could probably find him in a tavern, drinking to excess and loudly proclaiming his socialist agenda.

Benito's mother, Rosa Maltoni, was a Catholic teacher. Rosa's father was by no means a fan of the man to whom Rosa had become engaged. In fact, he did not want her to marry Alessandro, but the couple ignored his wishes. Some might find it curious that Benito was born into a Catholic household but grew up to become such an evil man. Clearly, Benito followed in his father's footsteps rather than his mother's.

From a youthful age, Benito Mussolini was extremely disobedient and aggressive. At school, he was known as the bully on campus. He would make fun of other students, harass them verbally and attack them physically.

Today we can see Mussolini's ideological descendants, Antifa, conducting this same type of behavior on campuses across the United States.

Mussolini was removed from a boarding school at the age of ten for stabbing another student. One could make the case that this incident, although horrific, was an outlier. He was young, he was dumb, and he was just a kid who had made a bad decision. But the problem continued as he grew older, and he came to be known for his violent fights. This sort of behavior continued into his early adulthood, when Mussolini traveled to Switzerland, joined the country's Socialist Party, and frequently clashed with the police. Altogether, Benito was arrested eleven times.

Later, Mussolini became the editor of a socialist paper called *L'avenire del lavoratore*. Through his writings, he professed his disgust for democracy and even degraded the Catholic Church. If this sounds similar to the preaching of today's left-leaning political groups, then my point is becoming clear. Numerous times, Mussolini called for widespread violence. He seemed to love nothing better than a good fight. He was also known as a great organizer who could get workers to strike on behalf of the socialist movement. His voice and leadership were so powerful at the time that he was even able to organize strikes in other countries.

You may be wondering: How did a man who was indoctrinated by his father at such a young age move from socialism to fascism? Let's take a look.

THE SEPARATION FROM SOCIALISM

By 1912, Mussolini was a major player in the Socialist Party. His political leadership landed him the editor's role for *Avanti!* the daily newspaper that was the voice of the Italian Socialist Party. This was a massive step up for Mussolini and his influence in Italian politics. Only two years earlier, in 1910, he had tried to divide the revolutionary wing of the Socialist Party by creating his own. Although unsuccessful at the time, after taking up his new role in 1912, he submitted a motion to the party congress and was granted new national party leadership.

With the help of *Avanti!* the Socialist Party grew exponentially. Mussolini became the face of socialism across the country until the First World War began. Italy chose to remain neutral in the war, a stance that Mussolini initially accepted. When he wrote that Italy should take an actively neutral stance during the war, many within the Socialist Party objected, and Mussolini was eventually removed from the party. It turned out that, with the world aflame with war, it was not time to play, "I want to be friends with everyone," and nationalism became favored over socialism.

After his removal from the Socialist Party, Mussolini's fortunes continued to decline. He was dismissed from his editor-in-chief position at *Avanti!* and began his own publication called *Il Popolo d'Italia*, which means, "The Italian People." In his writing, Mussolini sided with the Allies' position that Italy should intervene in the war. This was a major contrast to his professed neutral ideology, and there is no clear historical answer as to why he made this sudden dramatic switch. One theory at the time, put forth by the Socialist Party of Italy, was that Mussolini was selling out to fascism for monetary gain. This theory gained traction, since many observers wondered how Mussolini was able to finance his own paper with little income. Mussolini's detractors were surely dismayed when the *Il Popolo d'Italia* became an instant success.

This is an important part of the history of fascism. Mussolini did not have much money, and he did not have much power, but he did have a voice. He had an emerging ideology that he needed to express—one that he wanted others to join. It was not so much that Mussolini left socialism, but that socialism left Mussolini. Recall that socialism was the ideology that he had been taught to follow since his birth. He did not give up easily on that set of values and ideas. Mussolini required a rebirth of the ideology, and the result was the creation of fascism. Fascism was a new type of socialism that would eventually gain a massive following. With fascism in hand, and the power of his voice, Mussolini was able to gather the masses to his side.

Class and nationality were topics of great import to Mussolini's fascism. Mussolini saw that Italians had begun to identify less with socio-economic classes and held more affinity to their association with the nation where they lived. This phenomenon was happening during a time of war, when most Italians were living in poor conditions. There was not much difference between blue-collar workers and white-collar workers. Everyone was poor. Since most Italians seemed to be in the same situation, their ethnic identity was a stronger association than the identities associated with fading social classes. Over time, Mussolini came to agree with the nationalists, which in turn established the association of ethnicity over class as a tenet of fascism.

Having a strong hand in the resolution of this social-ideological struggle, Mussolini established the concept of National Socialism. You may have heard this term because it became synonymous with Adolf Hitler and Nazi Germany. Rather than the social classes determining the country's production processes, Mussolini and his friends decided the nation together, as a whole, would be the producers. Who decides what the producers produce? The state. To make this work, a centralized state must be initiated to control the means of production. Without a strong, centralized government, state control of the mechanisms of production would not work. It's easy to see how National Socialism was an attractive idea to those who yearn for power.

With a centralized state, the economy and various aspects of society can all be controlled by the government. Fascism then is a movement that puts the nation above the individual, is managed and directed by a centralized government, and is led by a dictator. That dictator is the one who decides what shall be produced, how money should be redistributed, how much food a family should receive, how much an individual is worth, and ultimately, how much a life is worth. If you do not kneel to the state, then you are against the state. If you go against the fascist state, then the state will kill you and your family, and I am not exaggerating.

With this simplified version of the history of fascism in mind, how can we define members of Antifa as true fascists? Is Antifa just an ideology, as claimed by Joe Biden and Joy Behar, or is Antifa a violent group of extremists? You must ask yourself: Which modern political side in America prefers that the federal government control things? Is it the conservatives, or the progressives and leftists? Do we see conservatives violently attacking people in the streets? Are conservatives burning down retail stores and community buildings in our cities? Do conservatives call for centralized government? No. It is Antifa and the leftists who fit these descriptions and who want fascism to win here in America. As their ideological ancestors did before them, they violently push their agenda and seek to attack those who oppose it.

FOLLOWERS OF FASCISM

As mentioned previously, in fascism it is the state that matters, not the individual. Thus, because one does not identify as an individual, they must identify as the state. If they do not identify as the state, then they are going against the state. This ideology, saying that there is no self, only the tribe, and the modern tribe is the state is primitive and tribalistic. What happens when someone does not agree with the state? Professor Robert Paxton states that fascism focuses on "internal cleansing and external expansion."[1] This internal cleansing uses violence to push out anyone who disagrees with the state.

How could the people of a country tolerate this kind of behavior? The fascists were not random people committing random acts of violence. These were people with a well-calculated agenda who manipulated the people into believing that others deserved the violence that was inflicted upon them. How did they do this? They pushed the idea that they were going to rid the state of any anti-national terrorists. If implying that someone was an anti-nationalist wasn't enough to justify punishment, attaching the crime of terrorism to their name made it a done deal.

By painting their opposers' attitude as evil, fascists were able to gain the trust of the people, to the point where they generally accepted a violent national cleansing. This was a crafty ploy to push an agenda on a people who loved their country and hated terrorists, and it worked. The Italian general public came to feel that the fascists would only attack those who deserved it; surely, no one who was truly innocent would be hurt. If the state said someone was guilty, he or she was guilty. It really was that simple.

In Italy, a group that would attack anyone who opposed them was Mussolini's Black Brigade, also known as the Blackshirts. This brigade was made up of veterans who wore black turtlenecks or black collared shirts and wore a badge that featured a Death's Head with a dagger in its teeth. The uniform and badge were meant to intimidate and evoke fear in all who opposed them. In the beginning, the armed group focused primarily on attacking socialist organizations. Before they were officially labeled as the Blackshirts, they were a fringe group of fascists. Their objective was to intimidate or get rid of socialist power and anyone who opposed Italy's involvement in the Great War. These men would commit brutal acts of violence in small towns, villages, and even in their own communities.[2]

To break the socialists' holds on labor and political organizations, the Blackshirts beat elected officials, broke up meetings, and destroyed newspaper offices. They were not opposed to murder and would sometimes surround a man's house with his family inside. If he refused to come out and surrender to them, they would storm the house and physically remove the family. The family would then be forced to watch in horror as their house was lit on fire and all their possessions burned. Other times, the Blackshirts would force those who opposed them to drink motor oil, and would then throw feces all over them, before sending them home to their families. As if that weren't degrading enough, they would make people defecate on manifestos, speeches, flags, and religious objects. Lastly, the Blackshirts would physically attack their opponents, stripping them naked and severely beating them.

Over time, the Blackshirts and fascists became the dominant political force in Italy. Moderate newspapers went so far as to praise the Blackshirts for their "patriotism" and their respect for law and order. In *Violence in Italian Fascism*, Jens Petersen writes that governments failed to appreciate the scope of the violence and believed that attacks against citizens were "limited and isolated."[3] This does not come as a surprise, since the newspapers frequently would either downplay the violence or not report on it at all.

By the end of 1922, fascists controlled almost every public administration. In the same year, Mussolini was appointed Prime Minister of Italy. At that time, many people saw Mussolini as a voice for the people. They thought he would end the violence and disorder that plagued the country. Instead, Mussolini appointed himself Minister of the Interior, which allowed him to take control of the Italian police. Under Mussolini, the violence was prolonged as the police were made to stand down while the violent suppression of the opposition by the Blackshirts continued.

By this point, I hope and expect that the connection between Antifa and fascism is becoming clear.

THE FASCIST CONNECTION

Roughly a century later, fascist groups are still prevalent throughout society. Today, there are outspoken fascists, though they are quickly condemned for their ideology and actions. There are also fascists who believe they are anti-fascists but follow both the actions and ideology of the Italian Blackshirts, whose history we just reviewed. It takes a special level of ignorance to believe you are going against an ideology while you are, in fact, advancing it. I am, of course, talking about the organization and ideology of Antifa.

Recalling the apostle Paul's warnings against people who preach false doctrines and act like they speak the truth, we should discern that Antifa's adherents masquerade as anti-fascists when, in fact, they are fascists. Just as the Blackshirts wore black and committed violence for the sake of advancing their agenda, Antifa's members are known to don black clothing, masks, weapons, and riot gear while they wreak havoc across the nation. The purpose of their attire is to intimidate and conceal their identity from criminal prosecutors. In *Why Antifa Dresses Like Antifa*, Rick Paulas states,

> These defensive methods work only if there are enough black-clad others nearby. A single person in all black and multiple face masks is an eye grabber. This effect of anonymity-by-mass has allowed for the offensive side of bloc tactics to flourish. The uniformity camouflages those who participate in illegal acts like property damage, refusing police orders or physical assault against white supremacists or Nazis. This willful protection of the group is embedded in the style's aesthetic.[4]

This fascist group wears black to conceal their identities as they engage in illegal behavior.

The writer craftly utilizes the term "bloc tactic" rather than "fascist tactics." This same tactic was used in the 1980s by several European anti-government movements and in the late 1990s for the World Trade Organization protests. This tactic is used to destroy property and commit violence as a means to express their rage. While it is interesting that a fascist organization calls itself anti-fascist and uses Blackshirt tactics but calls its actions bloc tactics is just another example of if you put lipstick on a pig, it's still a pig.

Cowardice is revealed when someone hides behind a mask while speaking out about something they supposedly strongly believe in. Those with truth stand up for what they believe in and do not hide behind a mask. The author of the biblical book of Hebrews writes,

> [A]nd others experienced mocking and scourging, yes, and also chains and imprisonment. They were stoned, they were sawn in two, they were tempted, they were put to death with the sword; they went about in sheepskins, in goatskins, being destitute, afflicted, tormented, (*men* of whom the world was not worthy), wandering in deserts and mountains and caves and holes in the ground. (Hebrews 11:36–38)

These are examples of people who were willing to die and be publicly shamed for what they believed in. Antifa covers their faces and wears black so they can commit evil acts of violence in anonymity, without having to own up to their actions or suffer any consequences. Daryle Lamont Jenkins, founder of the Antifa-related "One People's Project," told Erica Euse, writer for VICE,

> If anything, I wear something practical, like boots and jeans, things that can stand a little wear and tear. I try to be prepared in case there is some sort of throwdown. I don't want to wear the "Sunday's best," so to speak. This often means wearing things like a bandana or face mask in case there is tear gas or tight-fitting clothing so that they can't be grabbed.[5]

Doesn't this Antifa leader just sound like someone who is ready to follow the First Amendment and protest peacefully? Of course, I am being facetious. These Antifa members show up in unsuspecting communities ready to commit violence and property damage.

Antifa claims they exist to fight neo-Nazism, neo-fascism, white supremacy, and racism. Antifa also claims they fight against capitalism, the free market, the police, the government, and the United States.

In early 2017, conservative writer and speaker, Milo Yiannopoulus was scheduled to speak at the University of California, Berkeley. A group of Antifa members showed up to the event wearing black clothing and masks and carrying shields and weapons. Antifa members threw rocks through the windows of campus buildings, lit fireworks, and ignited a fire outside the building. Remember, though, according to Antifa, all that violence was justified because they were rightfully outraged.

Later in 2017 Antifa clashed with white supremacists in Charlottesville, Virginia. It must be noted that racism is evil and we all should do what we can to combat racism, but we can fight racism with our words and not with fists and weapons. Yet, according to Sheryl Gay Stolberg who covered the Charlottesville event for the *New York Times*, "The hard left seemed as hate-filled as the alt-right. I saw club-wielding 'Antifa' beating white nationalists being led out of the park."[6]

Just weeks later, a "Rally Against Hate" event happened in Berkeley, California. This rally was peaceful, even though right-wing demonstrators showed up to counter-protest. Whether an observer agrees with one side or the other, we should acknowledge that both sides have a right to protest peaceably. The irony is that Antifa showed up at an anti-hate rally intending to commit violence fueled by hate. They attacked and beat protesters who were Trump supporters, not because they were Nazis or fascists nor because they were neo-nationalists or white supremacists; they beat them because their views were simply different from Antifa's views.

Let me ask again: Who decides if you are an anti-nationalist terrorist? Within fascism, the fascists and the state decide. Because Antifa labels you as a racist, in their view you deserve to be violently beaten. It doesn't matter if they don't have any evidence to prove you are a racist; just the fact that they say you are a racist is enough to convict you. This is the exact same strategy the Blackshirts used on the Italian people. Antifa is blind to the fact that the vast majority of Trump supporters are patriots, just as Donald Trump is. In *Death of a Nation*, Dinesh D'Souza writes:

> Trump's nationalism is nothing more than traditional American patriotism, surrounded by the familiar symbols of the flag, the anthem, and soldiers' graves. It should be emphasized that nationalism is not a distinguishing feature of fascism or Nazism. Moreover, Mussolini and Hitler were not nationalists in the traditional or Trumpian sense. Mussolini once reviled the Italian flag as a 'rag" to be "planted on a dunghill." Traditional patriotism, Mussolini wrote, was a scheme for the capital class—the bourgeoisie—to win the loyalty of the people and protect its class privileges. Mussolini resolved to "remake" Italy much as Obama in 2008 resolved to remake America. Mussolini's allegiance was never to the nation in general but only to a fascist concept of the nation.[7]

The Blackshirts attacked the socialists in the early 1900s but eventually moved beyond their original target and began attacking anyone who disagreed with them. Antifa is doing the same thing today by first going after actual racists, and then spreading their anger to include anyone who disagrees with them. In August of 2018, Charlie Kirk and Candace Owens were eating at a Philadelphia restaurant when members of an Antifa group started harassing and throwing things at them. Their attackers were shouting, "Fuck white supremacy!" "No good cops in a racist system!" And "Cops and Klan hand-in-hand!"

What had Kirk and Owens done to deserve this? Nothing at all. They were definitely not racists. Kirk says, in fact, that he has been against racism for his entire life.

In fact, Owens, who serves as his communications director, is black. She said she thought that it was "bizarre that there are a bunch of white people saying, 'no racists,' or 'no good cops,' when every single cop here is black." Remember, this kind of violence can happen because *you* don't get to decide if you are racist; Antifa gets to decide that.

The attack on Kirk and Owens came mere weeks after California Democratic representative, Maxine Waters, encouraged supporters to harass Trump administration officials. Outside the Wilshire Federal Building, Waters said, "Let's make sure we show up wherever we have to show up. And if you see anybody from that Cabinet in a restaurant, in a department store, at a gasoline station, you get out and you create a crowd. And you push back on them. And you tell them they're not welcome anymore, anywhere."[8]

Her remarks were regarding immigrant children being held in cages.

It is important to note that, even though Obama administration officials built the cages, Representative Waters did not ask people to go after Obama administration officials when they were keeping immigrant children in cages.

More recently, in 2020, a group of Antifa members from Portland, Oregon, crossed the border into Washington to attack patrons at a local restaurant. Bob Price of Breitbart quoted Andy Ngô as saying that Antifa "attacked bar patrons on the way and confronted people at their homes."[9]

Doesn't this sound a lot like what the fascist Blackshirts did? Breitbart also reported that Antifa "brutally jumped this man earlier in Vancouver, Washington. He was on the ground and a group of people kicked him repeatedly."[10] By randomly attacking people and businesses, Antifa continually mimics the actions of Mussolini's Blackshirts.

Unfortunately, Antifa's violence didn't stop there. A member of Antifa also threatened the mayor of Portland, one of the most left-leaning cities in the United States. The Antifa representative sent a video message to the mayor, "Ted, we are asking for the last time that you resign. If you ignore this message outright, the destruction to your precious way of life is going to escalate. Blood is already on your hands, Ted. The next time, it may just be your own."[11]

The lack of self-reflection from Antifa members is truly astonishing. They went of their way to target a Democrat mayor who, for the longest time, supported the shenanigans of Black Lives Matter and Antifa. Remember, Antifa's adherents are the same people who destroy public and private property, set buildings and cars on fire, attack reporters and police officers, create autonomous zones, and promulgate destructive ideas. But they claim they are the anti-fascists, the anti-racists, the saviors of America, and they are the people who are fighting back for the greater good. Don't you believe it! The ideology of this group and movement is a cancer to the republic that will destroy us if left unchecked.

Two
ANTIFA'S FRIENDS IN HIGH PLACES

It would be easy to fill an entire book with stories of Antifa brutally beating Republicans, beating conservatives, beating business owners, lighting businesses on fire, and harassing people at their homes and elsewhere. Rather than doing this, I am including just a few examples to show that those who claim to be anti-fascist are promulgating fascist behavior, strategy, and ideology. Not only is Antifa promulgating this, but so are politicians like Democratic Congresswoman Maxine Waters, President-Elect Joe Biden, Michigan Democratic State Representative Cynthia Jones, Minnesota Attorney General Keith Ellison, and many others. We have already talked about Representative Waters telling her supporters to confront Trump administration officials in public. Her encouragement even led groups to harass Trump supporters outside of their homes.

In 2018, Antifa gathered outside of Fox News analyst Tucker Carlson's home. Carlson's wife, Susan Andrews, was home by herself when the group broke his oak door. One member of the Antifa group mentioned a pipe bomb, a comment that was picked up on Carlson's security footage. No pipe bomb was found, but you can imagine how frightened Mrs. Carlson must have been.

During a 2020 Election debate between Donald Trump and Joe Biden, Biden was asked if he would condemn Antifa. Biden replied that Trump's own FBI Director, Chris Wray, had stated that Antifa is not a group or an organization but a movement or an ideology. The media reported this as if Joe Biden were going against Antifa. But in fact, he was denying that the group even exists. As we can see, Antifa has caused a great deal of suffering and trouble for a group that doesn't even exist.

Michigan State Representative Cynthia Jones even threatened Trump supporters over a Facebook live video in early December 2020. Jones said, "so this is just a warning to you Trumpers, be careful, walk lightly, we ain't playing with you, enough of the shenanigans, enough is enough, and for those of you who are soldiers; you know how to do it, do it right, be in order, make them pay, I love you all."[1] If any conservative had said something like this, it would be front-page news, with the Democrats demanding public censure and condemnation. But nobody on the left reprimanded Representative Jones for her comments or called for her to apologize.

Ellison, who, as I said serves as the Attorney General of Minnesota, has shown his support for Antifa by posting a picture on his Twitter account of him holding up *Antifa, The Anti-Fascist Handbook*, written by Mark Bray. This book has been said to condone violence against those Antifa disagrees with. Ellison went on to post that the book should "strike fear into the heart" of Trump.[2]

Seattle Mayor Jenny Durkan has also supported the efforts of Antifa. Durkan went so far as to allow protesters, some of whom were Antifa members, to camp out around the Seattle Police Department's East Precinct. The protestors took over a portion of the area calling it the "Capitol Hill Autonomous Zone," or CHAZ, and made a list of demands which included: abolishing the city's police department, banning the use of armed force, removing officers from schools, eradicating juvenile jails and prisons, and distributing reparations to victims of police brutality.

These are just a few of the nonsensical demands made by people who are of the radical Left and supported by a radical mayor. This autonomous zone consisted of eight city blocks which law enforcement was not allowed to enter. Certain news outlets made it seem as if this behavior was acceptable. In her article for Vox titled, "Seattle's Newly Police-Free

Neighborhood, Explained," Katelyn Burns wrote about how peaceful everything was where "protesters set about creating peaceful and safe police-free neighborhood. And the officers largely haven't bothered to come back."[3]

The article shows images of people writing words in chalk on the pavement. Others decided to spray-paint city property—property that was paid for by taxpayers like you and me, and will now have to be repaired using taxpayer dollars. Burns goes on to describe how the protestors invited the homeless into the zone. They had movie nights, dodgeball games, and small groups of people sat in circles to smoke weed together. Burns wrote,

> CHAZ has since evolved further into a center of peaceful protest, free political speech, co-ops, and community gardens. Protesters have invited the city's houseless population, who had been subject to a mass 'clearing' of tent communities throughout the city, to come stay in the neighborhood. Movie nights have been held, including *Mississippi Burning*, about two FBI agents investigating lynching's of black people and activists in Mississippi during the civil rights era.

Burns does an excellent job of describing a kumbaya moment, but she leaves out the violence as if it were never there.

Antifa was smart to allow reporters to come into the zone during the daytime, because when nightfall came and the reporters left, the peaceful atmosphere gave way to violence, including fighting, rape, and shootings.

Just a few weeks later, Katelyn Burns authored another article for Vox titled, "The Violent End of the Capitol Hill Organized Protest, Explained." She wrote,

> On Wednesday, dozens of officers from the Seattle Police Department arrested more than 30 people and cleared out the

Capitol Hill Organized Protest (CHOP), formerly known as the Capitol Hill Autonomous Zone (CHAZ), at Mayor Jenny Durkan's order. The mayor's executive order came in response to a wave of nighttime violence in the four-block area, including four shootings and several alleged sexual assaults.[4]

It makes one wonder, what happened to the weed circles, dodgeball games, and movie nights? We were told that CHAZ or CHOP was a great idea where people could live free of police involvement. Just three weeks before the police moved in, Burns was telling the world how great CHAZ was, writing,

> In the meantime, protesters have managed to create a police-free space in which black people, indigenous people, people of color, queer people, and houseless people feel especially safe. It's even become somewhat of a tourist attraction for more affluent white, liberal families.[5]

I don't know about you, but CHOP doesn't sound to me like a great place to take your family for a vacation.

In another incident, Shawn Whiting, who was live-streaming on Twitch, was detained by others in the zone and not allowed to leave until he'd deleted his video. How could this be, when we were told by Burns and Vox that the zone was pro-free speech? This place was portrayed as being civil, peaceful, and a tourist attraction, but Whiting was grabbed from behind and threatened simply because he wanted to show the world what was really going on there. Afterward, he said he saw numerous people with knives and was worried that he would be stabbed.

Of course, the liberal mainstream media said nothing about this. Had Shawn Whiting been a leftist who was attacked by a bunch of right-wingers, you can bet they would have been all over it. When those who are acting out follow the leftist narrative, the leftist media turns a blind eye to their hostile, criminal behavior.

Today, Seattle is still a hot spot for the Left and Antifa. On February 14, 2020, Antifa thought it would be a great idea to block off the East Precinct by piling up snow. It was piled up so high that vehicles were not able to respond to emergency calls. The crowd of "peaceful protestors" went on to throw snowballs and shout slogans at police officers. It is egregious that these people were able to inhibit first responders from helping the citizens of Seattle. Remember, according to President Biden, Antifa is just an idea. But they sure do cause a lot of trouble for being nothing but an idea.

IT'S TIME TO GET TOUGH ON ANTIFA

As you and I both know, some politicians will say whatever they need to say in order to get elected. Many Democratic politicians speak out of both sides of their mouths: one minute, they condemn Antifa for their violence; the next minute, they say that Antifa is just an ideology. Politicians from all parties should be just as hard on Antifa as they are on any racist or extremist group.

Of course, politicians aren't the only ones who let Antifa get away with their criminal conduct. The media is also culpable. For example, Don Lemon of CNN has praised Antifa, saying the group is "fighting racist fascists" and "no organization is perfect" even though he acknowledges the group's violent behavior. In addition to accepting violence, former CNN anchor Chris Cuomo, said, "And please, show me where it says protesters are supposed to be polite and peaceful. Because I can show you that outraged citizens are what made the country what she is and led to many major milestones. To be honest, this is not a tranquil time."[6]

So, Cuomo thinks that Antifa is moving this country forward by rioting, looting, assaulting people, and burning down businesses? This, to me, is pure drivel. The First Amendment to the Constitution states,

"Congress shall make no law respecting an establishment of religion or prohibiting the free exercise thereof; or abridging the freedom of speech, or of the press; or the right of the people peaceably to assemble, and to petition the Government for a redress of grievances"

In mid-2020, riots broke out in Minneapolis during which Antifa members, Black Lives Matter members, and criminals burned and looted businesses. With buildings burning all around him, MSNBC journalist, Ali Velshi said, "I want to be clear how I characterize this, this is mostly a protest, it is not generally speaking unruly, but fires have been started."[7] This is what some in the media do; they downplay what is happening to push a narrative to the American people. Buildings were burning to the ground across the street from Velshi, but he was saying, in essence, "Nothing to see here folks, everything is fine." It is important to note that multiple buildings were on fire and were being looted, and the protests were not peaceful.

Miguel Marques of CNN was covering the Minneapolis riots when he said, "The first thing I want to make perfectly clear is that this has been almost entirely peaceful." Another CNN journalist covering a New York protest that turned violent told his audience, "It has been mostly a peaceful protest but then they [the NYPD] chose to move in."[8] At this moment, a protestor literally walked up to the camera and flipped off everyone watching. Again, these are just a few examples of the media telling the American people that the violence they are seeing on screen is not really happening, that things are mostly peaceful, and that they have nothing to worry about.

It is truly a remarkable thing to see footage of Antifa members brutally beating people, stomping on people's heads, lighting businesses on fire, and looting stores, all while leftist politicians and the media tell us that their actions are mostly peaceful. It would be different if these events were outliers and if the footage we were seeing was from small pockets of events. The problem is that these events are not outliers, and these events are not rare but widespread.

ANTIFA'S FRIENDS IN HIGH PLACES

NOT PROGRESSIVE ENOUGH

The Left's ideology doesn't just attempt to destroy America; it attempts to destroy itself. On the surface, this does not make sense. Why would a group, an organization, or in President Biden's words, "an ideology," try to cannibalize itself? The easy answer is that the Democratic Party is so progressive that it can never be progressive enough. The Left has dominated the Democratic Party in such a way that at times they are almost indistinguishable. It was once fairly easy to see the difference between the more radical Left and the Democratic Party, but in 2022 seeing the difference can be very difficult. This progressive push has turned the Left and the Democratic Party into an organization full of radicals. If you do not keep up with the ever-changing Left, then you become an outcast, no longer accepted, and fair game to be destroyed.

Antifa is one of the main groups of the Left that wants to destroy the United States. If you don't believe in their ideology, then you'll be dealt with. Their retaliation comes in many forms.

One of these is the destruction of property. Just hours after Joe Biden was sworn in as our forty-sixth president, a group of Antifa supporters broke out the windows of the Democratic Party headquarters in Oregon and wrote graffiti all over the building. Eight people were arrested, and the police found weapons on them, along with body armor and the signature black clothing.

The group had signs that read, "Fascist Massacres," "We Are Ungovernable," and "We Don't Want Biden, We Want Revenge!" It strikes me as odd that they carried signs complaining about "Fascist Massacres" when, in fact, they are fascists. And if "We are ungovernable" doesn't scream, "We can't be reasoned with," I don't know what does. Those who belong to Antifa are literally letting everyone know that they cannot be disciplined, obedient, orderly, or respectable.

This is not a group that is aligned with America's core values or foundational morals. It also does not make sense that they don't want Biden in office when Biden has been giving in to their demands.

Lastly, Antifa's claim that the United States is engaging in imperialist wars is an odd one. There is a good case to be made that American imperialism ended well over a century ago. The only thing that makes sense out of all this is the consistency of a nonsensical group writing a bunch of nonsensical signs.

Before I move on, let me remind you of some wisdom most of us learn very early in our lives: If something walks like a duck, quacks like a duck, looks like a duck, and swims like a duck, it is a duck. It's also true that if someone acts like a fascist, talks like a fascist, and looks like a fascist, he or she is a fascist.

Don't let Antifa fool you!

Three
THE MAINSTREAM MEDIA

One of the key enablers of the Trojan Horse is the mass media, also known as the mainstream media (MSM). There is no doubt that today's MSM is aligned with the political left. Not all MSM outlets are leftist and there are conservative news outlets, but one of the main differences is that the conservative news outlets acknowledge their bias. When you tune in to Fox News, you can be quite sure that you're getting the news from a conservative point of view. The same is true of The Daily Wire. On the other hand, CNN doesn't have any sort of disclaimer acknowledging that all their reporters and anchors view the world from a leftist perspective. They are not delivering news but commentary, but they don't admit it.

Ideally, the purpose and function of the media is to give all the facts and let their viewers make up their own opinions. Notice I said that people should be given *all* the facts, not *some* of the facts, not just the facts that serve the outlet's narrative. When someone decides what information to give and what information to leave out based on a bias, an intention has been inserted into the reporting.

The MSM has been known to use deceptive tactics in the past, twisting the words of conservatives and shading the details of events to push their agenda. In the biblical book of Psalms, King David wrote, "All day long they twist my words; / All their thoughts are against me for evil" (Ps. 56:5). There are those who will go to extreme lengths to twist words and actions, even if it means destroying lives. To twist the facts of a specific situation, push your opinion, and claim to be unbiased is just plain wrong. It makes all the difference when the media openly make known their political viewpoint before reporting—even if they proceed to report in a manner that supports their agenda and pushes their values. I find no moral issue with that. On the other hand, it is deceptive behavior when the media claims to be unbiased but proceeds to report in a manner that supports an agenda and pushes values. For example, I am a conservative, writing a book that presents a conservative viewpoint. I have been up-front about that from the very first page. I am not trying to mislead anyone.

This is not at all the case with many members of the mainstream media. In fact, MSM outlets have been known to communicate with one another in order to push a narrative to the American people and the rest of the world. In doing so, the MSM decides what information to present to the people and what information to conceal from the people.

There is a story in the Christian gospels that mirrors what is happening today. I will admit that this is a rough analogy, but poignant connections can be made. The disciple Matthew writes in chapter 28 of the book that bears his name:

> Now after the Sabbath, as it began to dawn toward the first *day* of the week, Mary Magdalene and the other Mary came to look at the tomb. And behold, a severe earthquake had occurred, for an angel of the Lord descended from heaven and came and rolled away the stone and sat upon it. And his appearance was like lightning, and his clothing as white as snow. The guards shook from fear of him and became like dead men. And the angel said to the women, "Do not be afraid; for I know that you are looking for Jesus who has been crucified. He is not here, for He has risen, just as He said. Come, see the place where He was lying. And go quickly and tell His disciples that He has risen

from the dead; and behold, He is going ahead of you to Galilee. There you will see Him; behold, I have told you."

And they left the tomb quickly with fear and great joy, and ran to report to His disciples. And behold, Jesus met them and said, "Rejoice!" And they came up and took hold of His feet, and worshiped Him. Then Jesus said to them, "Do not be afraid; go, bring word to My brothers to leave for Galilee, and there they will see Me."

Now while they were on their way, some of the *men from the* guard came into the city and reported to the chief priests all that had happened. And when they had assembled with the elders and consulted together, they gave a large sum of money to the soldiers, and said, "You are to say, 'His disciples came at night and stole Him while we were asleep.' And if this comes to the governor's ears, we will appease him and keep you out of trouble." And they took the money and did as they had been instructed; and this story was widely spread among the Jews *and is* to this day.

But the eleven disciples proceeded to Galilee, to the mountain which Jesus had designated to them. And when they saw Him, they worshiped *Him*; but some were doubtful. And Jesus came up and spoke to them, saying, "All authority in heaven and on earth has been given to Me. Go, therefore, and make disciples of all the nations, baptizing them in the name of the Father and the Son and the Holy Spirit, teaching them to follow all that I commanded you; and behold, I am with you always, to the end of the age." (Matthew 28:1–20)

At the time of the first coming of Jesus, the chief priests—the teachers of the Jewish law—were responsible for giving people truth and guidance. One might ask, "What is the truth the teachers of the law were supposed to speak?" They were only supposed to give the facts that were reported to them by the soldiers. It was not up to the teachers of the law to force people to believe in God and follow the laws as they themselves understood them. It was not up to them to twist the words of the soldiers. It was not up to them to craft narratives. They were not supposed to give their opinion on events and how the prophecies of scripture would be fulfilled. If they did any of these things, they would lead the people astray. In the same way, the members of the MSM are responsible for giving us the facts. They are not supposed to give us their personal opinions. It is not their job to twist people's words or craft narratives. When they do such things, they can lead people astray.

Over the course of the last three decades, the news has become infected by leftist ideologies. Media outlets have become news reporters in name and activists in function. These are people with a clear agenda who will stop at nothing to push their beliefs upon the American people. In doing so, they manipulate the people into believing something that either isn't real or isn't the entire picture. When someone does not have all the facts, it is hard for them to come to an educated opinion. This is not to say that one cannot form an opinion, nor to say that one cannot come to a correct understanding when facts are omitted, still many people have been led astray as a result of the media's agenda. Those who believe in what the MSM tells them to believe are in a condition that conservatives refer to as "being asleep." They need to wake up and see the full picture of what is happening in our nation today.

TRUMP VERSUS THE MAINSTREAM MEDIA

One prominent spokesperson who has brought attention to these news outlets' actions is the forty-fifth President of the United States, Donald

THE MAINSTREAM MEDIA

J. Trump. President Trump labeled these activist news sites, "Fake News," a term that has become widely used, both in seriousness and in satire. In fact, during the Trump administration, the phrase "Fake News" became synonymous with the MSM. The only problem was that Trump routinely used this term to describe all media, and it is silly to generalize that all media is fake news.

Trump has routinely called the media, "the enemy of the American people." I've wrestled with this statement for many months. I believe it is the job of the media to simply give their audience information that is complete and free of bias and let the American people form their own opinions about why things are or are not happening, but there are some media out there that are opinion outlets. If those outlets are open about their bias and let their viewers, readers, or listeners know from the start that they are handing out opinions, then there is absolutely nothing wrong with that.

After many months of considering whether the media is the enemy of the people, I've come to the conclusion that this is not the case. There are a few factors that have led me to this conclusion. The first is that we are all Americans. We have stuck together through good times and bad times. The media has historically gone after Republican presidents, not as harshly as they have gone after President Trump, but they have attacked every Republican president. A single exception occurred after September 11, 2001. In the aftermath of that infamous day, the people of the United States stood together—it did not matter if you were Left, Right, Center, Republican, or Democrat in your political leanings—the only thing that mattered was that you were American, and we agreed that no one is allowed to "mess" with the United States. Americans had a common enemy at that time.

The way I view the United States here in the 2020s is similar to the way I see the inner workings of a family. We are brothers and sisters who share the same house. We might not agree on how to do things, and we might not always like the way our "siblings" act. If you have brothers and/

or sisters, you undoubtedly know that your siblings can annoy you incessantly at times. There might be the occasional fist fight or wrestling match over something stupid, but at the end of the day you are family and will have each other's backs. You might even feel like you hate your sibling, but if someone from the outside says something bad about him or her, just watch out. Attacking a family member means "game over" for the outsider.

I believe it's the same way for the American people as a whole. Right now, we don't have a common enemy as we did after 911, so we squabble among ourselves—often over issues that may be important but are not worthy of violence. In the same way, the media is part of our national family. We may not agree with them, and we may notice that what they are doing is wrong. They may lie to us at times, some might lie to us all the time; but at the end of the day, they are a part of our family and not our enemies. We can disagree with the media, we can call out their mistakes, and we can criticize them, but we should not consider them our enemy. With that said, I also believe that those in the MSM who are engaging in wrongdoing need to be called out.

For example, in early December 2020, Chris Hayes of MSNBC lied to the American people regarding COVID-19:

> We now have more deaths today than on 911. This will continue every day, more or less, for three weeks or so, most likely. I can't really get my head around it, and I suppose no one can. It's wrenching and horrifying and enraging. All of this was predictable and predicted. As I've said, the failures are larger than just Trump and the GOP, but that is by far the largest cause of the failure. They actively chose this path. They chose to send tens of thousands to their graves. They knew what they were doing.[1]

To his credit, Hayes was entirely correct when he said COVID-19 has been wrenching and horrifying and also enraging. There are many elements of this pandemic and our society's response to it that are hard to wrap your head around, and it is true that there were aspects of the COVID-19 outbreak that were predictable and other aspects that were unpredictable. However, it is insane to say that Trump and the GOP actively chose the path that led to pandemic casualties. The statement, "They chose to send tens of thousands to their graves" is hard to wrap your head around. This is an example of fake news and a boldfaced lie to the American people. There is no evidence that supports this statement. Trump and the GOP did not devise a plan that ensured thousands of people would die from COVID. In reality, Trump and the GOP sponsored an unprecedented research effort to create and produce a COVID vaccine in record time, which would save populations across the entire planet. It is odd that Hayes puts the blame for the deaths caused by COVID on Trump but not China, the country where the virus originated. Early in the outbreak, China chose not to release information related to the virus and let people leave the country freely. Those actions directly led to millions of deaths across the world, and President Trump and the GOP had absolutely nothing to do with this fateful decision. Hayes's hyperbolic statement was fake news.

Another example of fake news occurred just a month later when the *Washington Post* had to correct a report about a phone call between President Donald Trump and Georgia elections investigator Frances Walton. The original story from the *Washington Post* reported that Trump told Frances Walton to "find the fraud" and that if she did so, she would be "a national hero."[2] This, of course, started a media frenzy portraying Trump as corrupt and unfit to stay in office. The Trump administration replied that this report was a hoax. A recording emerged on December 23, 2020 showing that Trump did not use the words that the *Washington Post* originally reported. What Trump actually said was that Walton would be "praised" when the "right answer comes out." Trump went on encouraging Walton to closely examine the mail-in ballots, because he thought discrepancies would be found there.

The *Washington Post* quietly published a correction stating,

> Correction: Two months after publication of this story, the Georgia secretary of state released an audio recording of President Donald Trump's December phone call with the state's top elections investigator. The recording revealed that *The Post* misquoted Trump's comments on the call, based on information provided by a source. Trump did not tell the investigator to "find the fraud" or say she would be "a national hero" if she did so. Instead, Trump urged the investigator to scrutinize ballots in Fulton County, Ga., asserting she would find "dishonesty" there. He also told her that she had "the most important job in the country right now."[3]

How does a major news outlet like the *Washington Post* make such a giant mistake? Reportedly, the quote was "based on information provided by a source." Enlightening, truly. This is the problem with the media today. When they find one single source that fits their overall agenda, they run with the story. This is a major departure from the journalistic standard of corroborating a story by finding multiple sources rather than just one. This is important because if a source is a single person, that person can lie or have an unreliable memory. Apparently, the leftist media no longer cares enough to find out if the source is legitimate, so long as the content fits the narrative they want to present. Their bias is so strong they think there is no possible way that their source could be wrong. In other words, they don't see how their source could possibly be wrong when it provides proof that Trump is an evil man.

After the *Washington Post* came out with their correction, President Trump said, "While I appreciate the *Washington Post*'s correction, which immediately makes the Georgia Witch Hunt a non-story, the original story was a hoax, right from the very beginning."[4]

THE MAINSTREAM MEDIA

As I write this, there is an ongoing investigation in Georgia into whether comments and actions by Trump regarding the 2020 election were criminal, and two grand juries will be seated next week. Basically, Trump contends that he has been severely damaged by this massive misquoting in one of the nation's largest, most widely read newspapers.

It is truly remarkable that the media continues to get away with this kind of misconduct, and all they have to do to "fix it" is publish a correction. (Often, the correction is hidden toward the back of the paper, while the erroneous original article appeared on Page One.) Basically, the *Washington Post* punched Trump in the face and then a couple of weeks later said, "Oh, sorry." It's not a big deal. The reporter didn't get fired, nor was the source's name leaked for giving false information. No one suffered negative consequences, other than Trump, who said,

> You will notice that establishment media errors, omissions, mistakes, and outright lies always slant one way—against me and against Republicans. Meanwhile, stories that hurt Democrats or undermine their narratives are buried, ignored, or delayed until they can do the least harm—for example, after an election is over.[5]

President Trump is absolutely right. The media are biased and lean far to the left. They serve as propaganda machines for the Democratic Party and seek to destroy the Republican Party. The media does not care if they get something wrong and have to issue a correction. As long as a story goes against the opposition, even if it's a lie, it is a newsworthy story. If the story centers on Joe Biden or any other Democrat, you bet they will do their job well, making sure to find multiple sources to corroborate it.

You might think that it would be a rare occurrence for a news outlet to publish a false story with only one source to corroborate it. But you would be wrong. In 2017, CNN published a piece citing an anonymous source, saying that the Senate Intelligence Committee was looking into the chief executive of a Russian investment fund worth $10 billion. The chief executive was cited as meeting with Anthony Scaramucci before the inauguration of President-Elect Trump. The report went on to say that two Democratic senators wanted to know if Scaramucci had indicated in the meeting whether the sanctions on Russia would be removed. This issue was important because it would have an impact on the investment fund. It turned out that this story was fake news and resulted in a correction by CNN as well as an apology to Anthony Scaramucci. This report also caused three CNN staffers: the reporter, Pulitzer-Prize nominee Thomas Frank; assistant managing editor Eric Lichtblau; and Lex Harris, the executive editor in charge of investigations, to resign.[6] At least in this egregious case, there were resignations for this type of reporting, but the pushing of fake news continues unabated.

After the retraction from CNN, other media outlets framed the whole incident on President Trump as an attack against the media. The Left love playing the victim, even when they caused the destruction. The MSM rarely ever admits to doing something wrong, and blame is almost always shifted. Isn't it amazing how the leftist media can screw up and then spin the story so they come off looking like the victim?

In yet another example of false reporting, the *New York Times* had to issue a correction to one of their stories that claimed all seventeen U.S. intelligence agencies confirmed that Russia had orchestrated hacking attacks against the United States. The correction by the *New York Times* read as follows,

> A White House Memo article on Monday about President Trump's deflections and denials about Russia referred incorrectly to the source of an intelligence assessment that said Russia orchestrated hacking attacks during last year's presidential election. The assessment was made by four intelligence

agencies—the Office of the Director of National Intelligence, the Central Intelligence Agency, the Federal Bureau of Investigation, and the National Security Agency. The assessment was not approved by all 17 organizations in the American intelligence community.[7]

On June 9, 2021, the members of the MSM were dismayed when the American public found out that a Trump photo op, which took place one year earlier, was not the reason the police had cleared out Lafayette Park near the White House in Washington, D.C. This story began when George Floyd died at the hands of police in Minneapolis on May 25, 2020, leading to people rioting in the streets, including Antifa and Black Lives Matter. This rioting resulted in St. John's Episcopal Church being burned.

On the morning of May 29, protesters made their way to Lafayette Park to protest the killing of Floyd. On June 1, 2020, at 6:23 p.m., police began using tear gas and rubber bullets to clear the park of protestors. Attorney General William Barr walked into the park and spoke to the park police incident commander, telling him that the president was coming later that afternoon for a photo op in front of the church. Later that day, President Trump walked from the White House through Lafayette Park and stood in front of St. John's Church with a Bible in hand. The president's appearance led to a frenzy of media attacks by the MSM. Here are some quotes that were highlighted on Fox News:[8]

> **Jim Acosta (CNN)** – "If the White House, president, and his team had to do it all over again, would they have gassed and pummeled protesters to clear the park so the President could have a photo op?"
>
> **Joy Reid (MSNBC)** – "Clear away protesters with tear gas and rubber bullets so that Donald Trump could walk across the

street from the White House and stage a photo op in front of a church with an upside-down Bible."

Erin Burnett (CNN) – "The president wanted this photo op and he wanted to disperse that crowd because he wants an image of all of these protests being one thing which is violent, which is not accurate."

Anderson Cooper (CNN) – "Why were they ordered to move on protestors at that moment? Obviously, the president wanted a photo op."

Daniel Dale (CNN) – "Van der Veen falsely claims the clearing of Lafayette Square last June happened to 'establish an appropriate security perimeter' from a 'riotous mob.' No. They cleared peaceful protesters out of the way for a Trump photo-op. The 'narrative' Van der Veen is mocking is correct."

Katie Rogers (New York Times) – "Protesters dispersed with tear gas so Trump could pose at church"

Joe Biden – "He's using the American military against the American people. He tear-gassed peaceful protesters and fired rubber bullets. For a photo. For our children, for the very soul of our country, we must defeat him. But I mean it when I say this: we can only do it together."

Kamala Harris – "Donald Trump just tear-gassed peaceful protesters for a photo op."

THE MAINSTREAM MEDIA

After all this negative media coverage, the Department of the Interior's Inspector General investigated the incident in order to determine what really happened. (One would think that the journalists themselves would have investigated the situation before they blasted it all over the airwaves, but apparently, that was too much to ask.) The DOI's investigation found that President Trump's visit to St. John's Episcopal Church had nothing to do with the protestors being cleared from the area. The report states:

> This report presents a thorough, independent examination of that evidence to assess the [U.S. Park Police's] decision-making and operations, including a detailed timeline of relevant actions and an analysis of whether the USPP's actions complied with governing policies. The evidence we reviewed showed that the USPP cleared the park to allow a contractor to safely install antiscale fencing in response to the destruction of Federal property and injury to officers that occurred on May 30 and May 31. Moreover, the evidence established that relevant USPP officials had made those decisions and had begun implementing the operational plan several hours before they knew of a potential Presidential visit to the park, which occurred later that day. As such, we determined that the evidence did not support a finding that the USPP cleared the park on June 1, 2020, so that then President Trump could enter the park.[9]

As previously stated, these are facts that the media could have uncovered earlier. They could have sent their reporters out to investigate the situation. All they did was take some footage of the protestors being cleared out, and of the president taking a photo op, and assumed the connection. No longer do we see days of waiting for a story to unfold. Gone are the days of unbiased news. Gone are the days of waiting for evidence. Gone are the days when the American people could trust the press and the MSM.

If the media has a story they can use to push their agenda, they will go to extreme lengths to do it. Why would a network lie to the American people? Because they can get away with it.

These days, pushing an agenda with the expectation of changing the viewers' perception of reality is more important than telling the truth. The media can publish fake news and have millions of people read or watch the story and believe it. Then hours, days, months, or years later, they quietly publish a correction. Many who watch these leftist news outlets have already made up their minds, but they are hardly given the opportunity to hear corrections. As a result, the public's perception of the story is not changed, and some people continue running around with fake news stories in their minds.

The MSM's poor practices have sparked the creation of a whole sector of news media, where conservatives like me have started channels and networks built around debunking the Left and exposing their hypocrisy. My YouTube show, *The Bald Brad Show*, exposes the Left's destructive ideology and the hypocrisy of the leftist MSM. My channel is only one of the hundreds of channels that do this. Major popular outlets are *The Daily Wire*, *Blaze Media*, and *Louder With Crowder*. Conservatives and Republicans flock to our channels and sites because they know they are getting news that has not been tampered with. Unlike CNN, we are open about our biases and work hard to present the news that is found trustworthy. If there is not enough evidence to form a clear opinion, then we explain that we need to wait until enough evidence is presented to have a justified view of the incident. Our goal is to give facts instead of rumors.

There is nothing wrong with waiting on a story or incident before giving your opinion about something. The American people value the truth, and the truth is something we all seek. Sometimes, we see information that is made up of 90 percent truth and 10 percent lies. Since most of the information is true, the viewer or reader may overlook the part that is invalid and believes the entire story. This type of "truth-telling" has been happening for ages, ever since the beginning of the Bible. Our enemy, Satan, is adept at telling partial truths in order to get us to swallow a lie. For example, you may recall the story of Adam and Eve from the book of Genesis.

In this story, Eve is tricked into eating fruit that God has forbidden. The Bible tells us that after the Lord created mankind, He created a garden in Eden, full of all kinds of trees. In the middle of the garden stood the tree of the knowledge of good and evil. The Lord took the first man, Adam, and put him in the Garden of Eden to work it and take care of it. The Creator also gave Adam the following command, "From any tree of the garden you may freely eat; but from the tree of the knowledge of good and evil you shall not eat, for on the day that you eat from it you will certainly die" (Gen. 2:16–17).

God went on to create a helper for Adam, the first woman, Eve. Within the garden was a serpent, Satan, who asked Eve,

> "Has God really said, 'You shall not eat from any tree of the garden'?" The woman said to the serpent, "From the fruit of the trees of the garden we may eat; but from the fruit of the tree which is in the middle of the garden, God has said, 'You shall not eat from it or touch it, or you will die.'" The serpent said to the woman, "You certainly will not die! For God knows that on the day you eat from it your eyes will be opened, and you will become like God, knowing good and evil." (Genesis 3:1–5)

Let the reader take note how craftily Satan is spinning his "elevator speech." Perhaps 90 percent of what he says is true, but one word is a lie (say 10 percent). The portion of the sentence that is a lie is the word "not."

Another problem is that Eve is not fully acquainted with the words of the command that she was given. God was very clear with Adam. He didn't say anything about not touching the fruit. But to be fair to Eve, the command was given before she had been created. She heard it second-hand, from her husband, who may have added a little emphasis of his own—or maybe she just heard it wrong. When Eve replies to the serpent, she is correct in saying that she may eat from any tree in the garden, but she is wrong when she says that "you must not touch it, or you will die." Satan picks up on the fact that Eve is not fully familiar with God's command. "You won't die," he tells her, and he's right if we're talking about just touching the fruit. But Eve, seeing how tasty the fruit looks, does more than touch it—and sin and death come into the world as a result. All of history is affected through Satan's twisting of a few words.

This story gives us a great illustration of how the MSM spins the news and manipulates the American people. Most Americans do not spend their days researching, reading, and understanding political and current events. This leaves the MSM free to concoct stories that are 90 percent true but have a few lies sprinkled in here and there. Just like Satan, the media knows what they are doing, and they see it working. Just as Eve was not fully familiar with the words of the Lord, the American public is not able to fully understand every event and situation that takes place in the United States today. Since the media knows this, they take the opportunity to obscure the truth and manipulate the minds of the American people, getting them to believe a version of current events that is false. Satan tried to destroy God's creation from inside the garden and the leftist news media are trying to do the same thing to our country. If we do not seek the truth of circumstances and history, and know it wholeheartedly, then we are susceptible to being led astray, just as Adam and Eve were.

We must not allow ourselves to be deceived by the leftist media outlets that are spreading misinformation. It is vital that we refrain from being gullible. Instead of believing everything we hear, we must instead do research into what we have heard. We must closely examine the information we have been given and sort out what is trustworthy and true. This takes time and patience, but it is vitally important.

THE MAINSTREAM MEDIA

THE LEFTIST PROPAGANDA MACHINE

Merriam-Webster's dictionary defines *propaganda* as "the spreading of ideas, information, or rumor for the purpose of helping or injuring an institution, a cause, or a person." This is exactly what the MSM is doing. It must be noted that there is a difference between doing this accidentally or on purpose. As I've said before, not all news outlets or journalists push propaganda, but some are complicit in this.

Consider CNN, for example. On April 13, 2021, a Project Veritas reporter recorded CNN's Technical Director, Charlie Chester, saying openly that CNN is pushing propaganda and fear. Chester said, "Look what we did. We (CNN) got Trump out. I am a hundred percent going to say it, and I one hundred percent believe it that if it wasn't for CNN, I don't know that Trump would have got voted out."[10] This is a clear example of propaganda that spreads information for the purpose of injuring a person while helping another. This does not come as a shock to anyone on the Right, since we watched CNN go after Trump beginning on the day he announced his run for president.

Project Veritas also showed a video of Charlie Chester talking about how CNN made it seem like Trump had health issues. Chester said,

> Yeah. I mean like Trump, we did it. Like when Trump was, I don't know, like his hand was shaking or whatever, I think. We brought in like so many medical people to like all tell a story that like . . . he was like neurologically damaged, that he was losing it. He's unfit to, you know, whatever.[11]

Just how bad was it for Trump during his first 100 days of office? A Harvard study showed that the news coverage of Trump was 80 percent negative and 20 percent positive. It was reported that "CNN and NBC struck a 93 percent negative tone on their Trump stories, with only 7 percent positive."[12] What was the result of the media pushing this type of propaganda? A poll was conducted in 2018 during Trump's presidency that showed that 26 percent of Americans thought the news media was the enemy of the people—51 percent of Republicans and 5 percent of Democrats.[13]

This propaganda poses a problem for the United States because it makes the president look weak, and if he looks weak then the country also looks weak. Of course, no American wants the United States to look weak in front of our enemies. There was a time when the media understood this. The best example of this is how they did everything possible to make Franklin D. Roosevelt look vigorous and strong though polio had left him paralyzed from the waist down. But because many in the MSM fervently disliked Donald Trump, they tried to make him look weak, crazy, and unfit to hold office.

In the Project Veritas video discussed earlier, CNN's Charlie Chester said, "We were, we were creating a story there that we didn't know anything about, you know? That's what—I think that's propaganda . . . . We had nothing else to run with at that time. We were like, just taking shots off the bow just hoping something would hit, you know?" These are the actions you might expect from an enemy of America. I believe that all Americans should root for the success of a sitting President, whether or not they agree with him or her. I strongly disagree with much of what President Biden does as president, but I pray for his success. His success as my president is success for America.

The MSM is capable of showing a president as being strong. This is what they have done for Joe Biden. Chester said, "The whole thing of him running . . . showing him (Biden) jogging, was obviously a deflection of his age and they're trying to make it like, oh, I'm healthy."

The reason why the MSM portrayed President Biden as being strong was not that they wanted America to look strong, but because they wanted Biden to be elected. The MSM's idea of America and Biden's idea of America go hand-in-hand. What is that idea? That America is fundamentally flawed and that it must be changed through government intervention.

Someone might say that Chester is just one bad egg within a vast pool of eggs, meaning that he is just one bad media person within thousands of good media people. The problem with this thinking is that I have found dozens of similar examples. I don't have the time or the space to go into all of them, but I will say that Chester does not stand alone in his efforts to use the media as propaganda to spread his progressive beliefs.

Clearly, the MSM wanted Joe Biden in office because he would push their agenda. Once in office, the propaganda would switch to something else. Chester is on camera saying,

> I think there's just like a COVID fatigue. So, whenever a new story comes up, they're going to latch onto it. They've already announced in our office that once the public is open to it, we're going to start focusing mainly on climate, like global warming—and that's going to be our next. I don't know. What's the word I'm looking for? It's going to be our (CNN) focus. Like, our (CNN) focus was to get Trump out of office, right? Without saying it, that's what it was right? So, our next thing is going to be for climate change awareness.[14]

Rather than waiting for events to happen naturally on their own and then reporting on them, CNN is artificially manufacturing stories to push a certain agenda; this agenda is to change public opinion regarding climate change, previously known as global warming. Can anyone really believe that news outlets like CNN are unbiased and truthful in their reporting?

ARE YOU A CONSPIRACY THEORIST?

Have you noticed how the MSM is quick to label conservatives and Republicans as "conspiracy theorists?" Any questioning of media stories by the Right is consistently knocked down and called disinformation, but when the Left manufactures stories and propagandizes news, no one bats an eye in protest. If a conservative questions irregularities in the election, he or she is called a conspiracy theorist. If he questions the necessity of government shutdowns because of COVID, he is a conspiracy theorist. On the other hand, the Left hails as credible news stories that come from media outlets like CNN, whose leader has been shown on videotape discussing how they craft, manipulate, and use propaganda to push a certain narrative.

Unfortunately, many Americans take the media's reporting as truth, regardless of which political side they are on. If you are on the Left, you are likely going to believe in CNN and MSNBC. If you are on the Right, you are likely to believe in Fox News and OAN. It seems in today's culture that neither side takes the time to research the things they are seeing and hearing to find out if they are true.

I once worked as an assurance and advisory accountant. In this capacity, I audited public and private companies to see if their financials were trustworthy and true. To give an extremely simplified version of what the job entailed, a public company has financial documents that it discloses to the public, and people can review them to determine whether they want to invest in the company. The problem is this: How does the potential investor know if the numbers and information are correct? This is where auditors come into it. They pull actual documentation from the company that sometimes is selected through random sampling. Auditors don't just ask the client for their calculations and accept whatever results they provide. Auditors do their own calculations and check the actual documentation to verify that what the company has reported is correct.

THE MAINSTREAM MEDIA

I believe that all Americans should be auditors of all the information we get from the news media. We should be doing our own research to find out if what the media is telling us is true. Someone may ask, "But isn't it the media's job to tell me what is true?" Of course it is, but the problem is that it's not happening.

Auditing the information provided by the MSM can be a daunting task since so much information is being presented to us daily. Trying to take it all in can be like trying to get a few sips of water from a fire hose. You can't take the time to research everything you hear. But, as I did in my job as an accountant, you can sample a large enough section to find out whether a particular media outlet is reliable. We need to be selective regarding what we choose to research. The media will always choose themes that they want to cover in the hopes of changing the public's opinion. Consider how the MSM tried to change the public's opinion during the Trump administration.

The themes were the character assassination of Trump, America's evil history and structure, rampant mass shootings, fake news, immigration, COVID-19, Russian collusion, police brutality, and the president's Twitter posts. The Left's position on most of these themes can be debunked on a statistical level. If you want to learn more about this, I recommend that you enroll in an Introduction to Statistics course which can be found for free online. Once you have this foundation, more than half of what the media says can be researched quickly with a simple online search.

A tactic of the media is to take a data set and use the outliers to make their case. An example of this would be the data they use to say that the police are hunting black men in the streets. An observational study conducted by the Skeptic Research Center found that half of liberals believed that the police killed over 1,000 unarmed black men every year. The survey also showed that roughly 35 percent of them believe that the police kill 10,000 or more unarmed black men a year. Even 66 percent of moderates and conservatives believed that the number is more than 100.[15]

According to the *Washington Post* database, a total of thirteen unarmed African Americans were shot in 2019—not ten thousand, not one thousand, not one hundred, not even fifty—only thirteen. In 2020, a total of eighteen unarmed African Americans were killed by police.[16] It is truly mind-boggling that a large subset of Americans believe 10,000 unarmed black Americans are killed every year, when the real number is only 13. It should be noted that of these thirteen, some could have been trying to run an officer over with a car, reaching for an officer's weapon, or trying to render a police officer unconscious. This enormous gulf between facts and perception shows the power of propaganda and the power of misleading the people.

Now, of course, one wrongful death is a tragedy. One death is one too many. My point here is not to say that black lives are not important. Of course, they are. But I want to show how facts can be distorted by the media and believed by a gullible public.

The biased media can manipulate reality to make the viewer think something is happening on a grand scale when it's not. Perhaps you remember what happened on January 18, 2019, when Nicholas Sandmann, a student from Catholic Covington High School in Kentucky was taunted by a Native American activist named Nathan Phillips. Sandmann and some of his fellow students had traveled to Washington, D.C. to take part in a protest against abortion. Some of the students were wearing Trump MAGA hats. In the plaza of the Lincoln Memorial, some Black Hebrew Israelites began shouting insults at the students, who responded by shouting and performing some of their school's sports chants. At the same time the students were shouting chants, there was an Indigenous People March taking place. Nathan Phillips, who was a participant in that march, felt like the students were mocking him and his people. Because of this, he proceeded to beat his drum in the face of Sandmann, which led to a few viral videos.

The media ran with the videos and thus slandered Nicholas Sandmann as well as Covington Catholic High School. An NBC anchor reported that the video showed, "some students harassing an older Native American man, a Vietnam vet, in the midst of a special ceremony." On January 21, a CNN anchor said, "It does look like that young man to me is taunting that Native American Vietnam vet." Then, on January 22, Chris Cuomo of CNN added fuel to the fire when he said, "The kid, Nick Sandmann, he doesn't seem to be afraid, but he did make a choice and that was to make it into a standoff."[17] The media took one clip out of many and crafted a narrative about race and how MAGA hat-wearing Trump supporters are racists.

There was a time when reporters researched their work in order to make sure that what they were reporting was the truth. Today, they just find short clips and run with a story without doing any extensive investigative journalism. As a result of their carelessness in this situation, the MSM had to consistently revise and make corrections regarding what they had reported. But their corrections couldn't do much to vindicate Sandmann, who had been portrayed as a teenage bully who was harassing a Native American hero. Why? Because this scenario fit the narrative that the MSM wanted their viewers to believe—that Trump supporters are bullies and thugs—and it's just not so.

This is what the media does best. When they see an event take place that fits into their overall narrative, such as teenage Trump supporters appearing to harass a Native American Vietnam veteran, they put it on the air, no questions asked. In today's media climate, the goal of the MSM is getting the story out first and making corrections later. The problem with this mentality is that the damage it causes cannot be reversed, and public perspectives rarely change. The media is fully aware of this which, I believe, is why they do it in the first place.

It turns out that this strategy has a flaw. Every now and then the person who is being slandered will rise up and fight back. This is exactly what Sandmann did. He sued CNN for $275 million and the *Washington Post* for $250 million. Both media companies eventually settled with their accuser. It is unclear how much Sandmann received, but the fact that that two major news outlets settled a lawsuit with a teenager gives an idea of how wrong they were.

As we have seen through just a few examples, the MSM is not in the business of giving the American public the news but rather opinions disguised as news.

There are two main reasons why the MSM exists: (1) To push their political agenda; (2) To make money and craft stories that will gather as many viewers as possible.

Just as CNN Technical Director, Charlie Chester, said, fear sells. The MSM is not giving you information but selling you a product. That product is propaganda and manipulated information. These media outlets have an overarching agenda, which is to make money and promulgate a leftist narrative. We, as Americans, must open our eyes to both left- and right-wing media outlets so that we are not sucked into this dangerous vortex.

The citizens of Troy welcomed the gift of the horse with open arms. They allowed the horse to be brought into their most sanctified area. Today we have let the MSM into our homes through our televisions and we've given them access to our open minds. The media is indoctrinating Americans into thinking a specific way through the manipulation of the information they provide, which will result in the degradation of our country. We have always guarded against an enemy or an adversary to come from the outside, but we have not expected an enemy from within. If we don't stay alert and vigilant, then we will cease to have a country. This might seem like an extreme statement, but that doesn't make it any less true. The destruction won't come overnight, but it will come incrementally over years and decades. We are seeing this happen in real time, which is why the country continues to become more divided year after year. The only way we can stop this decline is by researching, reading, and becoming auditors, to see if what we are hearing and listening to is trustworthy and true.

Four
THE SPECTRE OF RACISM

A core tenet of the leftist narrative and ideology holds that America is a racist country. The Left holds onto the history of slavery in America, a dark time when true injustices took place, and claims that inequalities of the same magnitude remain today. But the truth is that racism today is at an all-time low in this country. I am not saying that racism doesn't exist; it does, and anyone who claims otherwise is a complete fool. I question whether or not America is systematically racist, as the Left believes.

Liberals claim that our Founding Fathers never intended for African Americans to be included in the Declaration of Independence's statement that "all men are created equal." Very few leftists consider that maybe they were taught wrong about this. Why? Because if our founders truly meant that "all men are created equal" then their entire world view would come crashing down. This would be like a Christian finding out that Christ never existed, and the Bible was made up of lies. Everything that the Christian had been taught, how to live his life, the way he looked at society would change. For leftists, examining and accepting information contrary to their beliefs is too much of a paradigm shift.

Most recently, they have adopted a philosophy put forth in *The 1619 Project*, which teaches that America is the product of slavery and racism can be traced back to the founding of the nation.

I agree that racism has been a dark blot in America's history; there can be no doubt about that, and I do not intend to belittle the horrors it has caused. But I do not believe that America is systemically racist. I believe, instead, that from its very beginning, the United States has worked toward the elimination of racism.

The fact is that members of the Democratic Party were the true instigators of racism and white supremacy in the United States, and Republicans have fought against these two evils ever since the party was founded.

In this chapter, we will take a bird's-eye view of the creation of the nation, so we can appreciate the overarching story of America. Through this method, we will be able to debunk certain leftist narratives and see if the founders truly intended to encompass black Americans in the statement that "all men are created equal."

THE AGE OF EXPLORATION

The United States of America is the most successful country the world has ever known. Ironically, the story of the country that we know today began in Portugal, during the fifteenth century. This was a time for worldwide exploration, as men from countries throughout Europe fought for supremacy on the high seas.

During this time, the Portuguese made contact with the Arabs and Africans in coastal areas of Africa and established trading centers. From these centers they brought ivory and gold to Portugal and transported slaves to a variety of Mediterranean estates.[1] Wait a minute? You mean to say slavery was happening hundreds of years before America came on the scene? Yes, absolutely, even though leftists tend to blame the United States for the crime of slavery, as if it were all our fault. The truth is that people were buying, trading, and selling other human beings long before the first Colonial American was born. The trade routes that were established were conducted through Arab middlemen or African traders who exchanged men, women, and children for various goods such as fish, wine, and salt.

THE SPECTRE OF RACISM

In the late 1400s, Christopher Columbus made several presentations to various committees, monarchs, and other parties before King Ferdinand and Queen Isabella of Spain underwrote his journey across the Atlantic Ocean.[2] It should be noted that Columbus found little support—almost none, in fact. It was almost destiny that Columbus received his funding from Ferdinand and Isabella. Had he been sailing under the banner of England, France, or Portugal, he would have departed from the Azores or Bristol, which would not have allowed him to sail toward the Americas.

As the reader may remember, Columbus's fleet had three ships, the Nina, the Pinta, and the Santa Maria. Departing from Spain in August 1492, Columbus embarked across dangerous waters. Many explorers and seaman hugged the coast as they explored, but Columbus did not. He took his crew of ninety men directly across the ocean, which was both bold and unusual for the time. On October 12, they made landfall on the Watling Islands in the Bahamas. Columbus eventually made his way to Cuba, where he found people he referred to as Indians. His discovery paved the way for many other explorers to come to the new-found land.

In 1518, Hernando Cortes led an army of 1,000 soldiers to Tenochtitlan, where present-day Mexico City lies, and where emperor Montezuma ruled over the Aztecs. Liberals love to make it seem like everyone was living in peace and harmony before European explorers reached America. In reality, what was happening in the Americas before colonization resembled The Hunger Games. The Aztecs raided neighboring native groups and took captives to use as human sacrifices. They would drag their prisoner to a priest, lay him down on a stone table, and proceed to cut out his heart while he was still alive. Just how barbaric were they? In 1487, a four-day sacrifice took place at the order of the Aztec King Ahuitzotl. Some 80,400 captives were sacrificed by four priests. So many people were butchered that the priests took shifts. There were four killing tables where the priests cut out the beating hearts of the captives and then proceeded to kick their bodies down the pyramid. It is estimated that they went through people at the "killing rate of fourteen victims a minute over the ninety-six-hour bloodbath."[3] This is the history that the Left leaves out. They choose to ignore it because it does not support their campaign to convince people that America is the most evil country in history.

One of the major arguments leftists use to "prove" that America is evil is that Columbus's trip to the Americas eventually led to the deaths of millions of Indians. Many revisionist historians claim that "approximately 56 million people died as a result of European exploration in the New World."[4] To arrive at this number, the Left takes estimates that encompass the entire Western Hemisphere of 100 million people. Over the course of time and research, that number became excessively inflated. New research shows that the number of people in North America when Columbus reached its shores was somewhere between 1.8 million to 8.5 million. This research would mean that roughly 800,000 Native Americans died from either disease or the force of arms.[5] This number is significant, but it is a long, long way from 56 million.

As of writing this book, COVID-19, the "Chinese Virus," has supposedly killed 3.5 million people. According to the MSM, if you blame China for the virus, then you are racist and a bigot. On the other hand, when the Left calls Columbus a racist who committed genocide, they claim they are not being racist or bigoted. Once again, the hypocrisy of the Left can be seen in this double standard. Moreover, the Left act as if Native Americans had never caught a cold or seen any sort of disease in their lives, yet research has shown that many of them may have had a form of syphilis, and almost all historians agree that a variety of infections were widespread. Tuberculosis existed in Central and North America long before the Spanish appeared, as did herpes, polio, tick-borne fevers, giardiasis, and amoebic dysentery. Extensive epidemics swept through North America long before the Europeans arrived. This is not to say that the diseases the Europeans brought over did not have an impact on the native population.

But it was much less than the Left's revisionist historians would have us believe.

COLONIALIZATION

Following the Portuguese, Spanish, and the French, the English established their first permanent colony in the Americas at Jamestown in 1607. England had made attempts to plant colonies before then but without success. Many of the new colonists were adventurers and explorers rather than workers who would provide for the colony. There were attempts to trade with the Monacan and Chickahominy Indians, but this did not bring in enough income to support the colonists. The settlers of James Forte starved, with fewer than one third of the 120 colonists surviving a year.[6] It wasn't just starvation that swept through the settlement. Malaria was a disastrous disease that went unchallenged.

Liberals are correct to point out that the diseases the settlers brought to the New World had a massive effect on the Native Americans. They spread the diseases while they were raiding and attacking each other. Again, liberals want us to believe that the natives were all peaceful. The reality is that the tribes were continuously fighting, taking survivors as slaves, raping enemy tribes' women, and committing heinous crimes against men, women, and children.

The Left also loves to portray the leader of James Forte, John Smith, as racist. They say this because of Smith's attacks on various Indian tribes. Why did Smith do this? To help with food and supplies, Smith would sometimes command his men to raid Indian villages. These raids would bring back immediate returns of food and animals for the settlers. The raids were also carried out as a response to the Indian tribes who consistently harassed the colonists. During this time in history, it was common practice to attack and raid each other for food, supplies, and captives. The Native Americans were doing this to each other long before anyone ever set foot on the New World. Smith wasn't anti-Indian. Smith liked and welcomed some tribes as friends and trading partners, but he rejected others that he found to be untrustworthy. His decisions had nothing to do with race.

Smith even proposed a plan to place white males in Indian villages to intermarry with the natives. If Smith were truly racist, there is no chance that he would want the white race to intermarry with the natives. Furthermore, other settlers even created schools to help educate the natives. This is not the type of behavior one would expect from the racist stereotypes our liberal friends like to talk about.

By 1613, tobacco emerged as a highly desired crop. Due to high demand, a string of plantations cropped up along rivers where tobacco could be loaded onto boats and barges. Naturally, a high demand for a certain good or service brought a high demand for the labor required to produce it. The colonists had the idea of using indentured servants to cultivate the land and harvest goods. The difference between someone who was indentured and someone who was enslaved was that an indentured servant had a contract or an agreed-upon term of service in which the services provided would be used to pay off the costs of the servant's immigration to America. Once the debt was paid off, the indentured servant would be released.

It wasn't only blacks who were indentured servants. Whites served in this capacity as well. As early as the mid-1600s, black indentured servants were freed and purchased land, cattle, and their own black servants. For years, the culture of Southern colonialism in America preferred European servants over African servants. In 1640, Barbados had roughly 25,000 slaves and 21,000 of those were white. Oliver Cromwell alone shipped an estimated 100,000 Irish to the West Indies during his reign.[7]

Again, the Left doesn't ever talk about the slavery that was committed long before the colonists arrived in the New World. They don't ever want to hear how non-white people were buying and selling African slaves for hundreds of years before any European ever settled in North America.

Slavery is a dark moment for many cultures and countries, and in fairness, the finger should be pointed at every country that committed acts of slavery, not just America. It also should be noted that slavery still exists in some places around the world. Perhaps it's time to stop feeling so guilty about what happened in the past and do something about what is happening in the present.

This isn't the stuff you are going to read in any high school history book, nor is the teacher going to teach it. Moreover, you will not learn these facts in a general education class at a university. Why do our educators not tell us about these historical facts? Because many of our educational institutions align with the Left, and historical reality doesn't fit the leftist narrative that America is a racist country. If the Left taught this kind of history, it would show the American people that although America was wrong for having slavery, it was not the only country to do so, and several other countries could be considered worse in their practice of slavery.

But a question arises: Why was there a switch from using whites and Indians to harvest tobacco and rice, to having a mixture of whites, Indians, and blacks, then later to using predominantly blacks to harvest the crop? Unfortunately, there is not one clear answer to this question, but there were many factors involved in this transition. The best guess is that plantation supervisors and overseers would manage a group of slaves while they harvested the crop. While in groups, the whites and Indians would communicate with one another and revolt together against the overseers or plan an escape. Another reason is that the Muslim trade for blacks was heavily established, and it was easier to buy and sell African slaves. Another reason was that the African slaves who were shipped to America did not speak a common language, and thus were not able to communicate with one another on a level that was remotely comparable to the Europeans or the Indians. Since there was no commonality other than skin color among the slaves, historians hypothesize that the first-generation African slaves were disheartened, which resulted in infrequent rebellion.

Another question that needs to be asked is how could human beings enslave other human beings? This is a question that I've struggled to answer because the answer that is about to be given is one that we are almost unable to comprehend today. The colonists during that time did not believe that Africans were fully human. Many people today, and rightfully so, will ask how this was possible. This is another great question, but there are people here in the twenty-first century that do the exact same thing.

For example, millions of people don't think that a baby in a mother's womb is a human being but just a cluster of cells. As I was thinking about this recently, I saw a video of a robot communicating with a person. This robot seemed to display thoughts, critical thinking, and emotion. Technically, the robot did not have any of these traits, but it gave the appearance of having them. The connection I am trying to make is that the robot is not a human being. Even though the robot seems to have facial expressions, presents a caring personality, and communicates with us, it does not have any rights. The robot is merely someone's property. As horrible as it sounds, African slaves were thought to be more like robots than people. They had facial expressions, personalities, emotion, and thoughts; but since the culture did not view them as fully human, they did not have any rights. Slave owners and the culture of that time viewed slaves as property. This is a very rough analogy, but please understand that I am using a twenty-first century concept and relating it to a seventeenth century culture. The analogies are clearly not perfect and one would be hard pressed to try and make sense of the idea that a human being is not human, but somehow the leftists make that concept work with abortion.

Moving into the early to mid-1700s, the demand for slave labor was still high. By 1763, between 15 and 20 percent of all Americans were African Americans.[8] Much of that percentage resided in the South due to the agricultural demands there. The difference between the demand for labor in the North and South played a vital role in early America and the decisions people made at the time regarding slavery. By 1775, anti-slavery societies were forming in the northern United States. The world's first abolitionist group, the Quaker Anti-Slavery Society was established in Pennsylvania. When the leftists talk about slavery, they talk about it as if all Americans were racist and there was never a hard divide on this issue. They also leave out the fact the world's first anti-slavery group was created in the United States.

SLAVERY AND THE DECLARATION OF INDEPENDENCE

Embracing the ideas of Thomas Paine, John Locke, Thomas Hobbs, Baron de Montesquieu, Jean Jacques Rousseau, and others, Thomas Jefferson wrote the Declaration of Independence, one of the greatest documents in human history. The entire declaration encapsulates America's founding ideals with one of the most notable statements being, "We hold these truths to be self-evident, that all men are created equal, that they are endowed by their Creator with certain unalienable Rights, that among these are Life, Liberty and the pursuit of Happiness."

From these words, we can see that our Founding Fathers knew that slavery was wrong and that something must be done about it. Thomas Jefferson even had a provision in the original document that blamed Great Britain for importing slaves into the colonies:

> He [King George III] has waged cruel war against human nature itself, violating its most sacred rights of life and liberty in the persons of a distant people who never offended him, captivating and carrying them into slavery in another hemisphere or to incur miserable death in their transportation thither . . .. Determined to keep open a market where men should be bought and sold, he has prostituted his negative for suppressing every legislative attempt to prohibit or to restrain this execrable commerce [that is, he has opposed efforts to prohibit the slave trade].[9]

We do not see this indictment in the Declaration of Independence because South Carolina and other Southern states pressed to have it removed. After they etched their separation from the British into the history books, the next step for our Founding Fathers was to create a functional government. They didn't agree on everything, but they did agree that there would be no more kings.

They were embarking on a journey that few people had ever taken. The idea that people could actually elect their own leaders was a radical one. It was while they were establishing the shape and parameters of the new government that their disagreements over taxation and representation came to a head. Representation was based on population, and this meant that the Southern states would have fewer representatives than the Northern states. To remedy this, the Southern states wanted to count slaves as part of their population. This did not make sense to the Northern states, who insisted that since slaves did not own property, they did not have the right to vote.

A compromise was finally reached in which each slave was counted as three-fifths of a person. In other words, a group of 500 slaves would be counted as 300 people. James Wilson, who opposed slavery, was the one who proposed the three-fifths compromise.

Our founders had a difficult choice to make. They could accept the compromise and unify the country or refuse to compromise and tear the new nation apart before it could ever establish self-rule. We must remember that both sides wanted to establish states that were unified. If the North did not hold its ground, then the South could have run roughshod over them and further expanded slavery. The Northern delegates set aside their morality in favor of establishing a unified country. Thus, in 1787 the three-fifths compromise was agreed upon and placed in Article 1, Section 2, of the Constitution:

> Representatives and direct taxes shall be apportioned among the several states which may be included within this Union,

according to their respective numbers, which shall be determined by adding to the whole number of free persons, including those bound to service for a term of years, and excluding Indians not taxed, three-fifths of all other persons.

Now, many liberals point to this three-fifths compromise as an example of how racist the United States has always been. Although it is immoral to consider a person not whole, the reasoning for the unpalatable compromise is ignored by many progressives and leftists. Since America has almost always been divided between the North and South, the North wanted to abolish slavery while the South wanted to advance it. Whichever region had the most power would be able to advance their agenda. The South wanted more representation so that they could have more power to push pro-slavery laws and regulations. To succeed in this, the South wanted to count slaves as full people to gain more representation. The North wanted slaves not to be counted at all because they understood what the South was trying to do. This is an important concept, because the North understood that slaves were people and should be counted in full, but if they did count them then it would only hurt the anti-slavery movement rather than advance it. Talk about being caught on the horns of a dilemma.

Gouverneur Morris of Pennsylvania was one of those who opposed counting slaves for purposes of political representation. Morris said,

> The inhabitant of Georgia and South Carolina who goes to the coast of Africa, and in defiance of the most sacred laws of humanity tears away his fellow creatures from their dearest connections and damns them to the most cruel bondages, shall have more votes in a government instituted for protection of the rights of mankind, than the citizen of Pennsylvania or New Jersey who views with a laudable horror so nefarious a practice.[10]

Morris thought the state should buy all the slaves and then set them free. It is hard to say if something like that was even feasible, but it does show the North's zeal for abolishing slavery. Morris suggested that "instead of attempting to blend incompatible things, let us at once take a friendly leave of each other. There can be no end of demands for security if every particular interest is to be entitled to it."[11]

The South's response to Morris came from Pierce Butler of South Carolina who said, "The security the Southern states want is that their negroes may not be taken from them."[12]

By the start of 1801, there were approximately 5.3 million people in the American states and about 900,000 were slaves. Over the next thirty years, the number of slaves increased by 1.1 million.

MISSED OPPORTUNITIES

Our forefathers had multiple opportunities to end the progression of slavery in America. The first time was in 1619, when slaves were first being imported into the New World. They could have emancipated them then but did not. The second time was during Thomas Jefferson's first draft of the Declaration of Independence and lastly during the creation of the Constitution. We must understand that the framers wanted to end slavery, but their main objective was to establish a union with a functional government. Unfortunately, the abolition of slavery took a backseat to that monumental task.

UNCHARTED TERRITORY

In the late 1700s and early 1800s, North America was inhabited not only by those who considered themselves to be Americans, but also by Native Americans, the British, Spanish, and French. Much of the land had yet to be explored. Thomas Jefferson set his eyes on this uncharted territory, the lands on the other side of the trans-Appalachian West. Land was not even Jefferson's priority at the time. He was interested in boosting the economy and wanted a trade route that would allow goods to be transported down the Mississippi River to the Gulf of Mexico. In order for this to happen, Jefferson had to purchase the port of New Orleans, which was owned by the French. The French not only offered New Orleans but more than 800,000 square miles of land, stretching all the way to present-day Montana, for $15 million. The Louisiana Purchase nearly doubled the size of the newly independent United States.

To put the price of this expansion into perspective, the $15 million spent for all that land in Jefferson's day would be worth an estimated $2.8 billion today, and that wasn't the only cost of westward expansion. A high price was also paid in terms of Native American lives and property. Just as slavery was a dark moment in America's history, so too was the removal of native peoples from their inherited lands. Although many Native Americans assimilated into a European lifestyle, most of them wanted to stay on their ancestral lands. They did not view land as something to be bought or sold as the newcomers did but as a sacred object given for all to use. To them, the very thought of putting up fences to keep others out was preposterous. They were willing to fight and die for the land that had sustained their ancestors for centuries.

In the early 1800s, a powerful Shawnee chief named Tecumseh forged an alliance with several other tribes and the British in order to stop American expansion. Although he and his warriors fought valiantly, the alliance began to fall apart after Tecumseh was killed in the Battle of the Thames on October 5, 1813. Just a few months later, on March 27, 1814, members of the Creek Tribe, who were British allies, fought Andrew Jackson and his troops at the Battle of Horseshoe Bend. The Indians were outnumbered by three-to-one and suffered a devastating defeat.

Resounding American victories in these and other battles led to the Indian Removal Act which, over the course of twenty-five years, would exile Creek, Choctaw, Chickasaw, Seminole, and Cherokee Indians from their traditional lands. This removal paved the way for the Trail of Tears, in which an estimated 60,000 Indians were forcibly removed from their homelands in the southeastern United States and marched thousands of miles to the west, to land the government had designated as "Indian Territory." The journey was a long, difficult one during which thousands died from exposure, disease, and starvation. Thousands more died shortly after reaching their new "home."

As we've already said, this was a dark time in American history, and frankly, there is no excuse for the way our ancestors treated the Indian people, especially in light of Thomas Jefferson's words about all men being created equal.

I believe that it's important to recognize an evil that our country has committed. But at the same time, we must recognize that we are not alone in our guilt. As I mentioned previously, Native American tribes were raiding and pillaging each other's villages long before the Europeans showed up. Raiding parties would often take the other tribe's men, women, and children as prisoners. These prisoners would commonly be used as slaves to work the land. It was not uncommon for them to scalp the Indians they were attacking or savagely mutilate the bodies of their enemies. All too often the Left treats the natives as the peaceful characters we see in movies, where they sing with each other, smoke peyote, and live as one with the land.

Although there is some truth to this, it was not the everyday life of an Indian. Two statements can be true at the same time. What the United States did to the Indians was unacceptable, brutal, and inhumane. What the Indians did to each other was also savage, unacceptable, brutal, and inhumane. My goal is not to diminish the injustice that was done, but rather to point out that the situation was extremely complex.

Five
AMERICA'S FIGHT AGAINST SLAVERY

Between 1820 and 1849, America saw the Missouri Compromise enacted, the Alamo was overrun by Mexico's forces under Santa Anna, and Texas became an independent Republic after the Battle of San Jacinto. The Mexican American War took place in 1846, ending with the Treaty of Guadalupe Hidalgo and the annexation by the United States of California, New Mexico, Nevada, Utah, most of Arizona and Colorado, and parts of Oklahoma, Kansas, and Wyoming.

This expansion did not come without attempts to limit the scope of slavery in the United States. For example, the Missouri Compromise banned slavery in any territory that was bought in the Louisiana Purchase. Unfortunately, the compromise was declared unconstitutional in 1857 by the Supreme Court in its decision in the case of *Dred Scott v. Sandford*.

Chief Justice Roger Taney, who wrote the infamous decision upholding slavery, was a Southerner and a Democrat. Taney believed that our Founding Fathers did not intend Africans to be a part of the phrase "all men are created equal." His belief was based on the fact that many of our Founding Fathers, including Thomas Jefferson, had owned slaves. He reasoned that this meant they could not really have believed that all men, specifically black men, were created equal. Taney reasoned that, if they had believed this, they certainly would have set their slaves free.

This idea should sound familiar since the leftists and Democrats state the exact same thing today. In Dinesh D'Souza's book, *Death of a Nation*, he examines the Left's logic:

> Taney's reasoning in *Dred Scott* is identical with that of contemporary progressive critics of the founding. Like him, they agree that the framers were white supremacists who had no intention of including blacks in the Declaration of Independence. This is significant because of what came out of Taney's reasoning, namely his disturbing conclusion that the right to own slaves is "expressly affirmed" in the Constitution and that blacks have "no rights which the white man was about to respect." Moreover, "The Negro might justly and lawfully be reduced to slavery for his benefit." Was Taney's constitutional reasoning sound? If progressives today are right about the framers and the Constitution, it follows that Taney was also right about them, because his logic is the same as theirs. And if Taney was right, then *Dred Scott* was right in affirming that blacks have no constitutional rights and Congress has no power to restrict slavery in the territories.[1]

The Dred Scott case furthered the divide between the North and South as well as between the Republicans and Democrats. Many Americans saw the divide, including Abraham Lincoln, who said:

> A house divided against itself, cannot stand. I believe this government cannot endure permanently half slave and half free. I do not expect the Union to be dissolved—I do not expect the house to fall—but I do expect it will cease to be divided. It will become all one thing or all the other. Either the opponents of slavery will arrest the further spread of it and place it where

the public mind shall rest in the belief that it is in the course of ultimate extinction; or its advocates will push it forward, till it shall become lawful in all the States, old as well as new—North as well as South.[2]

When the Left and Democrats speak of the divide over slavery, they describe it in terms of the North against the South. They do this because they don't want to admit that it was also a battle between Democrats and Republicans. The Democrats were pro-slavery and the Republicans were pro-abolition. The leftists among us are quick to ask for reparations, but I've never heard them say that the Democratic Party should foot the bill. I find it ironic that the same people who say that America is a systemically racist, evil country are content to be members of the party of slavery.

WHITE MEN DIED FOR FREEDOM

Another thing these people ignore is the fact that thousands upon thousands of white men fought in the Civil War to liberate blacks from slavery. Approximately 326,000 Union soldiers died from combat, starvation, or disease. The brave men who marched into battle to make all men free sang these words from *The Battle Hymn of the Republic*:

> In the beauty of the lilies Christ was born across the sea,
> With a glory in His bosom that transfigures you and me;
> As He died to make men holy, let us die to make men free!

These soldiers believed that all men were created equal, just as the Founding Fathers did. If they didn't believe this, they would not have sacrificed their lives. If they didn't believe that black Americans were equal to white Americans, they never would have paid the ultimate sacrifice. To make sure these great men did not die for nothing, Lincoln issued the

Emancipation Proclamation, which was ratified by a Republican Congress, and read in part "Neither slavery nor involuntary servitude, except as a punishment for crime whereof the party shall have been duly convicted, shall exist within the United States, or any place subject to their jurisdiction."

The Thirteenth Amendment, prohibiting slavery, was passed into law 84 years after the signing of the Declaration of Independence. This might seem like a long time, but remember that it is not easy to put an end to something that has been around for thousands of years. America was among the first countries in the world to prohibit slavery, but the change took years and cost thousands of lives.

Today, we have come to expect change to happen in an instant. Thanks to the internet, we can access information, commodities, and services at the click of a button. At the time of the Civil War, 160 years ago, it took time for information to spread, as well as time to ingest that information. Today, we have time for leisure activities and to pursue self-transformation, but this was not true for our ancestors.

Nonetheless, the end of slavery was just the beginning. The Republicans' focus was to further achieve the goal of a nation where policies respect the ideal that all men are created equal. The Reconstruction had a government in place that supported the emancipation from slavery and equality for blacks. With Republicans leading the way, Democrats were fearful that it might be the end of their party and were losing hope that slavery could be brought back. During the Reconstruction, Democrats fought hard to save the plantation system, both literally and ideologically.

As Democrats were busy creating the Ku Klux Klan, Republicans passed three important amendments to the Constitution. The first one was the Thirteenth Amendment which abolished slavery. When the amendment came to a vote, only sixteen Democrats out of eighty voted in favor of it. The Fourteenth Amendment granted citizenship to all persons born or naturalized in the United States. This included formerly enslaved people and guaranteed all citizens equal protection of the laws. Lastly, the

Republicans passed the Fifteenth Amendment, which declared that "the right of citizens of the United States to vote shall not be denied or abridged by the United States or by any State on account of race, color, or previous condition of servitude." When both the Fourteenth and Fifteenth Amendments came to a vote, not a single Democrat voted for them. It is astonishing to me that the same party that claims that America is racist, was actually built on a belief of white superiority.

It was also during this time that Republican Hiram Rhodes Revels became the first African American elected to the United States Congress. Revels would not be the only black to serve in Congress during Reconstruction; he was joined by a dozen others. The amendments that Republicans passed would pave the way for the Civil Rights Act of 1964 and the Voting Rights Act of 1965. If we pause for a moment, we can see the tremendous strides the United States has made to live up to the famous words in the Declaration of Independence. The Left has blocked out this overarching story of how America extinguished slavery.

THE FIGHT FOR CIVIL RIGHTS

As the Reconstruction era came to an end, the Democratic Party and white supremacists started to regain control of the South. Democrats had control over the state legislatures and began passing Jim Crow laws that segregated whites and blacks in public transportation, schools, parks, cemeteries, theatres, public pools, phone booths, hospitals, jails, and restaurants. These laws also forbade blacks from living in white neighborhoods. In 1892, Homer Plessy purchased a first-class train ticket on the East Louisiana Railroad and insisted on sitting in the "whites only" section. Plessy, who was already known for his activism, was arrested and jailed. Plessy argued that he was seven-eighths white and one-eighth black but, because of Louisiana law, he was still considered black. He also said that regardless of his race, his treatment was unconstitutional. His case quickly rose to the Supreme Court, where the Justices were charged with ruling whether the Louisiana law requiring racially segregating railway coaches was constitutional.

This was the first test of the Fourteenth Amendment and its meaning, and the Court ruled in an 8–1 majority that the Louisiana law was constitutional on the grounds that the equal protection clause was not violated. The majority held that:

> It could not have been intended to abolish distinctions based on color or to enforce social, as distinguished from political equality, or a commingling of the two races upon terms unsatisfactory to either. Laws permitting, and even requiring, that separation in places where they are liable to be brought into contact do not necessarily imply the inferiority of either race to the other, and have been generally, if not universally, recognized as within the competency of the state legislatures in the exercise of their police power.[3]

The Court argued that if both groups were provided the same thing, then they were equal. The Fourteenth Amendment was created to make everyone equal under the law, but it did not eliminate distinctions based on a person's race. Justice John M. Harlan, who opposed the decision, dissented in his opinion:

> In the eye of the law, there is in this country no superior, dominant, ruling class of citizens. There is no caste here. Our Constitution is colorblind, and neither knows nor tolerates classes among citizens. In respect of civil rights, all citizens are equal before the law. The humblest is the peer of the most powerful... The arbitrary separation of citizens on the basis of race, while they are on a public highway, is a badge of servitude

wholly inconsistent with the civil freedom and the equality before the law established by the Constitution. It cannot be justified upon any legal grounds.[4]

Since *Plessy v. Ferguson* was the first case to challenge the Fourteenth Amendment, it established precedent for all future cases. The Court's decision left a big scar on America. One can see how hard it is to change the culture of a society. There is a case to be made that if the Court had ruled in favor of Plessy, the Civil Rights movement would have advanced more quickly.

A MAN NAMED WASHINGTON

Around the turn of the century, Booker T. Washington rose to fame. Washington was born a slave and, after being emancipated, he gained notoriety for being an educator. He founded the Tuskegee Normal and Industrial Institute, a normal school for African Americans. Washington was a Republican who believed in free labor, free markets, and free people. He also believed that blacks could obtain economic security by acquiring industrial skills. Washington's work in the black community caught the attention of President Theodore Roosevelt, who invited him to the White House. This dinner with the President enraged Democratic racists throughout the South. Why was this a big deal to them? They hated the fact that blacks were inching ever closer to equality with whites.

Another prominent African American at the time was W.E.B. Du Bois. A Harvard-trained sociologist and historian, Du Bois was undoubtedly America's leading African American intellectual. In 1903, Du Bois debuted his book, *Souls of Black Folk*, that strongly attacked Booker T. Washington for his message on black Americans acquiring industrial or vocational training. Du Bois accused Washington of being an Uncle Tom. He felt that the focus of the black community should be solely on civil rights and Washington's advocacy was too economically focused. Du Bois's critique of Washington was quite odd, in that Washington knew he did not have the power to change the political landscape or end segregation. Even though the men had their differences, their goal was still the same: to obtain a better life for African Americans.

As the push for "all men are created equal" continued, the NAACP was established by a group of interracial activists. During this time, the primarily Democratic Ku Klux Klan was experiencing a revival, thanks in large part to white supremacist Thomas Dixon's 1905 book *The Clansman*, and D.W. Griffith's 1915 film *Birth of a Nation*, which also extolled the Klan. This revitalized Klan was not just opposed to equality for blacks but also against full rights and social acceptance for Catholics, Jews, and foreigners. The NAACP called for a boycott of Griffith's film, but the campaign did not have the success the NAACP expected. Two years later, the NAACP started another campaign that included mass demonstrations to protest lynching and other violence against blacks. Thousands of people of all races took part in these protests.

Between 1920 and 1970, thousands of blacks left the rural South and moved to the urban North. Many chose to settle in Harlem, a thriving black community in New York City. By 1930, 72 percent of all blacks in New York City lived in Harlem, some 164,556 people. Living conditions in Harlem were far from stellar. The death rate was 42 percent higher than the city's average, and black-on-black violence rose 60 percent between 1900 and 1927. The lifestyle in Harlem led to novels being written that called the living conditions of blacks "primitive." An African American author, Claude McKay, wrote *Home to Harlem*, a novel that portrayed negative stereotypes about people of color. As a result of this and the Great Depression, the NAACP began to focus more on both economic and political problems facing African Americans, rather than just one or the other.[5]

By 1939, Adolf Hitler's aggression had touched off the Second World War. More than 3 million African Americans served our country in the military, with approximately 500,000 of them being sent overseas. Even as whites and black were fighting a common enemy, they were still segregated into different units. In July 1948, Democratic President Harry S. Truman finally integrated the U.S. Armed Forces by an executive order, mandating that "there shall be equality of treatment and opportunity for all persons in the armed services without regard to race, color, religion, or national origin."[6]

In 1954, under Republican President Dwight Eisenhower, the Fourteenth Amendment was used to challenge segregation in public schools. The Supreme Court gave a unanimous decision on *Brown v. Board of Education*, ruling that segregation based on race in public schools violated the Fourteenth Amendment's call for equal protection under the U.S. Constitution. Just a year later, in Montgomery, Alabama, Rosa Parks refused to give up her bus seat to a white man, resulting in her arrest for violating segregation ordinances. This led to the *Browder v. Goys* case, where the bus segregation seating policy was found to be unconstitutional under the Fourteenth Amendment.

Just ten years later, Martin Luther King would give his "I Have a Dream" speech at the Washington Monument, in front of 250,000 black and white people who had come to the nation's capital to protest racial discrimination. Dr. King's numerous nonviolent campaigns paved the way for the Civil Rights Acts of 1964 and 1965. The Civil Rights Act of 1964 prohibited discrimination on the basis of race, color, religion, sex, or national origin. This act eliminated the application of Jim Crow laws. The Voting Rights Act of 1965 aimed to overcome legal barriers at the state and local levels that had historically prevented African Americans from exercising their right to vote as guaranteed under the Fifteenth Amendment to the U.S. Constitution. A few years later the Fair Housing Act addressed the matter of racial discrimination in the sale, rental, or financing of housing. By the early 1970s, the Jefferson's idea that "all men are created equal" started to see its realization in America. Shirley Chisholm, the first African

American woman elected to the U.S. Congress, became the first female candidate to run for President of the United States America also saw a rise in African American musicians, actors, and politicians. Throughout the 1980s, African American artists and performers such as Michael Jackson, Eddie Murphy, Richard Prior, Debbie Allen, Prince, Emmanuel Lewis, Magic Johnson, Ice Cube, Tina Turner, Russell Simmons, Will Smith, Oprah Winfrey, and many others would rise to celebrity status.

In the 1990s America would be introduced to Denzel Washington, Tupac Shakur, Snoop Dogg, Shaquille O'Neal, Jaleel White, Arsenio Hall, Jamie Foxx, Michael Jordan, Martin Lawrence, Jada Smith, Brandy Norwood, Steve Harvey, Sinbad, Whoopi Goldberg, and others. Today, the list of black American celebrities who have made an impact on culture and are looked up to as role models by youth around the world is virtually unending.

If we take a moment to pull back and look at the big picture of the Civil Rights movement, we can see how things started very slowly, but then sped up to bring about massive changes in a relatively brief period of time. I believe that as technology and access to information advanced more and more quickly so did the level of cultural and social awareness in America. We witnessed the Civil Rights Movement in the 1960s, and then in the early 2000s, we saw some of the greatest changes in America's history. In 2008, Barack Obama was inaugurated as the forty-fourth President of the United States and the first black man to hold the office. Most recently, in January 2021, Kamala Harris became the first female and the first black woman to hold the office of Vice President of the United States.

AMERICA'S OVERARCHING STORY

The overarching story of our country's history is not that we are inherently racist, but rather that we have been making steady, consistent progress to eradicate racism from the time we became an independent nation. There can be no doubt that there were once many racist institutions in the United States. Shameful things were done in the name of white supremacy, but most Americans have joined hands to eradicate those racist organizations.

I am not denying that there is still racism in America. Unfortunately, this is the case. But we are making great strides toward racial equality and unity, and I believe our future in this regard looks very bright. I also believe that many people on the Left love to take the injustices of the past, ignore a few generations of progress, and throw those injustices in people's faces today when racism is at an all-time low.

I realize that some leftists genuinely believe there is more racism today than in the 1960s or before, but I believe they are wrong. One of these is historians, John Hope Franklin, said, "Jefferson didn't mean it when he wrote that all men are created equal. We've never meant it. The truth is that we're a bigoted people and always have been. We think every other country is trying to copy us now and if they are, God help the world."[7]

Historians like Franklin look at history with tunnel vision rather than standing back and looking at the big picture. Have you ever seen the famous collage of Abraham Lincoln, where hundreds of pictures are pieced together to make up a photo of our sixteenth president? Stand close to that collage, and you will see only a picture of Lincoln. But stand back a bit and you will see all the smaller pictures that make up the larger one. Only then can you understand the overarching picture. Progressives and leftists are standing too close to the collage and need to stand back to see how far we've come and understand what the Founding Father's intentions were. The fact is that Jefferson did believe that all men are created equal as well as that slavery should be abolished. Now that we have a big picture of America's history, we must examine our founders' philosophy to find out if the leftists are correct.

In the modern era, leftists claim that America's Founding Fathers never intended for blacks to be included in the phrase "all men are created equal." In order to see if this is true, we have to consider the fact that in the culture in which those men were raised slavery was commonplace. Slaves were being bought and sold throughout the world in the eighteenth century. According to Henry Louis Gates, over the period of 1525 to 1866, 12.5 million Africans were shipped to the New World through the transatlantic slave trade.[8] This is surely not an excuse for slavery, nor is it a "Get Out of Jail Free" card for our ancestors. But it does show that the United States is not alone with regard to its guilt over slavery.

Remember that the original draft of the Declaration of Independence had a provision that blamed the British for importing slaves into America, but the Southern states demanded that this language be removed. From the very beginning, many in this country have been opposed to slavery.

Some forty-one of the fifty-six signers of the Declaration of Independence were slaveholders, but others spoke out vehemently against slavery. In fact, one of the most famous founders, Benjamin Franklin, was head of the Pennsylvania Abolition Society. Franklin stated,

> That mankind are all formed by the same Almighty Being, alike objects of his care, and equally designed for the enjoyment of happiness, the Christian religion teaches us to believe . . .. [We] earnestly entreat your serious attention to the subject of slavery—that you will be pleased to countenance the restoration of liberty to those unhappy men who alone in this land of freedom are degraded into perpetual bondage and who…are groaning in servile subjection.[9]

Another founder, John Adams, said "every measure of prudence, therefore, ought to be assumed for the eventual total extirpation of slavery from the United States . . . . I have, through my whole life, held the practice of slavery in abhorrence."[10]

In addition, there were slaveholders who wanted to see slavery come to an end. For example, George Washington said, "I can only say that there is not a man living who wishes more sincerely than I do to see a plan adopted for the abolition of it [slavery]."[11] The writer of the Declaration, Thomas Jefferson, who was also a slaveholder, said slavery was a "moral blot" and a "hideous depravity."[12]

If the founders knew slavery was immoral and believed it should be eliminated, why did they hold slaves? One answer is that a person can know that something is a sin and still commit that sin. In the Bible's book of Romans, the apostle Paul writes, "For I do not understand what I am doing; for I am not practicing what I want *to do*, but I do the very thing I hate" (Rom. 7:15). In our everyday lives we often do things we know we shouldn't do. Our transgressions may not be as egregious as slavery, but still, most of us occasionally do things we hate. The founders knew slavery was evil, yet some of them still held slaves. Moreover, the cultural change to eliminate slavery started before the founding of the United States.

Northern reformers passed manumission acts beginning in the late 1700s. These acts allowed slaveholders to free their slaves at any time without the approval of the government. As I mentioned earlier, in 1775, the world's first abolitionist group, the Quaker Anti-Slavery Society, was founded in Pennsylvania. Northerners routinely freed their slaves or allowed them to buy their freedom so that there were only 3,000 slaves in all of the North by 1830, compared to more than 2 million in the South.[13] Roughly a year after the Quaker Anti-Slavery Society was formed, the Continental Congress reiterated a prohibition in the nonimportation agreement against the importation of African slaves, despite repealing the rest.[14] During the War of Independence, many proposals were sent to Congress asking for slaves who fought during the Revolution to be freed. As you might guess, the Southern Colonies blocked these requests.

Once the war ended, many Northern states submitted proposals to Congress. New Hampshire (1779), Pennsylvania (1780), Massachusetts (1783), Rhode Island (1784), and Connecticut (1784) all expressly forbade slavery in their constitutions, adopted immediate or gradual emancipation plans or had courts declare slavery unconstitutional.[15] In 1778, Jefferson put forward a bill that would ban the importation of slaves into the state of Virginia. His hope was that this would be slavery's "final eradication."[16] Jefferson also wrote in his *Notes on the State of Virginia* that he imagined a time after 1800 when all slaves would be free. The evidence suggests that Thomas Jefferson meant exactly what he said when he wrote that "all men" are created equal.

INDEPENDENCE VS. SLAVERY

Although many of our country's founders wanted to free the slaves, they felt that their first priority had to be achieving independence from England. They invested all of their energy into creating a republic but wisely wrote, "We hold these truths to be self-evident, that all men are created equal, that they are endowed by their Creator with certain unalienable Rights, that among these are Life, Liberty and the pursuit of Happiness." Their hope was that after a union was formed, all other problems, including slavery, would be resolved as time went on.

The Left cannot understand that the founders had to choose the lesser of two evils. The framers had to negotiate with one another and find ideals they could agree on, while working through others that they didn't agree on. The Left likes to pretend that our patriarchs had the choice of having a country based on slavery or having a country based on anti-slavery. The reality is that the only options were to have a country that would allow slavery for a brief time or not have a country at all. The Left's answer to the lesser of the two evils is to not have had a country at all. If our forefathers had chosen to do this, it is likely that the South would have formed their own union and would have created an economic stronghold where slavery would have endured in North America for many years beyond 1865.

The founders ultimately chose the wiser of the two options by deciding to have a country that was anti-slavery in principle, if not in practice. They imprinted the principle of anti-slavery in the Declaration of Independence. Lincoln saw the underlying principle that all men are created equal and devoted his life to making our forefathers' dream of abolition come true. Lincoln compared slavery to a man who has cancer "which he dares not cut out at once, lest he bleed to death; with the promise, nevertheless, that the cutting may begin at the end of a given time." Both Lincoln and America's early patriots saw slavery as a malignancy that must be tolerated for a time but ultimately must be removed. They were confident that slavery would not hold a permanent place in American society. The statements of our Founding Fathers and the documents they wrote would later be echoed by Lincoln and others in their fight against slavery.

It is not just conservatives and Republicans today who understand the compromise that had to be made. Ex-slave and abolitionist leader, Frederick Douglass, acknowledged the fact that it was a good decision, as it kept the South in the Union, which would allow the North to slowly chisel away at the South's pro-slavery agenda. Douglass said, "I am, therefore, for drawing the bond of Union more closely, and bringing the slave States more completely under the power of the free States."[17] It has always been astonishing to me that an ex-slave could see the big picture of what America was trying to do, but those who have never been enslaved cannot.

In his book, *Death of a Nation*, Dinesh D'Souza shares how Lincoln himself understood the overarching story of how the founders intended all men to be equal. Dinesh writes:

> Of the Declaration's assertion of equality, Lincoln said of the founders, "They did not mean to assert the obvious untruth, that all were then enjoying that equality, nor yet, that they were about to confer it immediately upon them. In fact, they had no power to confer such a boon. They meant simply to declare the right, so that the enforcement of it might follow as fast as circumstances should permit."[18]

Certainly, our Founding Fathers had their faults and transgressions. This does not change the fact that they laid the foundation for the greatest country the world has ever seen. History has proven that the founding documents encompassed ideas, and especially those ideas referring to personal liberty, which had never been tried before. With its founding principles in place, America would in time abolish slavery and establish equal rights under the law. The progressives and leftists love to call the founders white supremacists, racists, and bigots, but the truth is that, if not for the aspirations of those great men, this country's moral and political foundations would not exist. It's only because of them and their revolutionary ideas that we can live together as equals today!

THE PARTY OF SLAVES AND RACISM

The Left likes to say that the Republican Party is the party of racism and white supremacy, but that is simply not true. History tells us that the Democratic Party is the party of slaves, plantations, the Ku Klux Klan, Jim Crow laws, and racism. Our liberal friends have magically changed the story through the use of revisionist history, adding and subtracting events to fit their narrative, regardless of what really happened. But let's take a look and see who was really holding America back from abolishing slavery and eliminating white supremacy.

In 1793, Eli Whitney invented a machine that would revolutionize not just textile production but slavery. His innovative cotton gin was a device used to separate seeds from cotton. Prior to the arrival of the cotton gin, it would take a slave one hour to process a pound of raw cotton by hand; afterward, a slave could process anywhere from six pounds to ten pounds of cotton in an hour. Southern cotton production grew from 3,000 bales a year to 73,000 bales in just a decade. By 1810, cotton production would soar to 178,000 bales. The production boom and labor demand made slave labor more important to the Southern economy than ever.

As you can imagine, the increase in production meant an increase in capital. Southern cotton planters quickly became the richest people in the country. That amount of wealth came with great power, and the plantation owners knew they needed to protect their assets with political dominance. Why would the Southern plantation owners need political power if America was systemically racist? As shown previously, there were powerful anti-slavery movements already happening during the time of the revolution. The anti-slavery movement became so powerful that it even started to change the minds of Southerners. Virginian Founding Father, Patrick Henry, who famously said "give me liberty or give me death" urged his fellow Southerners to look for a time "when an opportunity will be offered to abolish this lamentable evil."[19] The Southern states even agreed to the Northwest Ordinance that prohibited slavery or involuntary servitude north of the Ohio River. How did the culture go from moving towards anti-slavery back to pro-slavery?

What happened was that Southern plantation owners banded together against the anti-slavery movement. Their mission was to stop the flow of information from anti-slavery advertisements. (Does this strategy sound familiar? It should.) This campaign was successful in swinging the culture back to pro-slavery. This shows how much power a group can have when they learn how to choke the flow of information. By the 1830s, Southern states had passed laws that prohibited teaching slaves and black people to read and write. If the law was violated, it could result in a fine, imprisonment, or floggings.

As plantation owners in the South became wealthier, they needed political security. The Democratic Party, which had been formed in 1828 by Andrew Jackson, represented the interests of slave owners in the North and South. The Democrats believed that enslavement was a "positive good." Robert Walsh, a physician and writer, expressed the idea that slavery was a benefit, writing "The physical condition of the American Negro is on the whole . . . positively good, and he is exempt from those racking anxieties—the exacerbates of despair."[20] Walsh was making the claim that slaves were happier being enslaved than they would be under freedom because they did not have to deal with the anxieties that a free laborer would. James Henry Hammond, Congressman for South Carolina, and a pro-slavery advocate, echoed this in an 1836 speech, saying,

> Slavery is said to be an evil . . . But it is no evil. On the contrary, I believe it to be the greatest of all the great blessings which a kind Providence has bestowed upon our glorious region.. . . As a class, I say it boldly; there is not a happier, more contented race upon the face of the earth . . . Lightly tasked, well clothed, well fed—far better than the free laborers of any country in the world . . . their lives and persons protected by the law, all their sufferings alleviated by the kindest and most interested care . . .. Sir, I do firmly believe that domestic slavery regulated as ours is produces the highest toned, the purest, best organization of society that has ever existed on the face of the earth.[12]

Hammond also makes the claim that slaves are happier than those who are free laborers. To this, I can only say, "Nonsense!"

No one was more outspoken about the benefits of slavery than Democratic Senator John C. Calhoun. Calhoun argued,

> Never before has the black race of Central Africa, from the dawn of history to the present day, attained a condition so civilized and so improved, not only physically, but morally and intellectually . . .. It came to us in a low, degraded, and savage condition, and in the course of a few generations it has grown up under the fostering care of our institutions.[22]

Calhoun and his fellow Democrats believed that blacks were an inferior race and did not have the intelligence to exercise their freedom properly.

In 1854, the Republican Party was created with the main goal of abolishing slavery. Unfortunately, the Republicans would have an uphill battle, especially after the *Dred Scott v. Sandford* case ruled in favor of slavery. Seven of the nine Justices on the U.S. Supreme Court were Democrats and all of them voted in favor of slavery. The other two justices were, of course, Republicans and dissented. Many historians regard the *Dred Scott* case as the instigator to the Civil War.

A Republican commander-in-chief would lead the Union to victory and fulfill the founders' principles. Once the war was won, many slaves secured their freedom, started new lives, and even ran for Congress. By 1900, twenty-two black Republicans had been elected to Congress. The Democrat Party did not elect a black person to Congress until 1935.

Republicans went on to create the Civil Rights Act, which declared that all people born in the United States were U.S. citizens and had certain inalienable rights, including the right to make contracts, to own property, to sue in court, and to enjoy the full protection of federal law.[23] Congress passed the Act but it was vetoed by Democratic President Andrew Johnson. Fortunately, Republicans had enough representation to override his veto. Republicans also wanted to give freed slaves access to education and give them land that had been confiscated from the Confederacy. This would be America's first attempt at reparations—and, yes, it was the Republicans who tried reparations and not the Democrats. These reparations would be historically remembered as "forty acres and a mule." Andrew Johnson later restored this Confederate land back to plantation owners, ultimately dissolving the promise of forty acres and a mule.

As the Republican Party continued to live up to the Founding Fathers' principles, Democrats formed an organization called the Ku Klux Klan. The Klan eventually expanded throughout every Southern state, and was the main force used to resist the Republicans. Historian Eric

Foner describes the Klan as a "military force serving the interests of the Democratic Party."[24] Members of the Klan created underground campaigns, similar to what Antifa does today, to intimidate and commit acts of violence against black and white Republicans. The Klan also tortured and murdered blacks who supported the Republican Party. As sick as it sounds, vast crowds turned out to view this "entertainment." They brought blankets, food, and drinks to watch while men were being brutally and publicly lynched. In 1871, Republicans passed the Ku Klux Klan Act that designated certain crimes committed by individuals as federal offenses, including conspiracies to deprive citizens of the right to hold office, serve on juries, and enjoy the equal protection of the law.[25] This political pushback crushed the Klan's activity and caused the organization to close its doors for a short time. It should be noted that during the same time the KKK sprang up, dozens of other domestic terror groups were established by Democrats—also known as Dixiecrats—throughout the South.

Slavery was over, and the Democratic Party needed to use whatever cards they had left to regain power. One of those cards was racism. If they could not be above the blacks through enslavement, Democrats made damn sure they would be above them in all other aspects.

As we've noted previously, by 1915, the Ku Klux Klan reappeared after the release of G.W. Griffith's film *Birth of a Nation*, which portrayed Klansmen as heroes, preserving genteel Southern culture against barbarian blacks. The new Klan was not just a scare tactic but also a weapon to keep blacks and others from voting and trying to exercise their other rights. Democrats didn't just stop at terror tactics but also attacked blacks with state-sponsored segregation. Every single segregation law passed in the South was done through a Democratic legislature, and segregation spread throughout the South.

Racism continued all the way into Franklin D. Roosevelt's presidency. This is quite interesting because even today Democrats champion FDR as one of the greatest, if not the greatest, presidents in American history.

Throughout FDR's presidency, he was friends with Klan members and campaigned for Klan members. In 1934, FDR campaigned for Mississippi Democrat Theodor Bilbo to win his Senate election race. Bilbo had been a member of the Klan for many years and FDR still supported him. Both FDR and Bilbo worked to subdue anti-lynching legislation and racial integration in the armed forces, and they worked together for the New Deal. It is not odd to hear about a Democrat supporting racism and white supremacy, but it is weird that Democrats today idolize a president who supported such things.

Roosevelt did not just assist congressmen who were in the Ku Klux Klan; he also nominated a member of the Klan, Hugo Black, to the Supreme Court. Black was not just a passive member; he joined rallies, parades, and spoke at nearly 150 Klan meetings. It should come as no surprise that Black also supported FDR's New Deal. Another pro-segregationist and supporter of the New Deal was democratic Senator Sam Rayburn. Rayburn not only supported segregation but also resisted civil rights for African Americans. One can see a common theme in the men FDR chose as his allies. They believed that blacks should be suppressed.

Although these are only a few examples of the men FDR worked with himself, Hugo Black hinted that there were many more when he said,

> President Roosevelt told me there was no reason for my worrying about having been a member of the Ku Klux Klan. He said that some of his best friends and supporters were strong members of that organization. He never in any way, by word or attitude, indicated any doubt about my having been in the Klan nor did he indicate any criticism of me for having been a member of that organization.[26]

Though many on the left say that FDR did not really know who any of these men were, the evidence suggests that this is not true. Why is all of this important? It shows that the Democrats were racist well into the 1930s and there is something behind the fact that these same Democrats were big supporters of the New Deal. They wanted to secure Democratic power, but they also wanted to suppress blacks. The answer to this was to create a welfare state, starting with the New Deal and carrying it on to today.

BLACKS IN A RACIST PARTY

Events throughout history show that the Democratic Party was still racist into the 1930s, a majority of black Americans switched to the Democratic Party during that time. The switch of blacks going from the Republican Party to the Democratic Party happened predominantly in just four years. In 1932, FDR received less than 33 percent of the black vote, but by 1936 he received 75 percent of that vote. You would be right to ask the question, "Why would blacks leave the party of anti-slavery, anti-segregation, the creators of the Thirteenth, Fourteenth, and Fifteenth Amendments, and join the party of white supremacy?" The short answer is that things were so bad during the great depression that the benefits of the New Deal attracted black voters. As the benefits expanded into LBJ's presidency, blacks gave overwhelming support to Democrats in exchange for governmental benefits.

The New Deal included relief and public works programs that were open to unemployed people of all races. The Works Progress Administration (WPA) was by far the most important program in the New Deal for blacks. The WPA gave black workers skilled jobs and fair wages. Furthermore, the WPA, PWA, and other New Deal public works programs made special efforts to focus on disadvantaged black communities by providing health clinics, hospitals, and immunizations as well as new schools, college buildings, and special courses; and recreation facilities, staff, and programs.[27] The welfare state continued to expand over the years and has allowed the Democratic Party to secure the African American vote for decades. The

Democrats who once were the party of the physical plantation, became the party of the metaphorical plantation.

One of FDR's successors was Lyndon Baines Johnson, who took office upon the assassination of John Kennedy. Just as they praise FDR, Democrats today praise LBJ for establishing his vision of "The Great Society." LBJ was indeed a racist. Many leftists would ask, "How could a man who helped and reformed various programs that helped the African American community be racist?" The first piece of evidence is that LBJ nominated Thurgood Marshall to the Supreme Court. There were other black candidates who were just as qualified, such as Judge A. Leon Higginbotham, but LBJ told a staffer, "The only two people who ever heard of Judge Higginbotham are you and his momma. When I appoint a nigger to the court, I want everyone to know he's a nigger."[28]

This was not the only time LBJ used this kind of language. There was an incident when LBJ was a senator when he not only called his chauffeur, Robert Parker, a nigger but also compared him to a piece of furniture. Parker said that LBJ asked him what he would like to be called, "boy, nigger, or chief?" Parker wanted to be called by his name, but LBJ lashed out at him, saying "Let me tell you one thing, nigger. As long as you're black, and you're going to be black till the day you die, no one's gonna call you by your goddamn name. So, no matter what you are called, nigger, you just let it roll off your back like water and you'll make it. Just pretend you're a goddamn piece of furniture."[29]

You might think that anyone who spearheaded civil rights legislation could not be racist, but remember that it's all about power; keeping the black vote while also holding them on the metaphorical plantation. In his book, *Inside the White House*, Ronald Kessler describes a conversation between LBJ and two governors. Allegedly, LBJ told the governors, "I'll have them niggers voting Democratic for two hundred years."[30] Somehow, it is okay for LBJ to use this kind of language, but if someone on the Right were to say such things, he or she would be labeled a racist. And rightly so.

The Civil Rights Act was passed because of Republicans. Revisionist historians and leftist history teachers do not talk about this in class. They say it was the Democrats who pushed the Civil Rights Acts through Congress. But the official Congress voting records show that 80 percent of Republicans in the House voted yes, and 82 percent of Republicans in the Senate voted yes. How about the Democrats? Only 61 percent of Democrats in the House voted yes and 69 percent in the Senate. To put this in perspective, if Congress consisted entirely of Democrats, this historic law would not have passed.

The fact is that LBJ knew that racism was on the decline in America. He knew the Civil Rights movement would be popular. Plus, the Democrats needed the black vote to stay in power. This is where the expanded governmental programs came into effect. LBJ could kill two birds with one stone. He could secure the black vote for years to come and keep the blacks suppressed. To do this, LBJ increased the budget to allow for food stamps, housing, health care, welfare checks, and retirement checks. In the black community, it was no longer a father or mother supporting a family but the government. This metaphorical plantation was so effective that we can still see it forty years later in Democrat-run areas.

During a Young America's Foundation speech, Dinesh D'Souza perfectly explained the correlation between the physical plantation and the metaphorical plantation. To make the connections Dinesh pulled from Kenneth Stampp's novel, *The Peculiar Institutions*, where Stampp lays out key attributes that an observer would see on a slave plantation: Number one, broken down, dilapidated, unsafe housing; Number two, broken families; Number three, a high degree of violence required to hold the place together—police power, whippings, overseers, fences, barbed wire; Number four, everybody gets a basic provision—you need food, you have healthcare, they call the doctor—but nobody gets ahead. There's no opportunity; nobody really advances.

The Southerners and the Democrats used to call slavery a "school of civilization" and Stampp says, "That's not a school from which anyone ever seemed to graduate. Finally, nihilism and despair. A feeling there is no future, that this is an intergenerational lasting way of life." (These five key attributes that D'Souza points out can be traced back to entirely Democrat dominated inner city areas such as Detroit, Baltimore, and Oakland.

These cities have been run primarily by Democrats for decades. It is not as if the federal government isn't trying to help. The federal government has spent trillions of dollars to improve things in these areas. The problem is that the federal government is giving the Democrats the money to fix problems the Democrats created. Despite all that has been done to help, these inner cities are just as bad, if not worse, than they were in the late 1960s. If the leftists, progressives, and Democrats are going to point to racism for the problems in these historically black communities, they better be pointing at themselves. History has repeatedly shown it is Democratic policies that have created a metaphorical plantation for those in the inner cities. These Democratic policies need to be changed to uplift those in the inner city rather than suppress them.

Six
THE ANTI-POLICE MOVEMENT

A recent tenet of the Left's Trojan horse is that the police are racist and should be defunded. In 2020, the United States saw a crime surge resulting from an economic collapse, rioting, and the lockdown order due to the COVID pandemic. Cities across America did not just see an increase in crime but also in homicides. At the end of 2020, Chicago police reported more than 750 murders, a jump of more than 50 percent compared with 2019. By mid-December, Los Angeles saw a 30 percent increase over the previous year with 322 homicides. There were 437 homicides in New York City, nearly 40 percent more than the previous year.[1] "We're going to see, historically, the largest one-year rise in murder that we've ever seen," said data consultant Jeff Asher, who studied crime rates throughout the United States. He also reported that it has been well over fifty years since a year-to-year murder rate jumped nearly 13 percent.[2]

There was also an increase in rioting during 2020. In the span of just four months, 10,600 demonstrations took place across the country. Some of these demonstrations were peaceful, but others involved arson, vandalism, and looting. An estimated $1.5 million in damage was caused by protests following the death of George Floyd. That number could be as much as $2 billion and possibly more, according to the Insurance Information Institute.[3] Strangely, the Left doesn't blame the rioters for the damage; they blame the police. "This rise in crime is not the fault of the movement. It's actually the fault of the police and this has been our point all along," said MSNBC contributor Brittany Packnett Cunningham.[4] Cunningham was formerly a member of President Obama's Task Force for Twenty-First Century Policing and the Ferguson Commission. This type of language does not come as a surprise from a former member of the Obama administration, which was one of the most anti-law-enforcement administrations in modern history. In 2015, while Obama was president, homicides in the country's fifty largest cities rose nearly 17 percent.[5] To put this increase in perspective, such an increase had not been seen in a quarter century.

Cunningham's statements are tame compared to those of other leftist critics who claim that the police are systemically racist. "I think it's difficult to come to any other conclusion than: there's deep systemic racism within the department, which doesn't mean that every officer is racist, but it does mean that the culture is." Said R. T. Rybak, who was mayor of Minneapolis from 2002 to 2014.[6]

Although Rybak was targeting the Minneapolis police department, this ideology was shared among other leftists throughout the United States. In late August of 2016, Colin Kaepernick, quarterback of the National Football League's San Francisco 49ers, dropped to one knee during the national anthem. When asked why, he declared,

> I am not going to stand up to show pride in a flag for a country that oppresses black people and people of color. To me, this is bigger than football and it would be selfish on my part to look the other way. There are bodies in the street and people getting paid leave and getting away with murder.[7]

As we saw in the previous chapter, leftists believe that America is systemically racist. Kaepernick believes that the police are murdering people of color and getting paid for it. He was also photographed wearing socks with pigs dressed as police officers. When questioned about his socks he answered, "There is police brutality." He added, "People of color have been targeted by police. So that's a large part of it and they're government officials. They are put in place by the government. So that's something that this country has to change."[8] Kaepernick was cheered by the leftist media and celebrities for standing up against the racist establishment.

I believe the campaign against the police is a culture war that cannot be taken lightly. The Left seems to have decided that if one police officer is guilty of an offense, then all police are guilty. But surely, no rational person would believe that because one black person committed a crime, all black people are guilty. The very thought of such a broad characterization is preposterous.

I understand that some people may be offended when I refer to the campaign against police as a war; that may sound too harsh. But it's not, because a war is exactly what it is. Now, briefly, I want to examine the riots that resulted from police shootings more closely. Let's examine the evidence and see if our policemen and women are systemically racist. Are they shooting unarmed black men for no reason? Are they hunting people of color in the streets? Should they be defunded? And what is the result of this leftist narrative?

WHAT HAPPENED IN FERGUSON?

On August 9, 2014, at approximately 11:50 a.m., eighteen-year-old Michael Brown was recorded on a surveillance camera stealing a pack of Swisher Sweet cigars from a convenience store. The video shows that as Brown was walking out of the store, a clerk tried to stop him. Brown shoved the clerk in the throat and walked out the door. Just as any business owner who just got robbed would do, the clerk called the police and gave a description of the perpetrator.

At 11:57 a.m., the police dispatcher relayed the description of the suspect to officers in the area: "a man in a red St. Louis Cardinals hat, a white

T-shirt, yellow socks, and khaki shorts, accompanied by another male."9 Just a few minutes later, Officer Darren Wilson spotted Brown and friend, Dorian Johnson, walking in the middle of the street.

According to Officer Wilson's testimony, he pulled his vehicle up next to the two men and asked them to walk on the sidewalk. According to one witness, Brown responded, "Fuck the police." Wilson told the two to "come here," to which Brown replied, "What the fuck you gonna do?" Johnson and Brown made their way up to Wilson's patrol vehicle. Brown got too close to the vehicle and Wilson told him to back away. This is a common strategy police use for their own protection. During questioning, Brown proceeded to assault Officer Wilson by punching him in the face multiple times. One witness, a black man in his fifties, said that he saw Brown "punching Wilson at least three times in the facial area, through the open driver's window of the SUV."10 Officer Wilson testified that Brown grabbed his gun. As the two men were fighting over the firearm, Wilson attempted to shoot but the gun jammed. He was then able to get a shot off but missed Brown. Brown continued to punch him before another shot went off, missing Brown once again. After that shot, Brown ran, with Officer Wilson chasing him. Multiple witnesses heard Officer Wilson yelling for Brown to stop.

One man said he saw Wilson chase Brown until Brown abruptly turned around. Brown did not put his hands up in surrender, but seemed to shrug his shoulders and then made a full charge at Wilson. Wilson reported that he thought his life was threatened and only fired when Brown was coming toward him.11 Another witness said she saw Brown run from the SUV, followed by Wilson, who "hopped" out of the SUV and ran after him while yelling "Stop! Stop! Stop!" She agreed that Wilson did not fire his gun as Brown ran from him. She reported that Brown stopped, turned around, and "for a second" began to raise his hands as though he may have considered surrendering but then quickly "balled up his fists" and "charged" at Wilson. The witness described it as a "tackle run," explaining that Brown "wasn't going to stop." Wilson fired his gun only as Brown charged at him, backing up as Brown came toward him. Another witness said there were three separate volleys of shots. Each time, Brown ran toward Wilson, Wilson fired, Brown paused, Wilson stopped firing, and then Brown charged again. The pattern continued until Brown fell to the ground, "smashing" his face upon impact. Wilson did not fire while Brown momentarily had his hands up. The witness explained it took some time for Wilson to fire, adding that she "would have fired sooner."[12]

Officer Wilson's testimony aligned with statements from other witnesses, who also said that Brown turned around and started to run at the officer, with one hand in his shirt and the other in his waistband. Wilson continued to yell at Brown to stop and get on the ground. Wilson fired multiple shots at Brown, but Brown continued to charge until he was killed by a shot to the head. A seventy-four-year-old black male who witnessed the shooting told the police that he "would have fucking shot that boy, too."[13]

Following the shooting, Brown's body remained in the street for hours before being removed. The reason for this was that detectives kept getting interrupted by protestors as they tried to process the crime scene. The result of Brown's death led to civil unrest, rioting, looting, and the pushing of false narratives. Rioters taunted police, stood on their vehicles, broke car windows, stole food, alcohol, and consumer products. A convenience store that was near the fatal shooting was burned down and other businesses were damaged and looted.

Dorian Johnson told the media,

> My friend stopped running—his hands immediately went in the air—and he turned around towards the officer face-to-face. He started to tell the officer that he was unarmed and that you should stop shooting me. Before he could get his second sentence out, the officer fired several more shots into his head and chest areas.[14]

According to multiple eyewitnesses, who were also black, this was not true. Time and time again, Johnson's testimony went against witness testimony and forensic evidence but that did not stop the media from spreading rumors about what actually took place on that day. President Obama felt that everyone in the community was telling the truth when he stated, "This is not just an issue in Ferguson, this is an issue for America . . . there are problems and communities of color aren't just making these problems up." This statement by the president was false. Multiple witnesses did in fact lie about their testimonies. Witness number 14 said as much. "You have to understand the mentality of these young guys," he said,

> They have nothing to do. When they latch onto something, they embellish it because they want something to do. The majority of them do not work, all they do is sit around and get high all day . . . . Within one minute of the shooting there were seventy or eighty people saying things that didn't happen and they started embellishing it when the stepfather showed up.[15]

This same witness stated multiple times that witnesses had lied about the events that took place. At least a dozen witnesses were proven to have lied about what they saw.

The media, celebrities, and social justice warriors took to social media to broadcast rumors that Michael Brown had surrendered to the officer with his hands up and said, "Hands up, don't shoot," and that Brown was "shot like an animal."[16] This false narrative of "Hands up, don't shoot" spread throughout the nation, but the Department of Justice destroyed this narrative by stating in their report,

There are no credible witness accounts that state that Brown was clearly attempting to surrender when Wilson shot him. As detailed throughout this report, those witnesses who say so have given accounts that could not be relied upon in a prosecution because they are irreconcilable with the physical evidence, inconsistent with the credible accounts of other eyewitnesses, inconsistent with the witness's own prior statements, or in some instances, because the witnesses have acknowledged that their initial accounts were untrue.[17]

To put it plainly, there was absolutely no evidence to support the "Hands up, don't shoot" narrative, but this did not stop the [resident and the media from pushing this version of events.

In September of 2014, President Barack Obama told world leaders at the United Nations that, "In a summer marked by instability in the Middle East and Eastern Europe, I know the world also took notice of the small American city of Ferguson, Missouri—where a young man was killed, and a community was divided.

So yes, we have our own racial and ethnic tensions."[18] This type of language is typical of a Democrat or leftist. The president was, in essence, making the claim that the shooting was racially motivated because Brown was black and Wilson was white. Black Lives Matter also stirred up violence in Ferguson by focusing on this fabricated narrative.

After the St. Louis County grand jury ruled that Wilson was justified in the shooting, riots broke out once again across the nation. In March of 2015, Attorney General Eric Holder said,

> This morning, the Justice Department announced the conclusion of our investigation and released a comprehensive, eighty-seven-page report documenting our findings and conclusions that the facts do not support the filing of criminal charges against Officer Darren Wilson in this case. Michael Brown's death, though a tragedy, did not involve prosecutable conduct on the part of Officer Wilson.[19]

As far as the Left was concerned, the evidence in the case did not matter. There must have been racism and at the very least a violation of civil rights law. Holder knew that Black Lives Matter and the media were spreading false information about the case, which is why he said,

> I recognize that the findings in our report may leave some to wonder how the department's findings can differ so sharply from some of the initial, widely reported accounts of what transpired. I want to emphasize that the strength and integrity of America's justice system has always rested on its ability to deliver impartial results in precisely these types of difficult circumstances—adhering strictly to the facts and the law, regardless of assumptions. Yet it remains not only valid—but essential—to question how such a strong alternative version of events was able to take hold so swiftly, and be accepted so readily.[20]

Holder needed to find a way to appease the Black Lives Matter movement and show the people that they are not crazy; that racism did exist. How was Holder going to pull this off? Right after the initial investigation, Holder executed a second investigation which would, "determine whether Ferguson police officials have engaged in a widespread pattern or practice of violations of the U.S. Constitution or federal law."[21] Undoubtedly, if Donald Trump had been president at the time he would have been shouting "Witch hunt!" And that's exactly what it was. On one hand Holder could cover his and President Obama's rear ends while, at the same time, helping the Left push their false narrative that the police are systemically racist.

Holder's second report stated, "Between October 2012 and October 2014, despite making up only 67 percent of the population, African Americans accounted for a little over *85 percent* of all traffic stops by the Ferguson Police Department."[22] If someone knew nothing about statistics, they would look at this and say, "It must be racism." The problem is that these numbers don't really tell us anything other than that African

Americans were being pulled over 85 percent of the time. The report also showed that whites made up 29 percent of the population but accounted for only 15 percent of all traffic stops. The report does not tell us why they were being pulled over, what specific traffic violations they were committing, or maybe most importantly, what the rate of traffic violations are between white and black drivers. In Heather Mac Donald's book, *The War on Cops*, she tells of research done in New Jersey and North Carolina which found that black drivers speed disproportionately. For example, on the New Jersey Turnpike, black drivers were twice as likely to speed (with speeding defined as traveling at 15 miles per hour or more above the posted limit).

Moreover, low-income car owners are less likely to update their vehicle registration and maintain required equipment, which means they are more likely to be pulled over for things like expired tags, burned-out headlights, faulty turn signals, and other "minor" violations. Are black drivers in Ferguson more likely to be poor? The *New York Times* itself says that: economic chasms separate black and white neighborhoods there, so this could be one reason why a disproportionate number of black drivers are cited.

Some people won't accept statistical data that doesn't support their preconceived ideas. They feel it can't be possible that African Americans are being stopped for traffic violations more often than other drivers simply because they are committing more traffic violations. In their view, because there is a disparity in race, it must mean that the Ferguson Police Department is racist. As always with leftists and Democrats, it is easier to shout racism than it is to conduct a proper study. If Holder really wanted to find answers, he would have conducted a study on the demographics of different roadways at various times throughout the day and the week. It should also be noted that all Holder did was conduct an observational study of traffic violations. He then proceeded to make cause-and-effect claims based on those observational statistics. The problem with this is that it's impossible to make cause-and-effect claims through observational studies. A properly designed experiment would have to be conducted in order to make the racial claims that Holder is alluding to.

Heather Mac Donald writes:

> The report also seized on the fact that blacks made up 93 percent of arrests by Ferguson police officers. It is unclear whether "arrests" here refers to arrests following a traffic stop or arrests for all types of crime throughout the entire city. Assuming the latter, this figure, too, is meaningless without knowing the black and white crime rates. Blacks made up 60.5 percent of all murder arrests in Missouri in 2012 and 58 percent of all robbery arrests, though they are less than 12 percent of the state's population. Such vast disparities are found in every city and state in the country; there is no reason to think that Ferguson is any different. New York City is typical: blacks are only 23 percent of the population but commit 75 percent of all shootings in the city, as reported by the victims of and witnesses to those shootings; whites commit under 2 percent of all shootings, according to victims and witnesses, though they are 33 percent of the city's population. Blacks commit 70 percent of all robberies; whites, 4 percent. The black-white crime disparity in New York would be even greater without New York's large Hispanic population. Black and Hispanic shootings together account for 98 percent of all illegal gunfire. Ferguson has only a 1 percent Hispanic population, so the contrast between the white and black shares of crime is starker there.[23]

Mac Donald does an excellent job of showing the correlations between cities. These types of statistics can be seen throughout the country, but the Left still insists that our police are systemically racist.

THE ANTI-POLICE MOVEMENT

The Ferguson decision led to unrest in the streets. How did the protesters show their anger at the police? They burned civilian cars and businesses: Walgreens, AutoZone, Little Caesars Pizza, JC Wireless, Public Storage, Beauty World, among others. In total, twenty-five businesses were destroyed, along with twelve cars in just one night of protesting. It cost the taxpayers a minimum of $5.7 million to pay for the massive police response in Ferguson. Becky Yerak of the *Chicago Tribune* stated,

> Last summer, Michael Brown, an unarmed black 18-year-old, was shot and killed by a white police officer in suburban St. Louis. Rioting ensued; the *St. Louis Post-Dispatch* said 28 businesses were reported to have been burglarized Aug. 10, the first night of unrest after the Brown shooting. One local insurance adjuster who processed three claims estimated damages were no more than $5 million. For comparison's sake, the newspaper said, a 2012 St. Louis hailstorm saw insured damages of about $1.2 billion."[24]

This is a remarkable comparison to make. A hailstorm is not avoidable, whereas social unrest, rioting and looting, is. Yerak also makes comparisons to prior riots such as,

> The costliest riots occurred in Los Angeles in 1992, according to data on the Insurance Information Institute's website. Those riots resulted in $1.3 billion in insured damages in 2013 dollars. Among the 10 costliest civil disorders on record, seven occurred in the 1960s, according to the industry trade group. One in Chicago in April 1968 cost what is now the equivalent of $87 million in damages. That incident ranks ninth.[25]

Yerak's point here is, "Oh, it's not that bad. Look at the damage other riots have caused in the past. Heck, the weather causes more damage than these protesters did. What's the big deal? The insurance companies will take care of it." Thus, the Left justifies the burning and looting of businesses, many of which had black owners. To me, this is excusing the inexcusable.

UNREST IN BALTIMORE

On April 12, 2015, Freddie Gray, a known drug dealer, was arrested by the Baltimore Police Department for possessing an illegal knife. While Gray was being transported to the station in a police van, he sustained a spinal cord injury and was transported to the hospital to receive treatment for his injuries. As news of Gray's arrest spread, protesters flocked to the Western District police station. They felt that Gray had been mistreated by the police and that information coming from the police was inconsistent. The next morning, Gray passed away and protesters took this opportunity to riot. They didn't wait for more information or evidence. All the Left saw was that the police had killed a black man, and the city deserved to burn.

As you might imagine, the leftist media took advantage of this opportunity to spread their false narrative of racism and police brutality. The *Baltimore Sun* showed two African American males bashing in a car's windshield. One is shown stomping his foot through the windshield while the other is hitting it with an orange road cone. Other outlets showed a picture of an African American male throwing a metal chair through a restaurant window. Is the reader to understand that civilian cars and restaurants are racist; that if they hadn't contributed to police brutality, then why vandalize them?

These protesters (*thugs* might be a better word) lit 144 vehicles and 15 buildings on fire. More than 250 small businesses were damaged, along with some residences. Numerous businesses were looted of their products and goods. There's nothing like stealing a 40-inch television for the sake of social justice. I am being sarcastic of course, but the leftists' logic seems to be that the rioters deserved that television because they have been oppressed by the system. If the system didn't keep them down, then they would have been able to afford that television.

As the dust settled in Baltimore, the expectation was that things would get better for the riot-ravaged city. It turns out that when you call the police racist, throw explosives at them, and attack them, they don't want to protect and serve anymore. The result of the riots was that the Baltimore Police Department began turning a blind eye to criminal behavior. Kevin Forrester, a retired Baltimore detective stated, "What officers are doing is they're just driving looking forward. They've got horse blinders on."[26] Can you blame them? I don't.

Of course, I believe that Freddie Gray's death should have been investigated. Authorities should have done everything within their power to determine the cause of his injury and death and see if wrongdoing was involved. But as we've seen, the Left didn't wait for information before they began burning and looting businesses and causing millions of dollars' worth of damage. This "rush to judgment" has become more and more typical of the Left, and it causes vast amounts of damage.

Brad Heath of *USA Today* wrote an article titled, "Baltimore police stopped noticing crime after Freddie Gray's death. A wave of killings followed." He found that from "2014 to 2017, dispatch records show the number of suspected narcotics offenses police reported themselves dropped 30 percent; the number of people they reported seeing with outstanding warrants dropped by half. The number of field interviews—instances in which the police approach someone for questioning—dropped 70 percent.[27] This is what the people asked for when they rioted in the streets and called the police systemically racist. It was almost as if the police in Baltimore were afraid to make an arrest.

In his article, Heath went on to say that,

> The surge of shootings and killings that followed has left Baltimore easily the deadliest large city in the United States. Its murder rate reached an all-time high last year; 342 people were killed. The number of shootings in some neighborhoods has more than tripled. One man was shot to death steps from a police station. Another was killed driving in a funeral procession.[28]

This is a common trend that happens when one accuses the police of being racist.

After the riots in Ferguson, city data showed that murders per 100,00 went from 9.5 in 2014 to 23.7 in 2015, 42.8 in 2016, and 52.9 in 2017. This trend in crime was across the board. Rapes increased from 9.5 per 100,000 in 2014 to 38.0 in 2015. Robberies surged from 241.8 in 2014 to 389.4. The overall city data crime index went from 411 per 100,000 in 2014 to 562 in 2016.[29] These are numbers that leftists refuse to look at when it comes to the results of their behavior. They are dead wrong if they believe that calling the police racists, pigs, and animals is going to help their communities. They may believe that their cities can do fine without the police, but this has not proven to be the case. The fact is that when the police turn a blind eye to violent crime, it dramatically hurts low-income areas.

After the death of Michael Brown, the Left quit calling for police reform and began to demand that the police be defunded and—basically—abolished. These calls became more prevalent after the passing of George Floyd.

MINNEAPOLIS

On the afternoon of May 25, 2020, George Floyd bought a pack of cigarettes from the Cup Foods grocery store in Minneapolis with a counterfeit $20 bill. Employees of the store followed Floyd to his car and asked him to return the cigarettes. Floyd refused, so the employees called the police and reported that he was paying for goods with fake bills. They also said that he seemed drunk and not in control of himself. When the police arrived at the scene, Floyd and some other men were sitting in a car, with Floyd in the driver's seat.

The officers asked Floyd numerous times to show his hands, but the suspect showed no sign of complying with the request. As Floyd opened his door, the officers again asked him to show his hands. Instead, he began telling the officers that he was sorry. But because he was still not showing his hands, one of the officers drew his weapon. It was at this point that Floyd listened and placed both hands on the steering wheel. The officer holstered his firearm and proceeded to grab Floyd by the hand, calmly asking him to step out of the vehicle.

The officers involved seemed to be acting professionally, even though Floyd was behaving strangely and not doing what the officers were asking him to do. He seemed to be crying and begged the arresting officers not to hurt him. The officers replied that they were not going to hurt him.

Once he was out of the car, Floyd began resisting arrest, so the police sat him up against the wall of a nearby building and asked him if he was "on something right now." Floyd replied, "No, nothing." But this was not the truth; he actually had a potentially deadly dose of fentanyl in his system.

Officer J. Alexander Kueng asked the suspect about the foam around his mouth. He then notified Floyd that he was being placed under arrest and walked him to the police vehicle. Floyd, who had been sitting in his own car with the window rolled up, suddenly claimed that he was claustrophobic and needed the window in the squad car rolled down a crack, which the arresting officers agreed to do.

Before trying to get Floyd into the vehicle, they asked him numerous times to face the car so they could search him. He kept saying that he was not resisting, but at the same time he would not listen to the officer's commands. A search of his pockets revealed what looked to be a purple-blueish pipe. In addition to asking to have the window rolled down, Floyd also asked the police officers to stay with him, and they agreed to do that as well. But even though his demands were met, Floyd would not get in the police vehicle—while insisting at the same time that he was not resisting arrest.

He began talking to a bystander who urged him to cooperate and get in the police car. Up until this point, the officers seemed to be patient and gentle in their dealings with Floyd, but that didn't seem to be working, so they finally began to push and pull to get him into the car. Once they got him into the car, he simply came out the other side, where Officer Derek Chauvin was standing. While Chauvin and the other policemen struggled to get Floyd back in the car, he began saying that he couldn't breathe. Floyd was literally lying in the back seat of the squad car with his feet dangling out saying he couldn't breathe.

After Floyd made his way out the other side of the car, the officers proceeded to place Floyd on the ground, but he continued to struggle. At this point Chauvin placed his left knee on the back of Floyd's neck and his right knee on his back. Remember that Chauvin and his fellow officers had just spent four minutes trying to get Floyd to get into their vehicle.

Floyd kept repeating that he couldn't breathe, which was what he was saying while he was in the squad car resisting arrest. Floyd stayed on the ground for more than eight minutes and Chauvin clearly should have let him sit up. After all, there were enough officers on the scene to deal with him if he tried anything. Floyd said sixteen times that he couldn't breathe, and nothing was done to help him. Finally, he lapsed into unconsciousness and paramedics were called to the scene. Floyd was loaded into the ambulance and CPR was tried but it failed to restart his heart.

After Floyd's death, the Left took the opportunity to pounce with full-blown coverage and push their narrative that the police are inherently racist. They began portraying George Floyd as a stand-up citizen, the kind of man any parent would want his or her children to pattern their lives after. The MSM made George Floyd out to be a saint who sacrificed his life for social justice. With all due respect for George Floyd and his family, this was clearly not the case.

Nancy Pelosi even said, "Thank you, George Floyd, for sacrificing your life for justice. Because of you—and because of thousands, millions of people around the world who came out for justice—your name will always be synonymous with justice."[30]

What was this sacrifice Pelosi spoke of? She took to Twitter to clarify: "George Floyd should be alive today. His family's calls for justice for his murder were heard around the world. He did not die in vain. We must make sure other families don't suffer the same racism, violence, and pain, and we must enact the George Floyd #JusticeInPolicing Act."[31]

Despite what Pelosi said, there was no evidence that pointed to Chauvin being racist or killing Floyd because he was black. Minnesota Attorney General Keith Ellison told *60 Minutes* that there was no evidence whatsoever that Chauvin was a racist, or that his killing of George Floyd was motivated by race. Ellison said, "We don't have any evidence that Derek Chauvin factored in George Floyd's race as he did what he did."[32]

The Left believes that any action a white police officer takes toward a black man is clearly racist. CBS news anchor Scott Pelly pressed Ellison on this: "The whole world sees this as a white officer killing a black man because he is black. And you're telling me that there's no evidence to support that?" Ellison responded that it's not necessary to prove Chauvin is a racist to show that "there is a social norm" in U.S. society that "killing certain kinds of people is more tolerable than other kinds of people."[33]

Like President Obama's Attorney General Eric Holder, Ellison apparently feels that he has to talk about racism, so the Left won't come after him. Ellison went on to tell Pelly that, "In order for us to stop and pay serious attention to this case and be outraged by it, it's not necessary that Derek Chauvin had a specific racial intent to harm George Floyd."[34] "The fact is we know that, through housing patterns, through employment, through wealth, through a whole range of other things—so often, people of color, black people, end up with harsh treatment from law enforcement. And other folks doing the exact same thing just don't."[35]

He's saying that there are statistical disparities which provide proof that systemic racism exists, and that the police are one of those racist systems.

According to the MSM, George Floyd was a role model for every African American in this country. Derek Chauvin, on the other hand, represents America's racist institutions, and how those institutions hold African Americans down. Joe Biden pushed this narrative by saying,

> I just want to say a few words about the horrific killing of George Floyd in Minnesota . . . . It sends a very clear message to the black community and black lives that are under threat every single day . . . . They speak to a nation where too often just the color of your skin puts your life at risk . . . George Floyd's last words, spoken to a nation where the color of your skin dictates the safety of you and your future . . . . I'm a white man. I think I understand. But I can't feel it.[36]

Biden was spreading the lie that black lives are under siege by the police on a daily basis. This narrative is false and will be debunked later on in this chapter. Moreover, CNN's Don Lemon and Chris Cuomo echoed this false narrative when Lemon said to Cuomo, "It is not incumbent upon black people to stop racism. To stop this, it is incumbent upon people who hold the power in this society to help to do that, to do the heavy lifting. And guess who that is? Who is that Chris?" and Cuomo replied, "white people."[37] According to the Left, white people are to blame—they are causing all the problems and so must be responsible for solving the problems.

Does that sound like a stretch to you? It does to me. It is a biased statement from two men who claim to be unbiased.

THE ANTI-POLICE MOVEMENT

Again, let me say that I believe George Floyd's death was an avoidable tragedy. I grieve for the man and his family. But Floyd was far from being a saint, a prophet, a social justice warrior, a symbol of justice, and a sacrifice. He was a troubled person with a serious criminal record. He was arrested nine times over ten years and had served several jail terms. Charges against him included delivery of a controlled substance (1997), two separate charges of theft (1998), failure to identify (2001), possession of a controlled substance (2002), trespassing (2003), another charge of delivery of a controlled substance (2004), possession with intent to manufacture or distribute (2005), and—most significantly—aggravated robbery with a deadly weapon (2007).[38] He was sentenced to five years in prison for this last charge.

A police officer's statement in this case read,

> At this time, a black Ford Explorer pulled up in front of the Complainants' residence and five black males exited this vehicle and proceeded to the front door. The largest of these suspects [Floyd] forced his way into the residence, placed a pistol against the complainant's abdomen, and forced her into the living room area of the residence. This large suspect then proceeded to search the residence while another armed suspect guarded the complainant, who was struck in the head and side areas by this second armed suspect with his pistol after she screamed for help.[39]

This doesn't sound at all like the George Floyd we've read about in the leftist media. This does not fit the description of George Floyd that is offered up by Black Lives Matter, Antifa, and Democrats. Floyd was a violent criminal who had a history of drug abuse and even overdosed at one point. The video of Floyd resisting arrest and being on a lethal level of fentanyl shows that he'd continued to break the law. This does not mean that he deserved to die, nor that the officers who arrested him were right in their actions. But it does show that the Left will take any case in which a black man is killed by a white police officer and push the notion that America is racist and that, as Joe Biden said, "Terrorism from white supremacy is the most lethal threat to the homeland today."[40] Spreading such falsehood brings the kind of consequences we have seen in Ferguson, Baltimore, and Minneapolis. Rather than waiting for a trial and a presentation of the evidence, people rush to the streets to burn their cities down.

The morning after Floyd's death, a makeshift memorial was set up at the scene of his death. Protestors quickly followed with signs that read, "Stop Killing Black People," "I Can't Breathe," and "Black Lives Matter." Similar signs were created for Michael Brown along with the lie of "hands up, don't shoot." These people saw a horrible video and quickly came to the conclusion that this was racially motivated, and the police were going out into the streets hunting black people. It is astonishing to me that the Left will craft an entire narrative regardless of evidence.

Remember that in Minneapolis, protests started just hours after Floyd died. The investigation into his death had not even started. The full video and body cam footage had not yet been released. But all of that did not matter to the Left. All that mattered to them was that the video showed a white police officer killing an unarmed black man. The media told them the police are racist and should be defunded. The president told them that white supremacy was the biggest threat today. Celebrities like Lebron James told them that black people are being hunted every day. Even Minneapolis Police Chief, Medaria Arradondo, added fuel to the fire when he said, "Being black in America should not be a death sentence."[41]

There is no evidence to support this claim that being black in America will lead to your death at the hands of the police. But again, evidence does not matter to the Left. The narrative is what matters. Chief Arradondo fired the police officers involved in the arrest of George Floyd before an investigation even started. My personal feeling is that the officers should have been fired, but I came to this conclusion only after a thorough investigation and a review of the evidence. I didn't just look at a video, see a white officer kneeling on a black guy's neck, and start shouting, "RACISM!" Neither did I hurry to the nearest office supply store, get myself a black sharpie and a large poster board to create my sign, drive down to East 38th Street and Chicago Avenue and start protesting. I did not think, "Hey, if the television tells me it's racism, it must be racism."

But with the false narrative ingrained in the minds of the protestors, all hell broke loose in Minneapolis. The police station was vandalized first, with graffiti scrawled on walls and windows shattered. A police vehicle also had its windows broken.

One would think that the police and city council would act to stop this criminal behavior, but that was not the case. City council member Jeremiah Ellison, who had been involved in protests against the police before he was elected, told the mayor not to interfere with protestors vandalizing police property. None the less, as the violence increased, the Police Chief was forced to order his officers to respond with tear gas and rubber bullets. Despite these efforts to curtail the violence, the "protest" morphed into a full-blown riot, with looting, arson, and violence—all in the name of "Justice for Floyd."

A famous video showed an Antifa member breaking the windows of an AutoZone and spray-painting the building. The store was then looted, vandalized, and lit on fire. Nothing like a riot for helping you get that windshield wiper fluid for free. Such "protests" continued for days in major cities around the country.

It was during these riots that MSNBC reporter, Ali Velshi, stated, "I want to be clear on how I characterize this. This is mostly a protest. It is not generally speaking unruly." Velshi was standing right in front of a building that was literally on fire. Throughout the riots the media continued to downplay the destruction that was happening in major cities. NBC News allegedly told their reporters not to talk about "riots," but "protests."

This prompted FoxLA's, Bill Melugin to tweet, "What kind of alternate reality is this where the mass looting and burning of businesses is not considered a riot by a news network? A protest is what we had here in LA last night. What's happening in Minneapolis is the textbook definition of a riot. Protesters don't loot. Period."[42]

Robby Starbuck also took to Twitter, writing, "NBC says that the riots are not riots. Those "protests" must have magically caused spontaneous combustion that lit buildings on fire, threw flatscreen TVs into the hands of innocent "protestors" and caused hands to slam hammers into cash registers. What a wild series of events!"[43]

Meanwhile, CNN's Don Lemon went as far as to compare the Minneapolis riots to the Boston Tea Party. "Our country was started because of the Boston Tea Party. Rioting. So do not get it twisted and think this is something that has never happened before and this is so terrible and these savages and all of that. This is how this country was started."[44] Really? When did burning down businesses and destroying both public and private property become patriotic?

This narrative really started during the Ferguson riots. *Rolling Stone* published an article titled, "9 Historical Triumphs to Make You Rethink Property Destruction," that tried to put a positive spin on what was happening in America's streets. "Workers had produced that tea, capitalists had risked investment on it, and it was not the colonists' to destroy, but they said 'fuck property rights' and did it anyway," the *Rolling Stone* article states. "Today's conservatives don't seem bothered by this inconvenient history, though, because think of the dress-up opportunities!"[45]

It should come as no surprise that one of the authors of the article is a well-known Antifa leader. It makes sense that a fascist would try to rewrite history to cater to his idiotic actions. *Rolling Stone* was not alone in its defense of those who were breaking windows and setting places of business on fire.

The Atlantic published an article title, "The Double Standard of the American Riot." Slate posted "Proportionate Response" and NPR produced a column under the heading, "As Officials Condemn Violence During Protests, This Professor Says Some Is Warranted." There is a strong case to be made that the media are complicit in inciting violence across America by promulgating lies to the public.

THE FINAL TOLL

By the time, the violence finally died down, some 1,500 buildings in Minneapolis had been lit on fire, looted, and/or vandalized—and several of those buildings had been reduced to piles of rubble. A man named Oscar Lee Stewart, Jr. died after being trapped in a pawn shop that was set on fire. Hundreds of injuries were reported. According to Axios, the total damage caused by the "protests" was between $1 and $2 billion.[46] This amount eclipses the original record, which was set in Los Angeles in 1992 after the Rodney King incident. Leftist politicians even allowed Antifa to take over an intersection in the area where George Floyd was killed, naming it, "The Free State of George Floyd."

According to area residents, the intersection quickly turned into a warzone,

> As neighbors of 38th Street and Chicago Avenue, also known as George Floyd Square or the autonomous zone, we are witnessing a revolution by day and a devolution by night," they said. "Prayer gatherings canceled. Rallies canceled. Visitors arriving with flowers in hand, only to retreat to their cars when greeted by the sound of gunshots. Neighbors ducking for cover behind our houses, children in tow.[47]

The zone especially affected low-income, largely minority residents. One neighbor told a local news affiliate, "People don't feel safe. They are selling their homes, they hear gunshots, they know the police are not coming into the neighborhood."[48] The Minneapolis Police Chief said, "I'm hearing overwhelmingly from community members who, quite frankly, are feeling hostage over there at the situation. And we cannot allow for the violence to continue to happen."[49]

Black Lives Matter claims to care about minorities and people of color, but their actions tend to hurt minorities rather than help them. Minneapolis Police ended up avoiding the area around Floyd Square as the protestors wanted the zone to be "police free" and a "no-go zone."[50] Despite this, the police did try to enter the zone to respond to emergencies, only to find themselves surrounded by hostile crowds. There were multiple 9-1-1 calls made in the area, and victims of drug overdoses, shootings, and other violence had to be dragged out of the zone, since first responders were not allowed past the barricades. As you might imagine, when police are not able to patrol areas, the crime rate in those areas surges. Violent crime at the intersection and in the blocks immediately surrounding it rose dramatically in 2020, though crime also increased citywide. There were nineteen nonfatal and fatal shootings in the area in 2020, including fourteen shootings from May 1 through August 31. That compared with three shootings in all of 2019 and none during the summer months that year.[51]

In the year after George Floyd's death, Minneapolis saw a surge in crime, including homicides. The homicide rate doubled and there was a 250 percent increase in gunshot victims. The rate of violent crimes also rose dramatically in Ferguson and Baltimore, where police were not being supported by their local communities and politicians. When support is not there, police leave their jobs. Fox News reported, "Nearly 200 Minneapolis police officers have left the force in the wake of the death of Floyd, with many officers filing post-traumatic stress claims due to the civil unrest that followed. Minneapolis has seen at least 31 homicides this year, not including this weekend's violence."[52]

The same exodus is happening in cities throughout the United States. A report issued by the Police Executive Research Forum (PERF), a nonprofit think tank, shows a startling 45 percent increase in the retirement rate and a nearly 20 percent increase in resignations between 2020 and 2021.[53] The survey shows that in the largest departments with 500 or more officers, the retirement rate increased by nearly 30 percent. Overall, new police hiring has dropped 5 percent.[54] Some of these retirements are due to morale, police reform, and calls to defund the police.

DEFUNDING THE POLICE

In the wake of Minneapolis, many Democrats and other progressives pushed a "defund the police" agenda. Their solution to end the supposed systemic racism of the police is to defund. Some have even called for abolishing the police. Musician Lizzo said on Instagram,

> Defund the police sounds radical until you realize we've been defunding education for years. Abolish the police does NOT mean Abolish law enforcement. Defund the police means give some of those BILLIONS of tax dollars to healthcare/workers, social services, communities that need funding, education etc. We can reimagine a better country where law enforcement does what it's supposed to do![55]

On one hand, Lizzo says we should abolish the police but then says this does not mean we should abolish law enforcement. The job of the police is to enforce the law, but we conservatives are supposed to ignore calls for them to become social workers instead? If you push back, then they call you a bigot and racist.

Actress Natalie Portman also took to Instagram to write a lengthy announcement in her support of defunding the police. She said:

> When I first heard #defundthepolice, I have to admit my first reaction was fear. My whole life, police have made me feel safe. But that's exactly the center of my white privilege: the police make me as a white woman feel safe, while my black friends, family and neighbors feel the opposite: police make them feel terror. And for good reason. Police are the 6th leading cause of death for black men in this country. These are not isolated incidents. They are patterns and part of the system of over-policing of black Americans. Reforms have not worked. Minneapolis, where George Floyd was murdered, is one of the most progressive police forces in the country, having undergone extensive anti-bias training, I am grateful to the leaders in the @mvmnt-4blklives who have made us question the status quo. And who have made us imagine, what a world could be like in which we invested in nourishing people—rather than putting all of our money into punishment. I've gotten to the age in my life, where if my gut feels uncomfortable, I take the situation as wrong. But this concept initially made me uncomfortable because I was wrong. Because the system that makes me feel comfortable is wrong. #defendblacklives #defundthepolice.[56]

Portman's statements are right out of the leftist handbook. When she uses the term *white privilege*, she is talking about "inherent advantages possessed by a white person on the basis of their race in a society characterized by racial inequality and injustice."[57] In short, this is the idea that the color of your skin doesn't mean that you don't have hardships, but your whiteness is not one of them. The Left thinks that the amount of melanin in your skin sets you above everyone else in society. If that sounds racist, that's because it is. Not only is it racist but it is also false. But remember, the Left can't be racist because they are the defenders against racism. Marginalized groups such as Japanese Americans, who for decades couldn't own land in some states, now outperform whites in income, education, examination scores, and incarceration rates.

According to median household income statistics from the U.S. Census Bureau, several minority groups substantially out-earn whites. These groups include Pakistani Americans, Lebanese Americans, South African Americans, Filipino Americans, Sri Lankan Americans, and Iranian Americans. Indians are the highest-earning ethnic group the census tracks, with almost double the household median income of whites. Furthermore, black immigrant groups such as Nigerians, Barbadians, Ghanaians, Trinidadians, and Tobagonians have a median household income well above the American average. Ghanian Americans, to take one example, earn more than several specific white groups such as Dutch Americans, French Americans, Polish Americans, British Americans, and Russian Americans.[58] The evidence simply does not support the idea that white privilege exists but that will not stop the Left from pushing the false narrative.

Portman, like many other leftists, pushes the idea that—because there is a disparity—there must be racism. Ergo, since disparity exists within law enforcement, then the police must be racist. If that is so, why would anyone give money to a racist institution? The vast majority of Americans do not endorse racism and would not support taxpayer dollars being given to a racist institution. While it's true that disparity exists, we cannot lay the blame on racism.

Lastly, Portman uses her "gut feeling" to decide if something is right or wrong. A person's feelings change throughout the day. Using one's feelings without also using one's head could lead to irrational decision-making.

Defunding or abolishing the police has had massive ramifications on local law enforcement, as well as on communities throughout the United

States. At least sixteen cities slashed their budgets. New York City cut $1 billion from its 2021 budget, and Los Angeles cut its budget by $150 million. Other major cities that followed suit included Seattle, San Francisco, Washington, D.C., and Austin. As cities defunded their police departments, police looked away from crime. The New York Police Department logged 45,000 fewer arrests in the wake of the death of George Floyd, a 38 percent decline. This was the case even though there were 100 additional homicides, an increase of 58 percent. After Floyd's passing, Chicago's police made 31,000 fewer arrests, a 53 percent decline while murders rose 65 percent. In Louisville, where massive unrest included the shooting of two police officers during a protest, homicides jumped 87 percent.[59]

From Los Angeles and Houston to New Orleans and Minneapolis, the political response to the unrest led to de-policing and resulting in record violence. Already bloody St. Louis hit a fifty-year homicide high, a rate of 87 per 100,000 residents—a rate three times higher than Mexico and Central America.[60] As Milwaukee announced slashing 120 officers from its police force, the city saw a 98 percent increase in killings.

Overall, major cities throughout the United States saw a 3 percent increase in homicides in 2020. After the Minneapolis City Council unanimously approved a budget that shifted $8 million from the police department to other programs, murders in Minneapolis, where Floyd was killed, rose 46 percent between December 11, 2020, and March 28, 2021, Portland Mayor Ted Wheeler trimmed the police budget by roughly 4 percent. According to city police data, homicides increased from six in the first five months of 2020 to 38 in the first five months of 2021, a more than 530 percent increase.[61]

These statistics show a convincing case for a correlation between defunding the police and a rise in crime. The Left will say that these stats are just that, a correlation. They are not wrong in their assessment, but it is time-consuming and costly to create a designed experiment that would show the cause and effect of defunding the police and an increase in crime.

Police departments did not just see cuts to their budgets. Departments saw a massive increase in early retirements and resignations. A survey conducted by the Police Executive Research Forum found that almost 200 police departments indicated that retirements were up 45 percent and resignations rose by 18 percent from April 2020 to April 2021 when compared with the previous 12 months.[62]

Darrell Cortez, a thirty-year veteran of the San Jose Police Department, said he's glad he's not a cop now. "Police officers are really feeling demonized, vilified, criticized in the court of public opinion, how can we do our job better and not be on the 6 o'clock news everyday as a headline? Officers did this and officers did that."[63] Police Chief David Zack said that "officers were pushed to quit because the protests were directed at them. They said that 'we have become the bad guys, and we did not get into this to become the bad guys.'"[64]

New York City saw 2,600 officers retire in 2020 compared with 1,509 the year before. Resignations in Seattle increased to 123 from 34 and retirements to 96 from 43. Minneapolis, which had 912 uniformed officers in May 2019, is now down to 699. At the same time, many cities are contending with a rise in shootings and homicides. Asheville was among the hardest hit proportionally, losing upward of 80 officers, more than one-third of its 238 strong force.[65]

Police morale across the United States is at an all-time low. The Select Board's Committee on Policing Reforms surveyed more than 100 department employees at the Brookline Police Department, which is more than 53 percent of the department's total employees. The survey showed that 86 percent called morale poor with only 3 percent reporting it as good or excellent.[66]

It's understandable that the police are growing tired and disgusted when forced to deal with these kinds of situations for years on end. Portland Police Officer Knute Aroonsuck told NBC News' Gabe Gutierrez, "Morale

I think is at an all-time low now. It all boils down to these three main concepts of being underfunded, understaffed, and under-supported."[67]

As departments continue to be defunded and understaffed, still-active police will have to fill vacancies by working overtime. This will increase fatigue and accelerate the decline in morale. This, in turn, will adversely affect minority communities because police won't want to go into low-income areas and may turn a blind eye to crimes like drug dealing and prostitution.

As crime continued to increase, leftist cities realized that defunding the police was a terrible idea. As of the writing of this book, desperate attempts are being made to reverse the cuts. After Minneapolis cut $8 million from its police department, they recently voted to approve $6.4 million in additional funding. The Los Angeles City Council agreed to restore $36 million to the budget after slashing $150 million. The Oakland City Council wants to restore $10 million in funding after cutting $25 million. Baltimore's Mayor Brandon Scott, a Democrat, proposed a $27 million increase in police funding after campaigning to slash the police budget by $22 million.[68] Most of these additions resulted from community members' complaints about the rise in crime.

The main function of the government is to protect its citizens. Politicians who fail to do what is necessary to protect their constituents should be ousted and replaced by others who will. Unfortunately, that is not always how it is. Leftist-dominated areas complain about crime resulting from decisions made by politicians, yet they continue to vote for the very people who promulgate those ideas that negatively impact their communities. Republicans and other conservatives have caught on to this theme, which has resulted in a mass exodus from leftist areas and states.

Seven
DEBUNKING POLICE RACISM

The outrageous murder of George Floyd shown over and over again by the MSM revived the Left's false narrative that law enforcement itself is systemically racist. This resulted in the creation of entire movements, such as Black Lives Matter. President Barak Obama tweeted that, for millions of black Americans, being treated differently by the criminal justice system because of race is "tragically, painfully, maddeningly 'normal.'" Mr. Obama called on the police and the public to create a "new normal" in which bigotry no longer "infects our institutions and our hearts."[1]

This type of language wasn't unusual for President Obama. During the unrest in Ferguson after the killing of Michael Brown, he stated, "We have made enormous progress in race relations . . . But what is also true is that there are still problems, and communities of color aren't just making these problems up . . . the law too often feels like it's being applied in a discriminatory fashion . . . . But these are real issues, and we have to lift them up and not deny them or try to tamp them down."[2] President Obama was simply pushing propaganda to his followers who believed in the lie that the police are racist as these claims are not supported by evidence.

Starting in 2015, the *Washington Post* began tracking more than a dozen details about each police killing, including the race of the deceased, the circumstances of the shooting, if the person was armed, and whether the person was experiencing a mental-health crisis. This information was gathered by culling local news reports, law enforcement websites, and social media, and by monitoring independent databases, such as Killed by Police and Fatal Encounters. In addition, the *Post* has created a data collection site of its own.[3] This statistical data will help support multiple theories regarding law enforcement.

Promoting the argument of systemic police racism, leftists say that police in America are hunting black men in the streets because of their skin color. The MSM has pushed this lie so much that Los Angeles-based *Skeptic* magazine published a survey indicating that roughly half of self-described liberal or very liberal respondents believe 1,000 or more "unarmed black men" are killed by police every year. The survey also showed that approximately 35 percent of respondents believe that number is as high as 10,000 or more. Even among self-described moderates, 66 percent believe "about 100" or more unarmed black people are killed every year, as well as 54 percent of self-described conservatives and very conservative respondents.[4] The fact that there are people who actually believe 10,000 or more unarmed black people are being killed by the police every year should be shocking to everyone. The broad acceptance of this baseless conspiracy theory is outrageous and testifies to the power of media suggestion.

According to the *Washington Post* database, eighteen unarmed black people were killed by the police in 2020, and thirteen were killed in 2019. While every death is a tragedy, 18 is a far cry from 100, 1,000, or 10,000 and the disparity between these facts and popular belief exposes the damage the Left's ideology has caused in America. In 2015, the *Washington Post* documented 991 fatal police shootings. Half the victims were white, and 26 percent were black.[5] These numbers are consistent with 2016, during which 959 people were killed by police—48 percent of them white, and 24 percent black. In 2017, 986 people were killed by police (47 percent white and 22 percent black). These numbers are consistent over the last few years. The data reveals virtually no change in the statistics. If the police were indeed hunting black men, we could expect to see the percentage of black people shot by police increase year over year. It should also be mentioned that the shooting of an unarmed person is not necessarily unjustified. There are cases of victims—like Michael Brown—reaching for an officer's weapon, attempting to render the officer unconscious, or refusing to follow an officer's directions, implying that a weapon was present.

On June 12, 2020, Atlanta police officer Devin Brosnan responded to a call regarding an African American male named Rayshard Brooks, who had fallen asleep in his car while in line at a Wendy's drive-through. Responding Officer Brosnan radioed for assistance at the scene. Officer Garrett Rolfe received the call and arrived within minutes. A breathalyzer indicated that Brooks' blood alcohol level was above the legal driving limit.

When the officers began to handcuff Brooks, a struggle ensued and took all three men to the ground. As the officers wrestled with Brooks, he grabbed Officer Brosnan's Taser and ran. Officer Rolfe pursued Brooks down the drive-through lane. Brooks turned and fired the Taser at Officer Rolfe's head. Officer Rolfe returned fire with his sidearm, striking Brooks twice. Brooks later died at the hospital. Rioting broke out when word spread that a white officer had killed an unarmed black man and, as a result, the Wendy's was burned down.

Officer Rolfe was fired the next day, and Officer Brosnan was placed on administrative duty. Rolfe was later charged with felony murder, along with ten other offenses. Officer Brosnan received charges of aggravated assault and two counts of violation of oath. It is perplexing that this could happen to officers who were doing their job and were endangered by the assailant. While Brooks was initially unarmed, he resisted arrest and attempted to Taser Officer Rolfe in the head, which could have done serious harm. This appears to be a case in which an unarmed black man was justifiably shot by the police. Brooks represented roughly 58 percent of black arrests not involving possession of a weapon. In 2019, 42 percent of cases where black suspects were arrested involved the possession of a weapon

The Left will point out that there is a disparity in these arrest statistics as blacks make up 13 percent of the population and should show lower percentages regarding arrests and the use of unreasonable deadly force. However, the proportion of a specific race to the total population should not be a component in determining racism. The Left wants us to believe that cops are arresting blacks for no reason while they are letting whites off the hook for similar infractions. But the data does not support this.

Statistics reveal that black citizens are committing crimes that result in arrests at a higher rate than whites. According to the Office of Juvenile Justice and Delinquency Prevention, black suspects were responsible for 51 percent of the murders, 53 percent of the robberies, and 33 percent of the aggravated assaults charged in 2019. For those who believe 2019 may be an anomaly, statistics prove otherwise. In 2018, black suspects were responsible for 53 percent of the murders, 54 percent of the robberies, and 34 percent of the aggravated assaults. From 1980 through 2019, these numbers were virtually the same.[6]

For forty years 13 percent of the population has been responsible for roughly 50 percent of the murders. This data substantiates neither police racism nor systemic racism. It does indicate poor decision-making by individuals. Depending on the year, white suspects make up roughly the other 41 to 52 percent of those who commit murder. Those committing these crimes live primarily in urban areas. Over the course of three decades, the increase in violent crimes has paralleled the rise in abandonment by fathers. State-by-state analysis by Heritage Foundation scholars indicates that a 10 percent increase in the percentage of children living in single-parent homes typically leads to a 17 percent increase in juvenile crime.[7]

This supports the findings of Wendy D. Manning and Kathleen A. Lamb, authors of *Adolescent Well-Being in Cohabiting, Married, and Single-Parent Families*. Their research showed that children who grow up in intact families, with both a mom and a dad, are the least likely to commit delinquent acts. These delinquent acts include attacking a person with or without a weapon, threatening a person, murder, and rape. Delinquent acts could also include covert actions, such as arson, vandalism, shoplifting, and selling drugs.

Juveniles who commit delinquent acts tend to continue this behavior into adulthood. Similarly, children from fatherless families carry their problems into their adult lives. These children are three times more likely to end up in jail by the time they reach age thirty than children raised in intact families. They also have the highest rates of incarceration in the United States.[8] These children, regardless of race, tend to put themselves into situations that result in the commission of a crime. Choosing to commit a crime increases the rate at which individuals will encounter law enforcement. Just by sheer probability, committing a crime and encountering law enforcement will automatically increase the chance of something unfortunate happening.

This reasoning follows a logical train of thought: If an individual does not commit a crime, the police will not be called, the person will not be arrested, nor will they have an encounter with the police that might lead to a shooting or to a show of unreasonable force. In the *Proceedings of the National Academy of Sciences*, researchers found that the more frequently officers encounter violent suspects from any given racial group, the greater the chance that a member of that group will be fatally shot by a police officer. They concluded that there is "no significant evidence of antiblack disparity in the likelihood of being fatally shot by police."[9] This study completely contradicts the leftist narrative.

As stated previously, the data does not support the claim that police are systematically racist and arbitrarily shoot black people. Any officer who intentionally and without cause shoots an unarmed individual, regardless of race, should be charged with murder and sentenced to life in prison. There have been cases of officers shooting unarmed individuals who posed no threat to law enforcement. These cases are extremely few in number and are vast outliers in the statistical data. There are also cases of racist police officers, but these, too, are outliers. If anything, the data suggests that an officer's chance of getting killed by a black assailant is 18.5 times greater than the chance of an unarmed black suspect getting killed by a cop.[10] If the Left were to accept the truth of this data, their world would be flipped upside down and inside out.

In conclusion, the role of law enforcement is to maintain law and order in local communities by protecting members of the public and their property. They are to prevent crime whenever possible and improve the quality of life for members of the local society. When police are not in uniform, they are ordinary citizens. They have husbands, wives, girlfriends, boyfriends, sons, daughters, moms, and dads. These men and women have extremely hard jobs. They put their lives on the line every day. Like you and me, they go to work each day and they want to do their jobs well and come home to their families.

The Left does not see these men and women in uniform as people but rather as vicious racists out to hunt black men in the streets and promote white supremacy. On the other hand, there are those who want to see our police officers dead. A total of 1,763 law enforcement officers died in the line of duty during the past ten years, an average of 176 per year. There were 306 law enforcement officers killed in the line of duty in 2020.[11]

It is frightening that some leftists, thinking that the police officers deserved to die, take joy in these statistics. Even though we can provide verifiable proof that the vast majority of police are not racists who are not randomly killing black people, the Left refuses to concede that this is true.

We do not have a problem with systemic racism in this country, but we do have a crime problem. To make the argument that arresting someone who commits a crime is racist is asinine. The poor choices the individual made that led to encountering law enforcement is the true problem. This is not something the government can fix. The family structure must fix this problem. As explained earlier, a two-parent family structure statistically gives a child a greater probability of making good decisions and staying out of prison. Corrections expert Steven Martin said, "Family is the solution and the work ethic. You show me people with intact families and those folks work—their chances of ending up in prison are zero."[12] The re-establishment of the nuclear family in American culture would not completely solve the issue of crime, but it would greatly reduce the problem. The rise of far-left organizations like Black Lives Matter has made a push to destroy the nuclear family. The support of Black Lives Matter can be seen as a fig leaf for those who are maintaining the modern metaphorical plantation.

When communities of color realize they no longer need to look to the government for help, the Left will not lose just the battle, but the war for the allegiance of black Americans. To prevent this development of self-sufficiency and true empowerment, the Left and the Democrats support organizations like Black Lives Matter, which wants to rid American culture of traditional family structures. This ideology will hurt people rather than help them. I hope the reader can see that defunding the police is not the solution. Rebuilding American families and funding the police to protect and serve stable, functioning communities across the United States is the answer. The leftist ideology that the police are systemically racist and must be defunded is an ideology that will destroy this country from the inside.

Eight
INDOCTRINATION

Indoctrination is a vital component of the leftist strategy to change America. If they can indoctrinate our children with their destructive ideology, then those same children will pass down that ideology to their children. To do this, the Left has infiltrated our educational system and established an indoctrination factory intent on producing leftists at an extraordinary rate. Rather than teach our children how to think critically, leftist educators weaponized the system, figuratively speaking, to propagate anti-American principles.

The Left has had a stronghold on higher education since the 1960s. This was disregarded by many Americans as college was seen as an opportunity to hear differing opinions and decide for oneself which arguments to embrace. Although the Left had an upper hand in higher education, conservatism still existed on various college campuses. In fact, in the early 1970s, roughly 25 percent of professors self-identified as at least moderately conservative. That substantial minority of conservative voices on college campuses began to diminish sharply in the late 1980s and early 1990s. The Carnegie Foundation conducted its faculty survey in 1999 and found that a mere 12 percent of professors were conservatives, down from 27 percent in 1969.[1] The decline in conservatives continued as time passed. In 2009, Higher Education Research Institute political scientist Samuel Abrams discovered that Republicans comprise only 4 percent of historians, 3 percent of sociologists, and a mere 2 percent of literature professors. Because of the lack of differing viewpoints, our higher educational systems are creating young adults that think Marxism, socialism, and even communism are good.

In 2019, a Gallup poll revealed that young adults had a positive view of socialism and government power. Lydia Saad, who wrote in her article for Gallup titled *Socialism as Popular as Capitalism Among Young Adults in U.S.* said,

> Since 2010, young adults' positive ratings of socialism have hovered near 50 percent, while the rate has been consistently near 34 percent for Gen Xers and near 30 percent for baby boomers or traditionalists. At the same time, since 2010, young adults' overall opinion of capitalism has deteriorated to the point that capitalism and socialism are tied in popularity among this age group.[2]

Young adults are being taught that socialism is beneficial to society, rather than learning about the social and economic atrocities brought about by socialism and its effects on countries and their populace. It is imperative that we investigate the American educational system to study how it has devolved to produce these disparities.

As we explore how the Left is destroying our educational system, I will share stories of the five-plus years I spent in education following my many years as an accountant. Although the stories are personal, they support the evidence presented throughout the chapter. We will also look at a brief history of the American educational system, critical race theory, affirmative action, indoctrination, and the removal of civics from the curriculum. It is my hope that, with this understanding, we can take back our educational system.

AMERICAN EDUCATION

When early settlers colonized the New World, an educational system was not an immediate priority. Education was primarily left to the family, and children were taught at home. Church and religion had a major impact on early literacy in America, as reading the scriptures was common practice. Due to this tradition, Americans had the highest literacy rate in the world. Today, America isn't even in the top ten. As of 2018, the United States ranked twenty-eighth in literacy out of 214 counties. One would think that, as we are the wealthiest nation in the world, we would be in the top five. However, according to the U.S. Department of Education, 54 percent of American adults aged 16-74 (about 130 million people) read below a sixth-grade level.[3]

For children during the 1600s, going to school was secondary to helping around the house and farm. As the colonists continued building communities and towns, schools began to sprout up. Modeled after a grammar school in England, the Boston Latin School was established in 1635. It was funded by donations from local citizens but later transitioned to become America's first public school.

By the mid-1600s, towns in the New England colonies were required to establish schools. As these schools were funded by tuition, most families couldn't afford to have their children attend. Only about 10 percent of children spent time away from home to receive an education. Those who could afford the expense typically sent only their sons. The vast majority of women and people of color were not allowed or were unable to attend. We would be hard-pressed to find a student today who would consider his or her education a luxury. Instead, most young Americans consider school a right rather than a privilege.

By the late eighteenth century, the colonies had established private academies that became feeder schools for Ivy League colleges. Schools used textbooks imported from England that were based heavily on theology and designed to bring the learner closer to God and family. These textbooks later evolved into instilling American values and morals that were included in the Constitution and the Bill of Rights. Students were taught civic duty, the function of government, the role of the church, the value of volunteering at state and local levels, and being a contributing member to society. This pedagogy is similar to that of many of today's private schools but is a far cry from what is taught in today's public schools.

Following the American Revolution, the philosophy of education shifted. Predominately private education morphed into a state-sponsored system. John Adams believed that citizens as a whole should be expected to bear the expense of education, stating, "The whole people must take upon themselves the education of the whole people and be willing to bear the expenses of it. There should not be a district of one-mile square without a school in it, not founded by a charitable individual, but maintained at the public expense of the people themselves."[4]

Thomas Jefferson, the founder of our first public university, endorsed Adams's stance. Jefferson supported spending public tax dollars on public education saying, "The tax which will be paid for this purpose [education] is not more than the thousandth part of what will be paid to kings, priests and nobles who will rise up among us if we leave the people in ignorance."[5] The founder believed, "no other sure foundation can be devised for the preservation of freedom and happiness."[6] Our founders believed that a society must be educated if it is to uphold its values.

By the nineteenth century, education became available to all. John Chavis was admitted to Washington Academy (now Washington and Lee University) in 1799, becoming the first African American known to receive a college education in the United States. Roughly twenty years later, Alexander Lucius Twilight attended Middlebury College and became the first African American known to have earned a bachelor's degree.

Sadly, while African Americans were widely educated in the Republican North, they were prohibited from receiving an education in the Democrat-run South. To counter this problem, during Reconstruction, Republicans established the Freedmen's Bureau, which built schools for blacks in the South. Many of the educators were women who favored abolition. Thirty-three percent of teachers were black. The Bureau received well-deserved recognition, as well as major Republican support for public education in the South. Republicans eventually gained enough power in Congress to establish public schools paid for by taxes.

In 1837, Horace Mann was named Massachusetts Secretary of Education. Well-known as an educational reformer, he became known as the Father of the Public School System. Borrowing from the Prussian style of education, he redesigned school structure, placing students in grades based on age. With this change, older students were no longer expected to instruct younger children. Instead, the European style of direct instruction through lecturing was introduced.

Mann's structure was widely adopted, and he is credited with developing the factory model of schooling. Many Americans today misrepresent the intent of the "factory model of schooling," misinterpreting that the goal of those schools was to create factory workers and that the schools themselves mimicked a factory atmosphere. Although many historians push that scenario, there is little evidence to support this claim. Despite the model's name, children were not typically taught the skills necessary for factory work. Remember, factories in the early nineteenth century bore little resemblance to the factories of today. There were—and are—aspects of our educational structure that one could compare to factories; however, that was not the purpose of the structure nor Mann's intentions.

With the dawn of the twentieth century, education boomed as cities grew and the Progressive Movement gained ground. John Dewey, an educational theorist, became a leading figure in the field. Dewey's pedagogy revolved around constructivism, with a student using both cognitive and social constructivism to learn. Cognitive constructivism is the idea that the learner actively constructs new knowledge by adding new concepts and perceptions to their pre-existing understanding of concepts. Social constructivism is a theory where development and understanding are constructed through social interactions with others and people can work together to make meaning of new information.

Dewey's ideas are still heavily used in today's classrooms. Dewey also found the bureaucracy of the educational system to be extremely regressive rather than progressive. The increase in bureaucracy within education was, in part, influenced by the Great Depression and President Franklin Roosevelt's New Deal.

As more and more Americans lost their jobs, tax revenue decreased, resulting in less funding for education. Many teachers continued working with little or no pay. Schools nationwide pleaded with Roosevelt to send federal financial support. The Civil Works Administration and the Federal Emergency Relief Administration were created to hire unemployed Americans in addition to building public schools. This relief provided employment for roughly fifty thousand teachers in rural areas. From 1933 to 1939, New Deal funds assisted 70 percent of all new school construction and prevented thousands of school closings by issuing emergency funds to pay teachers.[7] Yet, even as America was recovering from the Depression, segregation remained a problem.

In 1954, the United States Supreme Court issued a landmark ruling in *Brown* v. Board of Education. Chief Justice Earl Warren delivered the opinion of the Court, saying, "We conclude that in the field of public education the doctrine of 'separate but equal' has no place. Separate educational facilities are inherently unequal...."[8] The decision in *Brown* laid the groundwork for removing segregation in the nation's school systems and led to the equal rights movement of the 1960s. Today, this case is used as a tool of the Left to claim that our educational system is systemically racist.

The sixties also birthed the decline of teaching civics in our schools. Until the 1960s, high school students were typically required to take three courses on civics and government. Civics fell by the wayside as a result of budget cuts and curricula being narrowed to focus on core subjects. About 90 percent of students today take only one civics class. As a result, our youth learn little of how our government works or their role in society.

According to a 2016 survey by the Annenberg Public Policy Center, only 26 percent of Americans can name all three branches of government, a significant decline from previous years.[9] The majority of America's youth cannot speak to the functions of government and the limitations of power as assigned in our Constitution. I believe that these gaps in education have helped to bring about a leftward shift in our young people. They don't understand the basic principles upon which our democracy is built and their lack of understanding makes them prey to the criticisms and distortions of the Left.

The 1980s and '90s brought a move from traditional rating methods to using standardized test scores to measure the progress of students and schools. As America transitioned into the new millennium, Congress passed the No Child Left Behind Act requiring states to measure school progress through state exams and punish those schools not meeting the goals set. Instead of teaching a well-rounded curriculum, teachers were incentivized to "teach to the test" rather than risk penalties. I myself was a product of this style of education. State standards were the groundwork for instruction, but when the time approached to take the standardized tests, regular instruction came to a halt. We focused on scoring well on the tests, so the school would look good. This new approach to learning led to gaps in our grasp of basic subjects.

By 2015, the No Child Left Behind Act was replaced with the Every Student Succeeds Act signed into law by President Obama. This act gives schools more flexibility in measuring student performance. Again, the way students were taught saw a substantial change.

During the Obama administration, the Common Core State Standards Initiative spelled out what students were expected to know in mathematics and English language arts at the conclusion of each grade level.

Common Core state standards were designed to create the same standards across states, reflecting what students must know for entrance to college or the workforce. Common Core supporters pointed toward graduation rates as evidence that the initiative was successful. As an educator, I submit that graduation itself is not a good measure of success. Too many students obtain a high school diploma without even understanding eighth-grade mathematics.

I believe there is no better way to evaluate knowledge than by giving a student an assessment. "I am just a bad test taker" is simply an excuse. If a student knows the content, he or she will answer test questions correctly. Bad test-taking skill has long been used to justify poor understanding of the subject matter. A positive hallmark of Common Core is that it creates a system in which all students learn the same things and meet the same standards. Establishing common standards for content knowledge limits the leftist accusation that white children receive a better education than children of color.

Regardless of the textbook, math has not drastically changed for hundreds of years. With readily available technology and thousands of internet instruction videos, there should be no excuse for a student to fail high school math.

Although math textbooks have not changed dramatically, the same cannot be said for history texts. Progressives have long tried to inculcate targeted ideas to American youth. These targeted ideas include teaching that America is a terrible country responsible for every evil tragedy in the past few decades. This idea was aggressively promulgated by revisionist Marxist historian, Howard Zinn, in his book *A People's History of the United States*, which has been assigned reading in many high schools and colleges nationwide. Professor Sam Wineburg said, "In many circles, it has become the dominant narrative." The book appears on university reading lists in economics, political science, anthropology, culture studies, women's studies, ethnic studies, Chicano studies, and African American studies, in addition to history.[10]

The rewriting of American history is teaching our youth that our country is inherently wicked, patriotism is misplaced, and everything should be seen through the lens of race and gender. Our current educators were themselves educated in the 1980s with Zinn's work. They have gone from teachers to activists, teaching our children to hate rather than love America, that we are a fundamentally racist society and should be torn down. When viewed through this revisionist history, Republicans are racists and Democrats are the party of anti-slavery, which was the opposite of the reality in the 1800s. These revisionist critics have created a false narrative called "the big switch."

Revisionist historians insist that racist Southern Democrats switched to become Republicans and that blacks typically vote for Democratic candidates because they share the same ideals as the Republicans who switched to the Democratic Party. Author Dinesh D'Souza explains the myth regarding the big switch in his book, *Hillary's America: The Secret History of the Democratic Party*. Dinesh writes:

> Of course, many southern whites did switch from voting Democrat to voting Republican, helping the GOP become the majority party in the South, as the Democrats once were. But remember that racism declined sharply in the South during the second half of the twentieth century. There is quite literally a mountain of scholarly data that documents this. And this was the very period of GOP ascendancy. So as the South became less racist, it became more Republican … But many southern whites were not under the racist hold of the Democrats. As they became more prosperous, these whites came to see the GOP reflect their beliefs in economic opportunity and upward mobility. They also found Republicans more in tune with their patriotism as well as their socially conservative views. Quite naturally, they moved over to a party that better reflected their interests and aspirations. Remarkably, southern whites made the journey from Democratic to Republican for the same

reason that southern blacks switched parties from Republican to Democratic. In both cases, the switch occurred for economic—not racial—reasons. The black switch occurred first, in the 1930s, while the white switch occurred much later, in the 1960s and 1970s. In both cases, the timing is significant. Blacks clearly didn't switch for reasons of race because the Democratic Party was, in the 1930s, the undisputed home of racism. It remained so until at least the early 1960s. (I say "at least" because I believe that modern progressive Democratic ideology remains infused with racism, although this racism manifests itself in a new way.) So many blacks switched reluctantly, because they knew they were leaving the party of Lincoln for the party of segregation, lynching, and the Ku Klux Klan. Why did they do it? They did it because the Democrats promised them economic benefits. These benefits meant a great deal to blacks then living through the hardships of segregation and the Great Depression. Democrats offered blacks some of the same security that blacks had during slavery—in which the basic needs of blacks were met on the plantation—and blacks, during a desperate time, went for it.[11]

Leftist manufactured ideology, like the big switch myth, has resulted in a change in thought for half of America. This false narrative has persuaded 61 percent of Democrats that Republicans are racist, bigoted, and sexist.[12] No wonder our college campuses are filled with students who think their country is wicked. As long as progressive revisionist history is taught in our school systems, our youth will continue to be indoctrinated into the leftist mythos, setting off a snowball effect. More leftists will replace current leftist teachers and continue to teach our youth untruths—and the Trojan Horse will grow ever more dangerous.

TECHNOLOGY

The use of technology has dramatically changed how we teach our children. Today, there is a heavy emphasis on hybrid and blended learning. Hybrid learning allows some students to attend class in person, while others attend virtually. Primary education was conducted in this manner most recently during the coronavirus pandemic. Blended learning uses a combination of in-person and online instruction or software to complete exercises.

When the pandemic began, I used a combination of instruction using YouTube and Zoom to meet the needs of my students. This was not ideal, but it allowed me to take advantage of software and tools I would not otherwise have used if I had been in the classroom.

My school site finally returned to in-person instruction. However, in-class instruction time decreased from 200 minutes a week to 100 minutes. In other words, I was expected to teach a normal school year's worth of instruction in literally half the time. To achieve this, the math department combined blended learning and hybrid learning, as we still had students working remotely along with students physically present. We pre-recorded our lectures for students to watch before class as homework. When they came to class, we reviewed concepts they had struggled with before they worked on practice problems. This approach allowed me to teach all the content and, rather than students struggling with their math problems at home, I was able to assist them. I was also able to utilize various methods and concepts, such as John Dewey's constructivism theories in my instruction.

THE 1619 PROJECT

The goal of *The 1619 Project*, developed by Nikole Hannah-Jones, is to

> reframe American history by considering what it would mean to regard 1619 as our nation's birth year . . . that out of

slavery—and the anti-black racism it required—grew nearly everything that has truly made America exceptional: its economic might, its industrial power, its electoral system, its diet and popular music, the inequities of its public health and education, its astonishing penchant for violence, its income inequality, the example it sets for the world as a land of freedom and equality, its slang, its legal system and the endemic racial fears and hatreds that continue to plague it to this day. The seeds of all that were planted long before our official birth date, in 1776, when the men known as our founders formally declared independence from Britain.[13]

This project is built on pseudohistory and false narratives. I give Jones credit for openly stating that her goal is to reframe American history, instead of calling it what it is: revising American history. It is Jones's goal to portray America in the worst way possible by focusing primarily on its mistakes rather than concentrating on the principles she was founded on. The 1619 Project promotes the idea that 1776 holds no true significance, that America was founded in 1619, and every institution was built on racism and slavery. Even ex-slave Fredrick Douglass understood the overarching story of America instilling values through the Declaration of Independence.

Although our country did not live up to those principles in his time, he believed that one day she would.

Abraham Lincoln understood this as well, saying:

> Wise statesmen as they were, they knew the tendency of prosperity to breed tyrants, and so they established these great self-evident truths, that when in the distant future some man, some faction, some interest, should set up the doctrine that none but rich men, or none but white men, were entitled to life,

liberty and the pursuit of happiness, their posterity might look up again to the Declaration of Independence and take courage to renew the battle which their fathers began—so that truth, and justice, and mercy, and all the humane and Christian virtues might not be extinguished from the land; so that no man would hereafter dare to limit and circumscribe the great principles on which the temple of liberty was being built.[14]

Many great people rose through the years to express America's exceptionalism in these founding principles. On August 28, 1963, Martin Luther King Jr. gave his famous "I Have a Dream" speech in which he said,

> This note was a promise that all men—yes, black men as well as white men—would be guaranteed the unalienable rights of life, liberty and the pursuit of happiness . . . So even though we face the difficulties of today and tomorrow, I still have a dream. It is a dream deeply rooted in the American dream. I have a dream that one day this nation will rise up and live out the true meaning of its creed: We hold these truths to be self-evident, that all men are created equal.[15]

The American credo that all men are created equal is one that Jones and other leftists omit. Now knowing how progressives established the narrative in education, it is easy to believe that Nikole Hannah-Jones was indoctrinated into leftist ideology. What she learned in the classroom has resulted in egregious revisionist history. Nikole Hannah-Jones made the assertion to historian Leslie Harris that,

> One critical reason that the colonists declared their independence from Britain was because they wanted to protect the institution of slavery in the colonies, which had produced

tremendous wealth. At the time there were growing calls to abolish slavery throughout the British Empire, which would have severely damaged the economies of colonies in both North and South.[16]

Jones is basically saying the official creed of America did not fairly reflect the true intentions of the framers; that their true concern was protecting their slave holdings. She says the Revolutionary War was a ruse to push their slavery agenda, rather than a true fight to gain independence from tyranny. This assertion is absurd, as the founders were clear on the reasons we should rebel against the British as stated in the Declaration of Independence. The British imperial policies regarding taxation and the frontier were unfair to the colonists. The framers listed twenty-seven grievances against the king, including "for imposing taxes on us without our consent."

The 1619 Project also asserts, along with the majority of leftists, that slavery made America rich. In a PragerU video, Wilfred Reilly, Associate Professor of Political Science at Kentucky State University refutes this idea by stating:

> Slavery made some Americans rich—true enough. Eli Yale, for example, made a fortune in the slave trade. He donated money and land for the university that is named after him. But the institution of slavery didn't make *America* rich. In fact, the slave system badly slowed the economic development of half the country. As economist Thomas Sowell points out, in 1860, just one year before the Civil War began, the South had only one-sixth as many factories as the North. Almost 90 percent of the country's skilled, well-paid laborers and professionals were based in the North. Banking, railroads, manufacturing—all

were concentrated in the North. The South was an economic backwater.... Slavery did not make America rich.[17]

The false history being taught in today's schools is based on a subjective point of view and seeks to persuade our children to be ashamed of our country, that everything here is an outgrowth of racism, and that people of color will never fully receive their rights. The *New York Times*, which publishes the project, has produced educational material to be used as a resource that will "enhance traditional curricula, not replace them."[18] The 1619 Project is destructive and leads children of color to believe they are oppressed.

DO THEY KNOW WHAT THEY'RE PROTESTING?

During the 2021 Tokyo Olympics, a number of members of Team USA made a decision to protest on behalf of the oppressed. Hammer thrower Gwen Berry turned her back on the American flag during the medal ceremony. She also draped an "activist Athlete" shirt over her head and refused to face the flag during the anthem. She claimed she did this because she "represents the oppressed people."[19] It is not every day that the world sees an oppressed person win a medal at the Olympic trials.

Berry was not the only Olympian to protest. When Raven Saunders won a silver medal in the shot put, she lifted her arms over her head and formed an "X" with her wrists. She explained that the "X" is "the intersection of where all people who are oppressed meet."[20] The U.S. women's soccer team knelt to protest racism and discrimination before their game with Sweden. At no point did they mention who specifically was oppressed, who was oppressing them, or how they were oppressed.

One would think specificity would be important in order to do something about the oppression. I believe no evidence was presented because none exists. These vague demonstrations of solidarity with "the oppressed" are part of the false narrative learned from leftist professors and teachers instructing from documents like Zinn's and Hannah-Jones's revisionist histories or from the MSM, television, movies, or other leftist influences. Not all people of color believe this ideology, and not all black Olympians protest. U.S. Olympian Tamyra Mensah-Stock won a gold medal in Tokyo for wrestling. During a press conference before receiving her medal, she wrapped herself in the American flag. When a reporter asked how it felt to represent her country, she responded, "I love representing the U.S. I freaking love living there. I love it. And I'm so happy I get to represent USA!"[21] Does this sound like someone who is oppressed? If people of color had not received their rights, why would they love living in America? Only those who have been indoctrinated into leftist ideology believe they are oppressed even when they have achieved international fame and personal fortune.

The Left already has a stronghold over the educational system, which will continue to adopt leftist policy and curriculum. The less we teach children the principles and values that make this country great, the less we will have a country that is great. Ignorance begets ignorant actions. A study conducted among a thousand Americas asked what they were willing to sacrifice to work remotely from home. A "third of respondents even said they'd give up the right to vote in all future national and local elections. Gen Z was most likely—44 percent—to say they would give up their right to vote, while Baby Boomers were most opposed, with only 27 percent saying they would give it up."[22] Although this survey had a small sample size, the numbers regarding our youth's lack of appreciation of American principles are disturbing. In a span of only a few generations, Americans have become willing to give up something so sacred (voting) for convenience. Since the founding of America, thousands of people have sacrificed their lives to gain and safeguard our freedoms and rights, including the right to vote. To throw away this right in exchange for working from home illustrates how little they value democracy and their rights.

If false narratives like the 1619 Project are allowed to proceed unchallenged and become the "new normal," then we have lost. We cannot afford to lose this battle. Americans, especially conservatives, have been asleep far too long. This is not an easy fix, and the correction will likely take multiple generations to have an effect. We have only begun pushing back against destructive teaching.

The Left has turned our schools into tools of indoctrination. The 1619 Project is being used to support their ideology that America is systemically racist. A racist policy of affirmative action is being used to artificially create diversity within schools. Lastly, by limiting speech on campuses, differing opinions are silenced. The Left will not stop until America is torn down and rebuilt as a quasi-communist socialist country.

Nine

CRITICAL RACE THEORY: THE MONSTER IN OUR SCHOOLS

In 2021, many American families became aware of Critical Race Theory (CRT) for the very first time. By this time, CRT was already being taught by activist teachers in elementary schools, high schools, and colleges. This destructive teaching that all American institutions are extensions of racism and white supremacy gave birth to an opposing grassroots movement. CRT is similar to the 1619 Project in that the Left revised history and gave it a different label in an attempt to have it adopted by our educational institutions. Irate families across the country voiced their protests at local school boards.

The Critical Legal Studies (CLS), used by legal scholars and lawyers in the late 1970s, examined racial disparities in society and how they are propagated in our laws. By the 1980s, Professor Derrick Bell, a pioneer of CLS, set out to analyze various laws through the prism of race to show instances of oppressive racial structures. CRT was formed out of critical legal studies that asked questions concerning laws, policies, and regulations that were considered socially biased. According to Cornell Law School, "Proponents of CLS believe that the law supports the interests of those who create the law. As such, CLS states that the law supports a power dynamic which favors the historically privileged and disadvantages the historically underprivileged. CLS finds that the wealthy and the powerful use the law as an instrument for oppression in order to maintain their place in society's hierarchy. Many in the CLS movement want to overturn the hierarchical structures of modern society, and they focus on the law as a tool in achieving this goal."[1]

While there are legal scholars who promote CLS, there are also legal scholars who criticize it. Either way, we can see how CRT formed out of CLS with language like "favors the historically privileged" and "instrument of oppression." This is the common language of the Left in the twenty-first century. Nikole Hannah-Jones in her *Times* 1619 Project article even managed to link racism to traffic jams. Scholars supporting the CLS movement include Kimberlé Crenshaw, Mari Matsuda, Neil Gotanda, Stephanie Phillips, Richard Delgado, and others who attended the first annual CRT Workshop in 1989.[2]

Kimberlé Crenshaw, who coined the term, says that CRT "cannot be confined to a static and narrow definition but is considered to be an evolving and malleable practice. It critiques how the social construction of race and institutionalized racism perpetuate a racial caste system that relegates people of color to the bottom tiers."[3] In short, she is saying that we will keep the definition of CRT as generalized as possible so that any narrative we want to spin can be woven into CRT. Ben Shapiro of the Daily Wire wrote an eye-opening article, published in the *Daily Signal*, titled, "The Movement Against Critical Race Theory Is Deeply Necessary" in which he noted:

> It is a perverse worldview, unsupportable by the evidence, in which all of America's key institutions are inextricably rooted in white supremacy; it is an activist campaign demanding the destruction of those institutions. The founders of CRT have written as much. According to CRT founders Richard Delgado and Jean Stefancic, CRT is founded on two key premises: that "racism is ordinary, not aberrational—'normal science,' the usual

way society does business, the common, everyday experience of most people of color in this country"; second, that "our system of white-over-color ascendancy serves important purposes, both psychic and material." This means, according to Delgado and Stefancic, that "racism is difficult to cure or address" and that a formal commitment to legal equality on the basis of color-blindness is merely a guise for further discrimination. Furthermore, CRT founders say that whites are unable to understand racism, and that "minority status . . . brings with it a presumed competence to speak about race and racism.[4]

In short, CRT promotes the notion that your race is the most important characteristic that defines you as an individual, instead of your character, beliefs, values, and actions. CRT goes directly against Martin Luther King Jr.'s dream of how an individual should be perceived when he said, "I have a dream that my four little children will one day live in a nation where they will not be judged by the color of their skin, but by the content of their character."[5] We could only imagine Dr. King's outrage in placing such importance on an individual's race rather than on their character.

CRT goes a step further, insisting that racism is embedded in the minds of white people, either consciously or unconsciously, and that racism is inherent in all American institutions. It also declares that there is no way of removing that racism or white supremacy other than tearing down the institutions and rebuilding something different. When I say that the Left is destroying America, that's exactly what I mean. Since the Left believes all whites are racist, it follows that were the Left allowed to destroy and then rebuild our institutions, not a single white person would be involved in the planning. That, in itself, is racist.

We find ourselves with a Catch-22 in the definitional generalization of CRT given by Crenshaw and the concept that all social interactions produce evidence of racism. In a video titled, *What Is Critical Race Theory?*

Produced by PragerU, host James Lindsay presents a thoughtful experiment displaying this Catch-22 principal. In his video he says,

> Imagine you own a shop, and two customers enter at the same time—one white and one black. Who do you help first? If you help the black person first, Critical Race Theory would say you did so because you don't trust black people to be left alone in your store. That's racist. If you helped the white person first instead, Critical Race Theory would say you did so because you think blacks are second-class citizens. That's racist, too.[6]

One can see why CRT is so destructive. CRT proponents are looking for racism and will find it, even if it's not there. How does one find something that isn't there? By telling someone they are *unconsciously* racist, there is no need to produce any evidence with this tactic. You are racist because you have been told so.

CRT has expanded beyond a legal analysis into other disciplines, including history, economics, political science, and mathematics. History is the subject most protested by parents, as CRT is most likely to be taught in that context (or is already being taught).

Of course, American History cannot be taught accurately without covering the topics of slavery, race, and racism, and most Americans agree these issues should be discussed in the classroom, as long as the teaching aligns with history. Instead of covering the rise and abolition of slavery and the subsequent civil rights movements, the Left wants our children to be taught that we are systemically racist, that all white people are racist, that race is the most important characteristic that makes up a person, that all our institutions promote white supremacy, that all America's flaws are outgrowths of racism, and our nation's ideals and principals, along with its institutions, should be destroyed and made anew.

CRITICAL RACE THEORY: THE MONSTER IN OUR SCHOOLS

On August 6, 2021, Ben Shapiro and Malcolm Nance debated critical race theory on HBO's *Real Time with Bill Maher*. Ben Shapiro detailed CRT's beliefs. Malcolm Nance agreed, but later changed the definition. Nance made outlandish claims and blatantly lied in the debate. While the exchange is quite lengthy, I believe it is important to see how the Left blatantly lied about their narratives.[7]

Bill Maher: I gotta talk about these muzzle laws, there's these laws that have been introduced in a number of states to not talk about Critical Race Theory. Now Critical Race Theory, I must say to begin with, I hadn't heard the term probably a year ago, now I hear it every day. I think Americans are just starting to hear it and I think no one's exactly sure what it is. They know it has something to do with race and it's some kind of theory. Right? How would you describe it?

Ben Shapiro: I will admit that I read a lot of Critical Race Theory in law school. You know the work of Derek Bell or Jean Stefancic and Richard Delgado.

Bill Maher: This is the stuff no one knows other than you and six other people. What matters is what is it . . . what is it practically . . . it's being taught in schools or some form of . . .

Ben Shapiro: Yes, there's a certain sort of crystallized version of it that is a lot less complex than what Critical Race Theory actually is, but CRT essentially argues that racism is baked into all the systems of American society and that any sort of neutral system is in fact a guise for racial power, and so the argument is made by Derek Bell, for example, that *Brown v. Board of Education*, this is an argument he made in 1991, was actually a way for the white community to leverage its own power. It wasn't an attempt to end segregation in public schools; even things that are reportedly good in terms of race so long as they uphold these broader systems, things like capitalism or things like meritocracy, these things are actually just guises for power. And so what that boils down to in sort of practical terms is all disparity equals discrimination. If you can see any statistics where black people are underperforming white people, this means the system was set up for the benefit of white people and that white people have a duty to tear down these systems in order to alleviate the racism that's implicit in those systems. When it comes to schools, what tends to boil down is kids who are white have experienced privilege because the system was built for white people and we have to change the standards.

Malcolm Nance: I agree with everything he just said, and I appreciate you being honest and defining what it's like to be a black American. I agree with all of those suppositions because they are grounded in truth. The funny thing is it's not just African Americans, right? It's also the Scalp Act of 1749, where for three-hundred modern dollars you had to cut off the head or hair of an Indian to prove that you've got them out of the way to settle. That's a little bit of American history that people should know about. The Chinese Exclusion Acts of the 1840s, these are things we don't talk about.

Ben Shapiro: That's not true that people don't talk about these things. We all do.

Malcolm Nance: You don't want them talked about.

Ben Shapiro: That's not true either.

Malcolm Nance: You wanted to cancel them.

CRITICAL RACE THEORY: THE MONSTER IN OUR SCHOOLS

Ben Shapiro: No Malcolm, I'm sorry, but you're lying. It is lying. I have personally talked about many of the things you just mentioned. I define Critical Race Theory by citing the actual authors of Critical Race Theory, and you seem to be a pretty good beneficiary of the meritocracy because you have merit, Malcolm. So, if you are going to criticize the meritocracy as an outgrowth of white supremacy, then you're going to have to tear down the system that you've succeeded in because you have merit or do you not have merit.

Malcom Nance: You know, when my great-great-grandfather ran away from slavery to join the 111th US colored troops and fight against the South keeping human beings as slaves, he didn't think that in 150 years his great-great-grandson is going to have to sit on stage and argue with a guy that thinks all that is bullshit.

Ben Shapiro: All of what is bullshit?

Malcom Nance: I'm just saying there is no controversy. The controversy that's made up is people saying that this being discussed, this is being taught in school, and that kids should be kept away from it. It's not even a real controversy.

Ben Shapiro: Malcolm, the fifth largest school district in America, Clark County, just decided they were going to lower standards with regard to testing because they wanted to alleviate disparities in outcomes. That is an outgrowth of Critical Race Theory.

Malcolm Nance: Can you draw a straight line to it?

Ben Shapiro: Yes! 100 percent. Because when you say meritocracy is an outgrowth of white supremacy and then you suggest that I'm somehow denying that slavery took place, or your great-great-grandfather was a hero because I'm saying that I want people tested when they are in school to see if they are good at school, what you are purporting to push is just nonsense. It's just sheer bullshit, Malcolm. It's just bullshit.

Bill Maher: But I also think it's a leap to say that he thought that was bullshit because that's not what it is. Are we talking about 2021 or 1861?

Malcolm Nance: The point is, can we talk about 1861 and 2021?

Bill Maher: Yes, we can.

Ben Shapiro: You just did.

Bill Maher: I don't know who is against talking about history.

Malcolm Nance: Well, I mean I understand that they want to, you know, in Texas, they're talking about removing references to the Ku Klux Klan. How can you watch Forrest Gump without even knowing who Nathan Bedford Forrest is? I mean these are people who are historical figures who did bad things. No one is actually saying we want to go back and erase everything and restart and talk to you about these things. Critical Race Theory is a subject because the Republican right has made it a subject. No real school organizations are mandating this course on kids.

Ben Shapiro: Malcolm, I hope every Democrat in America takes your perspective. And they will be shellacked in the polls. Ruy Teixeira, *The Emerging Democrat Majority*, he just wrote a piece about what he called the Fox News fallacy, a tendency of people on the left to believe that just because Fox News mentions something, that it can't be real. The reality is, a lot of this stuff is taught in schools.

CRITICAL RACE THEORY: THE MONSTER IN OUR SCHOOLS

Malcolm Nance: You mean like viruses?

(Ben Shapiro and Bill Maher both are confused.)

Bill Maher: As far as what people are experiencing in their lives and in their schools, you are right that there are states from the old Confederacy that want to airbrush history. That's not, I think, the majority in this country. If you ask me, in CRT, if that means teach history unvarnished? I would say yes, then I'm totally for CRT. If you say, does it mean acknowledging that racism persists today? I would say yes, teach that. Should we have remedial means, that's like affirmative action, there's lots of people who are against that. I'm still for that. I still think when you read the statistics, and I have some of them here, blacks earn 40 percent less, 90 percent less family wealth, high poverty high schools, 72 percent to 31 percent white, live six years shorter, half as likely to go to college, eight times more incarcerated. These are real statistics. The question is, what do we do to address them? You think we should address them, right? The question is, what are we doing about it because if CRT means making children in school fixate on race; I am not for that. If it's about collective guilt, I didn't do anything to your great-great-grand father. I don't want to be responsible for that. If it's about, you know, a toxicity of just from being born white, if it's about dividing everybody into oppressed and oppressor, I'm not for that. So, there are things that are being taught and are going around that I am not for; if that was Critical Race Theory I wouldn't be for.

Malcolm Nance: I agree with you, and I don't think that's Critical Race Theory.

Ben Shapiro: The no-true-Scotsman fallacy is very tiring.

Malcolm Nance: I think what's happened here is this terminology, sort of like defund the police, has been hijacked and been framed around the Left, that they want to do all this. They want to rip down the entire social fabric of America, and they want us to be guilty about everything. I want you to teach history. I had a lot of people in the military, senior officers who had to make life-and-death decisions, who were total morons about the cultures and institutions in the countries where we are going into, and people died because of that. I don't need that here.

Ben Shapiro: So, I have a question. If we agree that history should be taught, then why are you defending Critical Race Theory, which is not history?

Malcolm Nance: Did I just not say a moment ago that I think that term has been hijacked and that's not what we're talking about.

Ben Shapiro: Then why are you defending it?

Malcolm Nance: I am going to go back and repeat that I didn't say that.

Ben Shapiro: You are literally defending Critical Race Theory by redefining it as just teaching history, which is a cheap semantic trick and you know it.

. . .

At the beginning of this discussion, Malcolm Nance agreed with Ben Shapiro's definition of Critical Race Theory. Nance then changed the terms of the definition, saying that schools should be teaching history. He did this by describing his great-great-grandfather, the Scalp Act, and the Ku Klux Klan scene in "Forrest Gump" as examples of Critical Race Theory.

CRITICAL RACE THEORY: THE MONSTER IN OUR SCHOOLS

Once Shapiro calls Nance out on his illogical stance, Nance suddenly says the term has been hijacked. The fact is that the Left wants to indoctrinate our youth with what Shapiro and I have stated regarding Critical Race Theory. The Left will use the smokescreen of "just teaching history" to disguise their true intent.

In economics, CRT urges teachers to show disparities in various structures of America to seemingly support the theory that racism exists. This is what CLS tried to prove that has expanded into the teachings of Critical Race Theorists. With race being the number one factor in what defines a person, activists dismiss other behaviors, such as personal responsibility, which could lead to disparities in social outcomes among races.

In an exchange between conservative Ben Shapiro and columnist Charles Mudede the moderator asked, "When does a disparity not indicate racism?" Ben Shapiro answered, "It's called evidence of racism. When there is no evidence of racism, it's probably not racism. When there is actual evidence of racism, it's probably racism." At this point, the crowd laughs at Shapiro's comment even though it makes sense. Shapiro goes on to say, "The fact is that everybody jumps to, "There is inequality and therefore there is inequity." Just because there was inequality does not mean there was inequity."

Charles Mudede responds as expected, saying, "But there has to be racism. You can't say there is no racism."[8] Mudede is supporting the idea that racism is intrinsic in all interactions, and, even when there is no evidence of racism, the deciding factor must still be racism. How does that make sense? It doesn't. When indoctrinated into the teachings of the Left, any disparity, whether economic or not, must be caused by racism. Those who are taught that there can be no explanation for disparity other than racism, are incapable of reaching outside that thinking.

In mathematics, Critical Race Theory teaches children that two plus two equals five. That isn't a typo; I meant to write five. How is this possible when we know two plus two equals four? The Left changes the impossible to be figuratively possible. Under these terms, if you do not conform to the idea that two plus two is five, or nine, or maybe even three, you are a member of white supremacy that is suppressing minorities or people of color. It is an understatement to say this is a crippling blow to our youth. This simple example has massive consequences for future developments in our nation.

This theory removes the factual knowledge of numbers and how they progress through a number line. Since the student does not need to acknowledge the factual understanding of the number line, their conceptual knowledge is completely disrupted. Both the factual knowledge and conceptual knowledge ultimately flow into procedural fluency, which is the solving portion of a mathematical problem. The reader must understand that this is foundational mathematics. If a house is built on sand, it will crumble, but a house built on rock will stand. The Left wants to indoctrinate our children with ideas that will crumble them and subsequently crumble our country.

Ten
DISCRIMINATION AND DISPARITIES

Since the very beginning of humankind, there have been vast differences between tribes, nations, groups, institutions, and individuals. The Left believes all disparities, such as gender wage gaps, blacks being incarcerated at higher levels, and differences in wages between the races, are evidence of systemic discrimination. The Left will say, "If Case A caused Case B, then every time you see B you can infer that A was the cause." There could be multiple factors that result in B, but the Left will completely ignore all other variables because an alternative narrative will cause their ideology to fall apart.

DISCRIMINATION

Let's start by examining the meaning of *discrimination*, as the Left often manipulates vocabulary to support their ideology. The definitions used here are from Thomas Sowell's book, *Discrimination and Disparities*. Sowell explains that there are two types of discrimination. Type I is "the ability to discern differences in the qualities of people and things, and choose accordingly."[1] Type II is "treating people negatively, based on arbitrary assumptions or aversions concerning individuals of a particular race or sex."[2]

The Left disallows the existence of Type I discrimination—examining people at an individual level regardless of grouping and making distinctions on the basis of consistent, quantifiable parameters. As discussed previously, the Left looks at the world and people through the lens of race, thus there is no individual. There are cases in which we make certain judgments based on individual characteristics that lead to a specific outcome. Sometimes the costs of a particular outcome must be weighed to determine a course of action.

To put this into context, Sowell describes a person walking down the street at night. There appears to be a shadowy figure ahead in an alley on the same side of the street. Based on the characteristic of being a shadowy figure, do you stay on your path and walk past the person, or do you cross the street? To make this decision, you have to weigh the costs of each alternative. If you choose to keep walking toward the person ahead of you, he might kill you, steal your possessions, or assault you; thus, your decision not to cross the street could very well cost you your life. The outcome of this decision would be based on the potential cost to you, not on individualism. Your judgment in this circumstance has nothing to do with race or gender but rather survival.

You could also judge a person based on individualism given certain pre-sorted events or the circumstances of your interaction. For example, I would treat that shadowy figure in an alley differently than I would if I were encountering them upon entering a classroom on the first day of school. The reason for this is based on the possible variations in the given interactions. As I enter my classroom I'm not encountering a random sampling of the general population (which has numerous variations) but rather a pre-selected population of students. I feel safe because I know the people around me are students who want to take the same classes I am taking and because a classroom is a much safer place than a dark alley.

Moreover, Sowell suggest that a person will not only make decisions based on cost analysis but also on "empirical evidence about groups as a whole, or about the interactions of different groups with one another."[3] Let's say there are two groups hoping to be hired by the same employer. In Group A, 60 percent are already working two jobs, while in Group

B only 10 percent are working two or more jobs. The employer needs to analyze the cost of hiring someone who is potentially overworked versus someone who isn't. This would result in roughly 60 percent of Group A not being hired. Hiring someone from Group B would result in better odds of finding someone working one or no jobs.

Hiring someone who is looking for a third who already has two jobs could result in the employee arriving late for work, calling in sick due to exhaustion, poor customer service, or the production of defective products—all resulting in a negative impact for the business. This scenario would not be classified as Type II discrimination since the decision is not based on personal bias or animosity toward a particular group, which falls under Type I discrimination, basing decisions on a group's empirical data. Sowell calls this decision making Type Ib, saying, "If judging each person as an individual is Discrimination Type Ia, we can classify as Discrimination Ib basing decisions about groups on information that is correct for that group, though not necessarily correct for every individual in that group, nor necessarily even correct for a majority of the individuals in that group."[4] This form of Discrimination Type I is the less ideal version, but it is a version that still must be considered.

Discrimination Type Ib can lead to harsher decision-making processes, especially when examining empirical data. Type Ib may result in a lack of developers willing to build in high-crime areas. Even if most of the people living in those localities are not criminals, the cost is too high for potential developers or business owners. If business owners choose to open businesses in high-crime areas, they may have to pay for better security, higher costs of freight, more expensive insurance premiums, compared to a low-crime area. These costs will ultimately be passed on to the consumer, which is why the price of goods and services tend to be higher in high-crime areas. There is also the potential of businesses closing and people losing their jobs.

In October 2021, Walgreens announced the closing of five stores in San Francisco due to organized retail theft. In 2014, Proposition 47 established a measure to reduce felony crimes to misdemeanors. This was created, in part, because the Left asserted that certain groups were being discriminated against and, thus, should receive lesser punishment. The referendum downgraded property theft valued up to $950 to a misdemeanor rather than a felony. Internet videos and newsfeeds showed thieves filling shopping carts, garbage bags, and duffle bags full of consumer goods and then walking out as if they had done nothing. San Francisco Police Chief William Scott said, "If it's a felony, our officers can take action, but if it's a misdemeanor, that arrest has to be a private person's arrest. And that makes a difference because they have to be willing to do that."[5] With this legislation in place, the majority of these thieves will never be put behind bars or face repercussions of any kind.

Phil Caruso, a Walgreen's spokesperson, said, "To help combat this retail theft, we increased our investments in security measures in stores across the city to 46 times our chain average in an effort to provide a safe environment. This is primarily a result of our participation in the city's 10B program to hire off-duty SFPD officers to have a presence in our stores."[6] Walgreen's decision to close stores because of the need for such expensive security measures illustrates how discrimination Type 1 takes effect in the real world. However, the radical Left labeled Walgreen's decision as Type 2 discrimination.

San Francisco city officials denied that Walgreens store closings were based on the increased level of retail theft. Instead, they blamed the departure on Walgreen's plan to close 200 stores nationwide as a cost-cutting measure after losing over a billion dollars during COVID-19 lockdowns. San Francisco supervisor Dean Preston tweeted, "So is Walgreens closing stores because of theft or because of a pre-existing business plan to cut costs and increase profits by consolidating stores and shifting customers to online purchases?"[7] This sleight of hand by the Left is crafty. Two things can be true at the same time. Walgreens could be closing stores due to COVID losses and include the five stores in San Francisco because of the high rates of security in the same plan. San Francisco officials do not want to admit that theft is the reason for the closings as it would underscore the negative effects of leftist policing policies.

Although Discrimination Type II was not present in the Walgreens example, it does exist. Multiple examples of Type II discrimination have taken place throughout human history. This is not to suggest that either form of discrimination is acceptable simply because it has always existed; quite the contrary. The problem is that the Left almost always equates statistical disparities in outcomes with Discrimination Type II. As I mentioned earlier, the reason for this mental roadblock is that the Left does not believe in seeing people as individuals but rather as members of a particular group.

HOUSEHOLD INCOME

Disparity in household income is one of the Left's so-called examples of discrimination. They see that the median household income of black Americans is less than that of white Americans and conclude that white Americans make more money on average because of racial discrimination, white privilege, and white supremacy. The Left's argument goes straight to Type II discrimination of dealing with groups rather than looking at the individual variables that would result in such an outcome.

The notion that America is racist because whites are making more than blacks is false and has been debunked time and time again. As of 2020, Asian Americans have the highest median household income in the United States at $94,904 per year. White Americans follow at $74,912, with Hispanic Americans at $55,321 and then black Americans at $45,870. Type II discrimination would suggest that this data reveals that Asian Americans have more privilege than white Americans.

These groups can be broken down even further into subgroups. The group of Asian-American includes people from the following countries:

China, Korea, Japan, India, Pakistan, Thailand, Vietnam, the Philippines, and others. According to the 2019 Census Bureau population estimate, there are 18.9 million Asian Americans living in the United States.[8] Even among the Asian population, there are disparities in income. Indian Americans have the highest income among Asian American subgroups, with a median income of $100,000. Filipino Americans follow with a median income of $80,000, then Japanese with $74,000, and Chinese with $70,000. A report from the Pew Research Center shows that income inequality in the United States is rising most rapidly among Asian Americans, as Burmese Americans make a median income of $36,000.[9]

To parallel the Left's argument, which of these Asian subgroups holds privilege over another? If one does hold a privilege, what is it and how does it differ from second and third-level privileges? The different levels equate to a hierarchy in privileges. For example, in median-income households among Asian American groups, Indian Americans are at the top of the hierarchy, followed by Filipino. Thus, Indian Americans would have first-class privileges, and Filipino Americans would have second-class privileges over Japanese Americans. The Left struggles with this answer because it is not so much privilege as it is culture. Each of these groups has its own established culture. This is not to say that some groups don't share some cultural traits, but there are differing traits that result in income disparity.

There are reasons why Asian Americans have a higher household median-income. One reason is the occupancy size of the household. It is common for an Asian household to have multiple generations living under one roof. "In 2017, Asian Americans on average had a household size of 3.04, compared to the national average of 2.65."[10] As one would expect, the more working people you have under one roof the higher the income level for that specific household.

Income levels also depend on the area in which one lives. Coastal areas are vastly more expensive to live in than certain parts of Middle America. Data shows that Asian Americans tend to live in areas with higher costs of living, such as Los Angeles, New York, and San Francisco. This cost of living would result in higher wages and higher household income. To break it down even further, an Asian American could be a teacher in California making $75,000. An African American teacher doing the exact same job in Texas could be making $40,000. Is one privileged over the other for making the decision to live in a different locality? Or could there be other reasons for the choices these individuals have made? The latter is the most logical.

There are also disparities in income among African Americans. Census Bureau statistics define a black or African American as "A person having origins in any of the black racial groups of Africa. It includes people who indicate their race as 'black or African American,' or report entries such as African American, Kenyan, Nigerian, or Haitian."[11] Within the grouping of black or African American, there are U.S.-born blacks and black immigrants. In 2013, the median household income for foreign-born blacks was $43,800. In comparison, the median American household income was $52,000.[12] According to the Pew Research Center, "Foreign-born blacks have a higher median income than U.S.-born blacks. U.S.-born blacks have a median household income of $33,500, a full $10,000 less than that among foreign-born black households. Among black immigrants, the group with the highest median annual household income is South Americans at $55,000. For African and Caribbean immigrants, both groups have a median household income of $43,000, while Central Americans have a median household income of $41,400."[13] The Left uses this disparity within the black community as proof of systemic racism, saying that U.S.-born citizens have lived here longer and have succumbed to the powers of supremacy and oppression. They disregard the variables that could contribute to this type of disparity.

Disparities might be attributed to individual decisions and culture. Like U.S.-born Asians and Asian immigrants, 83 percent of black immigrants live in a family household. "This group is made up of 50 percent who live in married-couple households, 24 percent in female-headed households, and 10 percent in male-headed family households." Among foreign-born blacks, 53 percent of Africans and 53 percent of South Americans live in married-couple households. Forty-nine percent of Central-American black immigrants live in married-couple households, as do 46 percent of black immigrants from the Caribbean.[14] Roughly 60 percent of Americans live in married-couple households. These numbers drop when it comes to U.S.-born blacks, with only 36 percent living in married-couple households.

Another variant is the education level of U.S.-born blacks compared to black immigrants. As of 2013, 30 percent of American adults aged 25 and older had a bachelor's degree or higher. Black immigrants were just under the national average with 26 percent of adults holding a bachelors or advanced degree. This gap narrowed in 2016, with the number of black immigrants holding college degrees rising to 28 percent compared to the national average of 31 percent. There are additional disparities among black immigrants. In 2016, Pew Research revealed that 59 percent of Nigerians have attained a bachelor's degree or an advanced degree, followed by Kenyans with 47 percent. Other countries include Ghana, 37 percent; Ethiopia, 31 percent; Guyana, 27 percent; Jamaica, 23 percent; Trinidad, 21 percent, and Haiti and the Dominican Republic with 18 percent each. Every one of these nations has its own established culture with those cultures narrowing further depending on family values.

The 2013 data shows 28 percent of U.S. immigrants adults ages twenty-five or older hold a bachelor's degree or higher. Black immigrants were close behind with 26 percent. Both percentages were comparable to the U.S. population with 30 percent. However, just 19 percent of U.S.-born African Americans in the same demographic have at least a bachelor's degree. As one would expect, higher educational degrees tend to offer more economic opportunity, as well as more career choices.

These disparities in household income have vastly more to do with decision making than racism or Type II discrimination. We always find it easier to blame some faceless figure than to blame ourselves or a family member for a decision that could impact generations. It should be noted that there truly are African American families in the United States that have been impacted by Discrimination Type II, and those effects have modern-day results. With that said, it only takes one generation of good decision making to fork a family tree and move up the income ladder.

Democrats and leftists have worked together to establish a system that forces certain environments to eliminate specific disparities. One of the environments they chose to focus on is education, with the adoption of affirmative action.

AFFIRMATIVE ACTION

The examination of various disparities across different environments resulted in the Left forcing institutions to enact policies to narrow or eliminate those inequalities. Affirmative Action is one of these policies. The term "refers to a policy aimed at increasing workplace or educational opportunities for underrepresented parts of society."[15] In an attempt to alleviate the disparities of minorities, the Left has only hurt them.

Harvard University was sued in federal court regarding discrimination against Asian Americans and the use of an affirmative action program in the student admissions process. The argument is that Harvard implements quotas on the number of Asians that can be admitted into the university. The Left calls this a diversity quota by which every race should be equally represented in all institutions. Harvard was not the only university to allegedly discriminate against Asian Americans. The U.S. Department of Justice and Department of Education opened an investigation into Yale's admission process to look for potential discrimination against Asian Americans.

Princeton conducted a study in 2009 that revealed Asians needed to score 140 points higher on the S.A.T. than whites to have the same chance of admission to top universities. *The New Yorker* reported that the "Supreme Court upheld the constitutionality of the University of Texas at Austin's affirmative-action program, which, like Harvard's, aims to build a diverse class along multiple dimensions and considers race as one factor in a holistic review of each applicant. Justice Anthony Kennedy, writing for the majority, approved of a university's ability to define "intangible characteristics, like student body diversity, that are central to its identity and educational mission."[16]

It's not only Ivy League schools that are pushing affirmative action policies. Heather Mac Donald wrote, in *The Diversity Delusion*, that Duke University "admits black students with SAT scores on average over one standard deviation below those of white and Asians (blacks' combined math and verbal SATs are 1275; whites' are 1416; and Asians' 1457)."[17] The Left has created more of a disparity in terms of GPA and the success of black students at universities where affirmative action was applied.

Peter Arcidiacono, Esteban Aucejo, and Ken Spenner conducted an analysis on racial differences in GPA and choice of majors, and found that blacks' grades were dramatically lower than other ethnic groups. The explanation given is that blacks are being accepted into institutions that are harder academically. In addition, they are being encouraged to pursue a STEM (science, technology, engineering, math) major for which they are ill prepared. As a result, many affirmative-action students change their majors after the first two years to humanities or social sciences.

Arcidiacono, Aucejo, and Spenner also discovered that

> The convergence of black/white grades is then a symptom of the lack of representation among blacks in the natural sciences, engineering, and economics. Over 54 percent of black men who express an initial interest in majoring in the natural sciences, engineering, or economics switch to the humanities or social sciences compared to less than 8 percent of white men. While

the similar numbers for females are less dramatic across races, they are nonetheless large: 33 percent of white women switch out of the natural sciences, engineering, and economics with 51 percent of black women switching.[18]

There could be many reasons for the switch, but one is placing students in courses for which they are not ready.

Any student, regardless of race, who performs poorly in mathematics in high school will likely struggle with math in college. That student will most likely have gaps in their academics that they will have to fill in while students who were correctly placed have already mastered certain prerequisites. In an attempt to rid schools of racial disparities, the institutions have unintentionally created more disparities. Some universities have taken note of this and have implemented policies to reduce the prerequisites required for entry level courses.

As of fall, 2018, incoming freshmen at California state universities did not have to participate in the standardized entry level mathematics exam and the English placement test. Chancellor Timothy White said that the reason for the change was to double the graduation rate from 19 to 40 percent by 2025.[19]

The chancellor's reasoning might seem sound, but we also see another reason for the decision. Over the past decade, minority groups have continued to score lower on the SAT exam.[20] The College Board found that "more African American and Latino students in the Class of 2019 failed to reach SAT benchmarks for college readiness than on the previous year's test." In 2018, 31 percent of Latino and 21 percent of black test takers achieved a combined score of 1030, but the numbers dropped to 29 percent and 20 percent in 2019.[21] White and Asian students were twice as successful on the exam as were African American and Hispanic students.

These numbers are not as much of a shock when we learn that students struggled to pass their high school exit exams. During the course of four years, students have multiple opportunities to take their exit exam. By the end of their fourth year, 92.2 percent of black students had passed the exam. A deeper analysis shows that in tenth grade, only 59.5 percent of blacks were able to pass the exam. This 30 percent jump caught the eye of Michael Watkins, the superintendent of the Santa Cruz County School District and the first African American to hold the post. Watkins said, "I did note that among African American tenth graders only 59.5 percent passed the exit exam, but by twelfth grade it was 92 percent. That tells me a couple of things: those who stayed in school became more familiar with the test and were able to pass it, but there is a significant dropout rate between the tenth and twelfth grades. Watkins also noted that the exit exam is the minimum standard for graduation. The fact that African American students are not passing the test earlier indicates to him that they are ill-prepared to attend a four-year college.[22]

Watkins correctly points out that the increase in the number of those passing the exam is partly due to students having multiple opportunities to take it. Moreover, there is also a significant drop-out rate among black students, which alters the population of black students taking the exam. Eliminating students who struggled in school would obviously result in a positive trend in the passing rate.

This sampling can be extrapolated across the entire United States. Some states have removed the high school exit exam altogether. California and roughly thirty-eight other states have passed legislation which says that students no longer have to pass the exam in order to receive a diploma. Those states say the exam did not fit or adhere to the common core standards and, thus, was not a sufficient exam. They further claim that the test created educational disparities by race, income, and disability. In reality, removing the exam boosted graduation rates, even if students haven't met basic standards.

In a scene in the movie, *National Lampoon's Vegas Vacation*, Chevy Chase's character notices water coming out of a hole in the wall at the

Hoover Dam. He asks his daughter for her gum so he can plug the hole. He does so, but the water starts coming out of other holes. Chevy chews more gum and tries plugging another hole, which only results in more holes. The analogy here is that the Left is artificially trying to remove disparities but, in doing so, has only created more disparities and more harm.

According to the Left, the student who studied hard, got good grades, and made good decisions should not have an advantage over the student who did not study, got average grades, and made poor decisions. They insist the person who did not study and made poor decisions deserves to be admitted into a university, even if stronger, more qualified students are refused admittance.

Does this make sense to you?

NEEDED: A GENTLE PUSH FORWARD

We've already seen how a black person who did not study hard, got average grades, and made poor decisions, is often accepted into a university over an Asian person who studied hard, got good grades, and made good decisions—simply because of the color of his or her skin. Isn't that racist and discriminatory? Again, the Left will turn a blind eye as long as these discriminatory policies rid the nation of any so-called disparity.

The solution is to establish qualifications that must be met to enter college. If someone, regardless of race, does not meet the qualifications, they should not be accepted. College admissions need to be based on good decisions that were made on an individual level. Each individual has three years of middle school to learn good habits for schooling. If they can't figure this out on their own, their parents have the responsibility to instill those habits in them. Students also have four years in high school to work toward meeting the qualifications necessary to be accepted by the university of their choosing.

The Left claims those who oppose affirmative action are bigots and that some children don't have the same resources and opportunities as others. While it's true that not all students are afforded the same resources, there are virtually an unlimited number of resources at a student's disposal. Mathematics has not changed much in the past hundred years, but how we solve problems is different. There are thousands of used textbooks parents can find to help their children study. Hundreds of used, free copies of SAT prep books are available. People should not wait for resources to come to them but should seek them out.

We should be encouraging all kids to try hard and persevere. Are they going to study? Are they going to study harder than everyone else? Will they seek after resources and opportunities? I'm not suggesting that all moms and dads should become "Tiger parents," but it is certainly important to help our youngsters make wise decisions.

In the end, race should not be a factor in determining acceptance into a university. The Left may have good intentions, but empathy can be harmful. In their attempts to help some, they hurt others. Research shows that disparities are created when people are allowed to make their own choices. There will always be those who succeed and those who don't. We should help those who are failing to succeed, but we must do it in a way that doesn't hurt anyone else. Affirmative action within education is racist, discriminatory, and needs to end.

WAGE GAP

Just as we've seen with affirmative action, if the Left sees any disparity in wages between races or genders, they want to put a policy in place to eliminate it. There is truth in the fact that women, on average, earn less than men. According to the Bureau of Labor Statistics, in 2020, women's annual earnings were 82.3 percent of men's. As is almost always the case, this truth is exaggerated. Many have heard that women earn 70 cents for every $1 men earn. Another well-known myth said that a woman would earn 59 cents for every $1 a man brings home. Many leftists and even moderate Democrats accept this untruth blindly.

If these myths were true, why would any employer hire men (and pay them a dollar) when they could hire women to do the same work for 70 cents? Corporations would only hire women so they could maximize their profit. Rather than examine the data further, the Left immediately goes to the discrimination argument. They point to racism, sexism, and how the world was built on patriarchy. When we examine the facts, we find that women are sometimes paid less than men because of their lifestyle choices, which affect their ability to earn. The Left chooses to ignore this.

When we examine the data provided by the Bureau of Labor Statistics or the U.S. Census Bureau, we find that the wage gap is calculated on median earnings data. In other words, it is based on univariate data, which is a study conducted on a single characteristic or attribute. Anyone who has taken a basic-level statistics course would know this is not an appropriate statistic for this argument. We should analyze the variables that contribute to women earning less or earning more.

One of the variables affecting the gender wage gap is the choice to have children and stay home to raise them. The Left does not necessarily believe that women choose to have children and stay home with them, but rather that men force them to do this. This comes from assuming that the world is based on patriarchy.

The Pew Research Center found that roughly one in ten mothers who hold a master's degree or Ph.D. stays at home to care for their families. The research center *also* found that, "among mothers with professional degrees, such as medical degrees, law degrees or nursing degrees, 11 percent are relatively affluent and are out of the workforce in order to care for their families. This is true for 9 percent of master's degree holders and 6 percent of mothers with a PhD."[23] The most recent research shows that the growth of stay-at-home moms comes from those with less education.

These high-income earners would negatively affect the gender pay gap for women.

Some mothers say they were pushed out of the workforce because of work/family conflicts, mainly as a result of employers being unwilling to create flexible schedules. This may seem coldhearted, but it isn't the employer's fault an employee had a child. Having a child may impact the performance of certain duties agreed upon in holding a position. This is not the fault of the employer but a result of the decision of the parents. On the other hand, a mother may have already had a child and then accepted a job in which she agreed to certain responsibilities only to find she could not keep that commitment. Either way, the decision to have children and stay home to raise them impacts a person's wage-earning potential.

Career choices also matter when comparing wage disparities. The type of occupation each gender chooses creates a disparity. Georgetown University put together a list of the five highest paying college majors. They then showed the percentages of men and women majoring in those fields. Petroleum engineering was the highest paying major, with 87 percent of students being male. Pharmaceutical science was second, with females at 52 percent of those in that major. Mathematics and computer science were in third place with 67 percent of students being male, followed by aerospace engineering with 88 percent male and, lastly, chemical engineering with 72 percent male. The data shows clearly that men choose these majors disproportionately more than women. Georgetown University also disclosed a list of the five lowest-paying college majors. Women comprised the majority of those studying four of those five.

Even when men and women have the same profession, they often make different career choices. Men tend to work longer hours and take less time off than women. Men lean toward different specialties within their professions that result in higher pay. Factoring in the different choices men and women make by conducting a multivariate study on gender pay shrinks the pay gap from 18 cents to roughly 6.6 cents. The American Association of University Women conducted this exact study. What about this 6.6 cents gender gap? What variables make up this gap? No clear answer can be supported by research. We don't know, but one thing can be expected: the Left will attribute this differential to racism, misogyny, discrimination, bigotry, or another negative descriptor.

THE WAGE GAP IN SPORTS

To explain why there are instances when men and women should not be paid the same, let's look at sports. In 2020, soccer player Megan Rapinoe was used as an example for pay disparity. In an NPR interview, Terry Gross interviewed Rapinoe to discuss equal pay and the meaning of the U.S. flag. Gross said,

> You've helped turn women's soccer into a very popular sport in the U.S., and you've helped pave the way for more equity in women's sports. Give us a sense of some of the disparities between how men and women have been paid in soccer and how they've been treated.

Megan replied,

> The amount of money that we could possibly earn in our contract compared to the amount of money that the men could possibly earn in the contract is very different. I think a lot of—a lot is made about the guaranteed money in our contract and the different compensation structures that we have. But when you look at the possibility of money for each team, ours is vastly, vastly lower than the men.[24]

Gross went on to correlate Rapinoe's wins and championships as a justification for pay that is equal to men's soccer. There is just one problem: men's sports and women's sports are not the same.

Society seems to find men's professional sports more entertaining to watch than women's professional sports. On the whole, men are physically faster and stronger than women. Look at the world record set in each sport and the differences are obvious.

The Left does not believe in biological differences between men and women. I am not sure they even believe in the idea of men and women anymore, but I digress. I'm not saying that women's sports are not entertaining. Women's figure skating, gymnastics, and tennis are popular sports. I'm talking about the hierarchy of entertainment that society enjoys and is willing to shell out hard-earned money to watch.

When comparing the revenue figures of women's sports versus men's sports, we find a massive disparity There are very few things that women's sports can change or alter to equalize their revenue earnings with the men. Athletes like Rapinoe will blame their contracts and their employers for this disparity, but let us remember that Rapinoe agreed to the terms of the contract she signed. Decision-making again comes into effect. If she honestly thought she was worth more than she was being offered, she should never have signed the contract. Why not negotiate with another team for a better contract? The market has a limit for sports athletes regardless of gender, and the market determined her pay.

Unfortunately, society is not willing to pay the same amount of money to see Megan Rapinoe play soccer as they would Cristiano Ronaldo. Since the consumer is paying less to see Rapinoe, her team makes less revenue than Ronaldo's team. The employer can only offer so much to Rapinoe and her teammates. It is not so much a gender problem as it is a numbers problem.

We can also look at the NBA to show the huge disparity in revenue between men and women. In 2018, the NBA made $7.4 billion in revenue compared to $60 million by the WNBA. To put this in perspective, the WBNA made 0.8 percent of what the NBA generated. The WNBA did not make even 1 percent of what the NBA makes. And they should be equally paid? Right or wrong, society is willing to pay more at the box office to see NBA stars over WNBA stars. The average ticket price for an NBA game was $89 compared to $17.42 for the WNBA. In 2019, the NBA finals drew 15.14 million viewers compared to the WNBA's 2018 ratings of 231,000. The number of games played is another factor in earnings. The NBA plays 1,230 games, and the WNBA plays 204.[25] We could devote an entire book to sports disparities between men and women, but we only need a few examples to understand why there would be differences in pay. I encourage the reader to examine other resources to further understand these pay differences.

If anyone, regardless of race or gender, wants to make more money; they must make the decisions that enable them to earn more. It is a lot easier to complain about the world and its injustices than it is to persevere and make decisions that allow you to rise above.

Eleven
ABORTION

As the wooden horse stood outside the gates of Troy, the Trojans looked on in amazement. The majestic piece of artistry and carpentry built by Epeius was a gift from the Greeks, a gift the Trojans welcomed into their city with open arms. As we have seen, the "horse" that sits within America's walls is made up of leftist ideologies, such as fascism, racism, slavery, colonizers, propaganda, the MSM, and many more. The Trojan Horse is believed to have been built with various pieces of wood, with each board having its own different length and width.

One of the largest panels of those that make up the "horse" of the Left is abortion. Behind this panel we find something barbaric and evil, yet these words alone do not describe the abomination of abortion. The Left believes it is a woman's right to kill an unborn baby. Abortion goes against the morality and creed this country was built on. The Left wants to strip both the unborn and born of their right to pursue life and liberty. This destruction of morality will inevitably lead to the collapse of America. John Adams said, "Our Constitution was made only for a moral and religious people."[1] Sadly, the importance of religion in America has been dwindling for the past five decades.

In 1952, Americans were asked to rate the importance of religion in their lives. An astonishing 75 percent of Americans surveyed said it was not just important but "very important." By 2018, that number dropped to 51 percent.[2] Oddly enough, between 1952 and 1978, the importance of religion dropped almost 25 percent. I believe this decrease can be linked to abortion. While the value of religion was dropping in America, the push for abortion had never been higher. On January 22, 1973, the Supreme Court ruled in a 7–2 decision that the right to an abortion was guaranteed by the United States Constitution. Although no one can prove a direct connection between the decline in the importance of religion and the endorsement of abortion rights, it seems clear to me that there is a correlation.

In this chapter, we will look at the history of abortion, various Supreme Court cases, and the arguments the Left has made in favor of abortion. The Court's decision in *Roe v. Wade* fundamentally changed our electoral democracy. For centuries, our democracy has left policy issues to the legislative representatives elected by citizens. For some reason, the Supreme Court decided that the matter of abortion was an issue that should not be left up to the American people and their elected representatives but rather to the authorities of the Court.

We must return to our moral and religious roots. If we don't, there is a good chance that more appalling rulings will come from the Court and continue to weaken the United States from the inside out.

HISTORY OF ABORTION

As an entire book could be written on this topic, we will only look at the foundation of the history of abortion, which crosses time, cultures, and religions. In *Medical History of Contraception*, Dr. Norman Himes writes how "primitive societies by tribes and continents shows that several had crude contraceptive knowledge, but that more commonly the volitional checks were abortion and infanticide."[3] Himes notes that the earliest written records of abortion date to Egypt in about 1500 BC. Abortions were performed by inserting sharp objects into the mother and extracting the baby. In addition to the Egyptians, the Romans, Greeks, Persians, and other societies performed abortions.

ABORTION

In ancient times, herbal remedies were used to alter a woman's menstrual cycle. The crown jewel of herbal remedies was the silphium plant. Silphium was in such high demand that it was harvested to extinction. Not everyone could afford herbal remedies at the time, which resulted in more drastic measures. Drawings found in ancient ruins depict pregnant women having their abdomens beaten with a mallet. As ancient and barbaric as this practice was, it is still utilized in Asia today.

Circa 300 BC, physicians in Greek and Roman societies advised women not to use sharp devices to induce miscarriages but to carry heavy objects, jump up and down, attempt fasting, and bloodletting. Protecting the baby was not their concern but fear that vital organs would be injured. As Himes mentioned, these practices were used by various civilizations on different continents. As civilizations became more advanced and moved into the classical period, philosophers grappled with the question of whether a baby in utero was a human being or something else just as significant.

"When is it a life?" was a topic of debate hundreds of years before Christ walked the earth. From the study of various writings and symbols, we can see that acceptance of abortion depended on the society of the time. Aristotle meditated on life and when it began. The dialogue of many religions, faiths, and philosophers centered on the idea of ensoulment—when the human body gains a soul. Some believed ensoulment happened at conception. Others believed the soul entered when the baby moved in the womb. Still others claimed it didn't happen until birth. Aristotle's opinion of ensoulment is quite unique in that he depicts the development of the human soul as something that evolves. According to the philosopher, there were three types of human souls: nutritive soul, sensitive soul, and intellective soul.

In chapter three of book two of Aristotle's *DeGeneratione*, he writes how the nutritive soul takes place at the very beginning and is possessed by all living things. This first stage can be correlated to plants and is designated the bottom tier of the soul hierarchy. The next stage separates plants from animals. The sensitive soul is what allows animals to move and gain senses that permit them to interact with the world. The intellectual soul separates the animals from the humans. Aristotle presents the intellectual soul as that which allows humans to reason and think critically. Regardless of a baby's level of ensoulment, it is a human life with the potential to reason and think critically.

Unlike today, most ancient civilizations performed abortion as a means of population control. Aristotle strongly opposed this strategy. He believed that if population control was to be established, the number of children per couple should be fixed.

Some philosophers believed that a baby did not become formed in the womb and begin to live until forty days after conception for males and eighty to ninety days for females. The argument centered around the inferiority of females compared to males and the idea that this delayed the development of the female baby. Philosophers came to the "forty-day" mark by analyzing babies. They determined that babies began to take on a human appearance by the fortieth day. At this time, the eyes formed, along with the ears and nose. Most Roman Catholic theologians including St. Thomas Aquinas, St. Augustine of Hippo, and St. Jerome, espoused the view that the fetus is ensouled at around day forty.[4] These philosophers' viewpoints greatly impacted the thinking of the early Church regarding abortion.

The Church grappled with the stages of ensoulment with most of the world's foremost religions addressing the question of when life begins. Early Jewish and Christian doctrines have shifted between a formed fetus versus an unformed fetus. Over time, the consensus agreed that formed or unformed was irrelevant. Conception and development were part of a divine process and thus should not be aborted or terminated by human intervention. Not until the late 1500s did the Catholic Church declare abortion to be murder. For hundreds of years, the Church wrestled with this issue. In the late 1800s, Pius IX ruled that all abortions would be classified as murder, a belief that stands today. Throughout history, many religious scholars and philosophers struggled with the aspect of ensoulment and the question of when life begins. It wasn't until the age of science that this struggle between ensoulment and the beginning of life faded.

Before scientific tests were available, doctors relied on movement in the womb to determine life. In modern times, with the invention of ultrasound and high-frequency endovaginal transducers, life can be detected as early as eight to twelve days. The majority of scientists and doctors agree that life begins at conception. Over the last couple of decades, scientists have been able to observe more detail during the first twenty-four hours of human life. According to the American College of Pediatricians, many consider the time of cell membrane fusion when the embryo gives evidence of being a different kind of cell than either oocyte or sperm, to be the beginning of a new human life since within minutes the new embryo acts to prevent the merger of another sperm with itself and starts the business of self-replication. The single-celled embryo is a very different kind of cell than that of sperm or oocyte and contains a unique genome that will determine most future bodily features and functions of his or her lifetime.[5]

This science is not subjective but rather objective—something anyone can observe with the use of technology. With these advancements, scientists have been able to track the different stages of development by the hour.

The Carnegie Stages of the Human Embryonic Development is the gold standard in embryonic science and shows that, from the very beginning, the human embryo specifically produces human enzymes and proteins. He or she continually forms specifically human tissues and organ systems. Unless prevented, a new human being (a human embryo) will continue to grow and biologically develop until death (fetus, infant, toddler, child, teenager, and adult human being).[6] Science can now show the development of a human being on a micro-scale verifying that life begins at conception. It is an objective fact that abortions terminate human life. The issue is that Americans no longer agree on objective facts.

The lack of agreement on scientific facts has led to modern-day movements, such as pro-abortionists and pro-lifers. Planned Parenthood describes pro-abortionists as people who "believe that everyone has the basic human right to decide when and whether to have children. When you say you're pro-choice you're telling people that you believe it's okay for them to have the ability to choose abortion as an option for an unplanned pregnancy, even if you wouldn't choose abortion for yourself."[7]

This is slightly misleading, as some abortionists support aborting a baby even when he or she is planned and the mother has already given birth.

As one would expect, the pro-life movement is anti-abortion and believes life begins at conception. These two sides battled over abortion laws for many years, until *Roe v. Wade* led to an unprecedented ruling by the Supreme Court in 1973.

ROE V. WADE

Before *Roe v. Wade*, early regulations primarily dealt with drugs administered to women to induce abortions. As one could imagine, drugs that have the potential to kill a human being in the womb could also kill the mother. Even so, women still chose to take the drugs despite the risk. Abortions were legal in the United States until Connecticut passed a statute banning them in 1821. Many states followed suit and soon every state had some form of legislation regarding abortion. Interestingly, at the same time states began shaping legislation regarding abortion, the first National Woman's Rights Convention was held in Worcester, Massachusetts, in 1850.[8]

The Woman's Rights movement laid the groundwork that led to the *Roe v. Wade* decision. Margaret Sanger, a pioneer for woman's rights, fought for the right to birth control. Sanger worked as a nurse, serving many immigrant women who had unwanted pregnancies. She witnessed women performing self-induced abortions or giving birth to children they did not want. Speaking with these women, Sanger found that many of them did not have access to information that could help them avoid an unwanted pregnancy. She believed that giving women information that could prevent them from getting pregnant would lead to greater empowerment for them and liberate them from a life of drudgery. How could she inform women about contraception when the federal government outlawed such actions? Without finding a way around the law, Sanger issued pamphlets through the mail. She was ultimately caught and indicted for violating federal Comstock Laws, a series of federal laws passed in the late-nineteenth century that were designed to regulate morality. Despite her arrest, Sanger's popularity grew, as did the birth-control movement.

In 1929, the National Committee on Federal Legislation for Birth Control was created to influence government decisions to overturn contraception restrictions. This committee helped reverse the Comstock Laws, the very laws Sanger had violated. Through her notoriety, she became the lead spokesperson for the Birth Control Federation of America, later to be called Planned Parenthood. In the 1950s, Gregory Pincus and John Rock created the first birth-control pills.[9] Sanger believed the pill would give women the right to choose when they wanted to have children and thus give them more power over their lives.

The creation of the birth control pill led to protests and some states passed laws prohibiting their sale, even to married couples. This led to the Supreme Court case *Griswold v. Connecticut* in which the Court ruled a state's ban on the use of contraceptives violated the right to marital privacy.[10] The plaintiffs were the executive director of Planned Parenthood League of Connecticut, Estelle Griswold, and Dr. C. Lee Buxton, who had been found guilty of prescribing birth control devices to married women. The two appealed the ruling claiming the law violated the U.S. Constitution. The state stood its ground and upheld the conviction. Griswold and Buxton then appealed to the United States Supreme Court.

The Supreme Court ruled in a 7–2 decision that the law violated the right to marital privacy. Justice William O. Douglas wrote for the majority and suggested "that specific guarantees in the Bill of Rights have penumbras [shadows], formed by emanations from these guarantees that help give them life and substance."[11] In layman's terms, the Bill of Rights has a source that creates an umbrella effect that establishes shadows where new rights can be discovered. According to Douglas, these rights had always been there, unbeknownst to our Founding Fathers, and had eluded elected legislatures for over 176 years. Within the "shadow," Douglas argued that a "zone of privacy" emanated from the First, Third, Fourth, Fifth, Ninth, and Fourteenth Amendments.

In the shadowy field of penumbra, Douglas magically found the right of association within the First Amendment. To make his argument, he cited various cases such as *Meyer v. Nebraska*, *Pierce v. Society of Sisters*, and *NAACP v. Alabama*. The Court found that the First Amendment protected such collateral rights as the right of association, the right to educate one's children, as well as "the right to read . . . and freedom of inquiry, freedom of thought, and freedom to teach."[12] In short, Douglas reverted to cases to support rights that he found in the penumbras of the Bill of Rights. He would go on to say that the Third Amendment, which places restrictions on housing soldiers in any house without the owner's consent and forbidding the practice in peacetime, could be absorbed by this so-called "zone of privacy." He also attached the Fourth Amendment prohibiting unreasonable searches and seizures, along with the Fifth Amendment privilege against self-incrimination.

Somehow this "zone of privacy" was transformed into the "right of privacy" by changing the word *zone* to *right*. Three other Justices utilized the Ninth and Fourteenth Amendments in their concurring opinions with Justice Douglas. The Ninth Amendment states, "The enumeration in the Constitution, of certain rights, shall not be construed to deny or disparage others retained by the people."[13] Justice Arthur Goldberg used this to argue that the Court can rule the "right of privacy" or "the fundamental right of marital privacy" without having to find it in a specific constitutional amendment. Justices John Marshal Harlan II and Bryon White used the Fourteenth Amendment to support the inclusion of the right of privacy in the due-process clause, which has traditionally been protected by American society.

I agree with the suggestion that it appears as though these justices were engaging in mental gymnastics. As you will recall, *Griswold v. Connecticut* was about birth control. Somehow, birth control became attached to the ban against quartering soldiers in private homes. I question how Connecticut's birth-control law is related to unreasonable searches and seizures. According to the Court, this is all found in the shadows of the Bill of Rights. The way the Court sees it, the Ninth Amendment grants the freedom to scour these shadows to find rights that are not listed in the Constitution and magically attach those newly found rights to pre-established rights. This is not how the law was intended to work. It has paved a way for justices to rule on a policy outcome they favor. The seven justices who agreed in favor of Griswold found (in the shadows) that the right to privacy was fundamental and substantive. Oddly, just twenty-eight years prior to *Griswold v. Connecticut* in *West Coast Hotel v. Parrish* (1937), the Court rejected the idea that the Constitution protects substantive rights. In this case, the Court found that the Fourteenth Amendment does not protect substantive economic rights against the state, such as the right to freely negotiate contracts and wages.[14] The court would later rule in *Griswold* that in non-economic areas such as "the right to privacy," these "substantive rights" do exist. Over the next decade, the Supreme Court would expand the "right to privacy" beyond the marital context. In *Eisenstadt v. Baird* (1972), the Court found that the state could not ban an individual from using contraceptives.

These cases laid the groundwork for a case that changed our electoral democracy. On January 22, 1973, the Supreme Court issued a 7–2 decision that the United States Constitution protects a woman's right to choose an abortion. Prior to *Roe v. Wade*, state legislatures decided the laws governing the practice of abortion. As a result, various states passed differing abortion laws. In 1969, Norma McCorvey, pregnant with her third child, decided she didn't want to keep the baby and sought a place that would perform an abortion. At that time, Texas law did not allow abortion.

Insistent on an abortion, McCorvey was referred to Linda Coffee and Sarah Weddington, attorneys eager to represent women seeking abortions. Her case progressed to the United States Supreme Court with Norma McCorvey using the name Jane Roe. Henry Wade was the district attorney of Dallas County at the time. The district court of Texas ruled that the state's abortion ban was illegal. The reasoning given by the state was that it violated the constitutional right to privacy. This was eventually appealed to the U.S. Supreme Court.

The U.S. Supreme Court struck down the Texas law banning abortion. With this ruling, abortions effectively became legal across the nation. The Court found that it was the woman's choice if she wanted an abortion during the first trimester. During the second trimester, the government was able to regulate abortion but not ban it. This allowed for the protection of the mother who may have health concerns. In the third trimester, if the fetus could survive on its own outside the womb, it should be protected by the state. The only exception to this would be if the mother's life were endangered. All of this fell under the "right to privacy" protection given by the Fourteenth Amendment.

In writing the opinion for the majority, Justice Harry A. Blackmun performed the same mental gymnastics as Justice Douglas. During *Griswold v. Connecticut*, Justice Douglas invented new rights from the shadows that emanated from the Bill of Rights. Justice Blackmun took those invented rights and ruled that the "due process" clause was included in the "right to privacy." The Fourteenth Amendment was not intended to create new rights, but to secure to all persons, notably including freed slaves and their descendants, the rights and liberties already guaranteed by the Constitution.[15]

ABORTION

The framers of our Constitution were not cognizant of abortion. If there was a "zone of privacy," a "right to privacy," or a "right to abortion," they would have included them in the Constitution. If this is a right American society wants and supports, we should elect politicians who will pass an amendment to guarantee it.

For *Roe v. Wade*, our Supreme Court acted against our constitutional system. Under our system, most policy issues have been left to our elected officials. This puts the power in the hands of the people, not the government. In *Roe v. Wade*, the Court decided that the people no longer have such authority. Anyone can scour the Constitution trying to find any sort of reference to the "right to an abortion" but will find no such right, let alone the word *abortion*.

The *Roe* decision has been criticized by many legal scholars, justices, and lawyers. Edward Lazarus, a former law clerk of Justice Harry Blackmun, stated, "As a matter of constitutional interpretation and judicial method, Roe borders on the indefensible. I say this as someone utterly committed to the right to choose, as someone who believes such a right has grounding elsewhere in the Constitution instead of where Roe placed it, and as someone who loved Roe's author like a grandfather." Professor Geoffrey Stone of the University of Chicago Law School and a clerk for Justice Brennan stated that "everyone in the Supreme Court, all the justices, all the law clerks knew it was "legislative" or "arbitrary." Yale Law School Professor John Hart Ely observed that *Roe v. Wade* "is bad because it is bad constitutional law, or rather because it is not constitutional law and gives almost no sense of an obligation to try to be."[16] At least six U.S. Supreme Court justices have criticized the Court's ruling on *Roe*. These include Byron White, William Rehnquist, Antonin Scalia, Clarence Thomas, Anthony Kennedy, and Sandra Day O'Connor. We have only covered a few reasons why *Roe v. Wade* was bad constitutional law, but scholars have written entire books on the issue.

DEBUNKING PRO-ABORTION ARGUMENTS

Pro-abortionists argue that the fetus is a "clump of cells," thus, not a person but a "potential person." This language allows them the freedom to kill something that is not human. Some refer to the baby as a "parasite." Many pro-abortionists go a step further and claim a baby isn't a human until the mother gives birth. They do this even though it is a scientific fact that the fetus in a mother's womb is indeed a human life with innate potential. Hymie Gordon, Professor Emeritus at the Mayo Clinic, says, "By all the criteria of modern biology, life is present from the moment of conception." Micheline Mathew-Roth of Harvard Medical School agrees, saying "It is scientifically correct to say that an individual life begins at conception." Between the moment the sperm joins with the ovum (egg) to form one cell and by day fourteen, the baby will already have the complex genetic blueprint for every detail, including gender, eye color, height, and skin tone. This code is separate from that of the mother.

A specific genetic blueprint generates the development of each individual human being. This is synchronous with the findings of Micheline Mathew-Roth and others. During the third week of its existence, the human being has its own nervous system. Amazingly, this happens before most women even realize they are pregnant. According to the American Pregnancy Association, the majority of women discover they are pregnant around weeks four to seven.[17] By the fourth week, the heart has begun to beat, and the arms, legs, and ears can be seen. By week eight, the baby has its own fingerprints and is able to sense touch and feel pain.

The idea that a fetus is a clump of cells has some truth to it. All species of animals are multicellular and are, thus, a clump of cells. As stated earlier, negligently embracing the notion that the human being is only a clump of cells allows abortionists to believe they are not committing murder or taking a human life. They have to deny or ignore the science or their viewpoint would be shattered. Ultimately, they would have to accept the fact that they were accomplices to murder. For years we have been told to "follow the science" by the Democratic Party, the MSM, and the progressive Left. Yet, when science, data, and statistics are introduced that contradict their beliefs, they no longer want to follow the science.

Pro-abortionists stand on the platform of a woman's right to choose and insist that pro-lifers want to control women's bodies. There is some truth to the belief that a woman has the right to choose. Women have the right to choose their own career paths, where they live, whom they date, and so many other life choices. No woman—let alone *any* person—has the *universal* "right to choose." There are limitations. If we had a universal right to choose, the entire planet would be destroyed by lawlessness and anarchy. Most people would agree that no one has the right to kill an innocent human being. That's not a choice someone should be allowed to make. The case for the "right to choose" would have to be defended universally rather than for one specific argument.

What is keeping the U.S. Supreme Court Justices from finding the "right to choose" within the same "shadows" where they supposedly found the "zone of privacy" in the Bill of Rights? As mentioned in the section on *Roe v. Wade*, the Court essentially established a universal right to privacy. In both cases, the concept of *universal* is elastic; it will expand and contract to fit the beliefs of those who are in the position of judging. Of course, this is not what the Founding Fathers intended, but the Court's decisions in *Griswold v. Connecticut*, *Roe v. Wade*, and other cases set a terrible precedent. If we were to use the same so-called reasoning that was used in the cases discussed in this book, the U.S. Supreme Court could find the "right to choose" within the penumbras of the Bill of Rights and attach it to the Fourteenth Amendment. The fact is, a woman, or any person, does not have a universal right to choose nor does anyone have the right to kill an innocent human being.

Pro-abortionists take this "right to choose" and attach it to "my body, my choice" or "pro-lifers want to control my body." The pro-lifers' argument is not regarding the woman's body but rather the child's body. The child has its own unique DNA. No can have one DNA at birth and then later develop a different DNA. The only way two humans could possibly have the same DNA is same-sex siblings who were created with the same selection of chromosomes. The probability of this taking place is hard to fathom. Theoretically, same-sex siblings could be created with the same selection of chromosomes, but the odds of this happening would be one in 246 or about 70 trillion.[18] The fact remains that everything we use to differentiate one human being from another can be applied to a mother and the child in the womb.

Another argument pro-choice defenders use to justify abortion is that of pregnancy occurring as a result of rape or incest. According to the Guttmacher Institute, one percent of women obtain an abortion because they became pregnant through rape, and less than 0.5 percent do so because of incest.[19] To say this is an outlier in the data is an understatement. About one million abortions are performed every year in the United States. Using outliers is a dishonest way of pushing a narrative. For example, if I have 240 students in my class and only 2 or 3 of them fail, would I use the grades of the latter to describe all 237 students' grades? The answer is a resounding no. The pro-abortion movement and the Left use outliers to describe an entire data set. This is not to say that rape and incest are okay. It is horrific to think there are monsters who commit these heinous crimes. With that said, the sins of the father do not justify the death of an innocent child. This child, regardless of how it was created, should be afforded the protections the rest of us receive.

Despite all the talk about rape and incest, the truth is that the primary reason why abortions are obtained is because having a child is deemed inconvenient. A study from BMO Harris reported that the cost of caring for a child ranges from $9,540 to $25,000 a year. The Guttmacher Institute found that 75 percent of abortion patients in 2014 qualified as poor (having an income below the federal poverty level of $15,730 for a family of two) or low-income (having an income of 100 to 199 percent of the federal poverty level). Clearly, it would be almost impossible to raise a child with that type of income. But can this be blamed on the child? People who are old enough to have sexual relations know that pregnancy is a possible outcome, but rather than giving birth to the child, trying to raise it, or putting it up for adoption, they would rather kill it. This falls in line with the Left's philosophy on so many issues that someone else should have to pay the consequences for the actions of others. In this case, it is not reparations, it is not higher taxes, it is not affirmative action but rather the death of an innocent child.

In addition to the inconvenience argument, pro-abortion advocates include the health risks of being pregnant, such as high blood pressure, depression, emotional distress, general stress, chronic hypertension, cardiovascular disease, and stroke. The list is quite extensive and is almost reminiscent of TV commercials that catalog all the side effects of a drug being advertised. It would be irrational to downplay the toll pregnancy places on the human body. Even with this extension of the inconvenience argument, how is this in any way the baby's fault? The short answer is it is not, but it is still the unborn baby who has to pay the ultimate price.

Even if protection was used, the man and woman still take a level of risk when having sex. Failure of contraception should be a part of the discussion before having sex with someone. If a woman gets pregnant, with or without contraception, the parents have the responsibility of caring for that child. If they are unable to do so, the child can be given up for adoption. The remedy for this situation is simple. If you can't afford to have a child, don't want to take on the health risks of having a child, or don't want to deal with whatever the "inconvenience" may be, then don't have sex.

Democrats, the progressive Left, and abortionists take no responsibility for their actions. This lack of responsibility has led states like New York to allow abortions all the way to full term. New York's policies on abortion mirror those of the Democratic Party. Both Joe Biden and Nancy Pelosi have been denied communion by the Roman Catholic Church for their stance on abortion. To put this in more perspective, almost every Democrat in the U.S. Senate and House of Representatives stands with their party in support of abortion rights, while almost all Republicans reflect their party's position against abortion. This support from Democrats and leftists has led to the deaths of roughly 63 million children since *Roe v. Wade*. The same party that says they want to help the black community and support Black Lives Matter has supported the killing of roughly 19 million innocent black children. It is abhorrent that the same party that wants to protect children in schools from mass shootings allows over one million innocent children to be murdered each year because they're "inconvenient."

Epilogue
TIME TO TAKE A STAND AGAINST THE TROJAN HORSE

The story of the Trojan War has been passed down from one generation to another. This ancient war involved over 200,000 men, 1,200 ships, the destruction of dozens of cities, and led to thousands of deaths. The war persisted for ten years, ending in the most unexpected way.

Toward the end of the war, the Greeks devised a plan to sail to a nearby island, leaving behind a victory gift for the Trojans. The gift, a hollowed-out wooden horse, was hand crafted by a master carpenter to resemble the Trojans' most sacred animal. Dozens of Greek warriors hid inside the giant horse, waiting for the right moment to make their move.

As expected, Troy accepted the gift with open arms and dragged the massive horse into their city. The citizens of Troy, along with their army, celebrated with dancing, drinking, and feasting. After the festivities, when the city was asleep, the Greek soldiers poured out of the horse. Opening the gates, they signaled the waiting army to attack. The city of Troy and its people were destroyed by the Greeks that evening, leaving nothing but utter devastation.

Today, this story can be used as a metaphor for the United States of America. We have seen through this book that a Trojan Horse sits within our walls: a horse made of ideologies with the capacity to destroy this nation from the inside out. We must awaken our fellow countrymen to what already lies within our walls. If we don't, we may follow in the tragic footsteps of the ancient Trojans. Except, in our case, our republic and democracy will be forever lost. Ronald Reagan said, "Freedom is a fragile thing, and it's never more than one generation away from extinction. It is not ours by way of inheritance; it must be fought for and defended constantly by each generation, for it comes only once to a people. And those in world history who have known freedom and then lost it have never known it again."

Who is going to defend and fight for America? American patriots hold dear the values and creed that were enshrined in the Declaration of Independence and the United States Constitution. What are these values? They are the Judeo-Christian ideals and beliefs that were embedded within the foundation of this country by our Founding Fathers. What is our creed? That we hold these truths to be self-evident, that all men are created equal, that they are endowed by their Creator with certain unalienable rights, that among these are life, liberty, and the pursuit of happiness.

The destructive ideologies of the progressive Left shroud themselves and crouch inside the horse. The Left insist that America is racist, defunding the police is a must, socialism is good, and more. Seeking to destroy this country from the inside, they indoctrinate our children with values and creeds that are at odds with what makes America great. They say they believe all men are created equal, yet they push for segregation in schools, affirmative action, and having the injustices of the past be paid for by present-day citizens who did not commit those past injustices.

Some leftists swear an oath to uphold the Constitution while spending their time trying to subvert what the Constitution says. In April 2022, the House of Representatives passed legislation to ban certain semi-automatic guns. This is a clear infringement of American citizens' right to bear arms. Continually chiseling away at our rights paves the way to a future where we have no rights.

TIME TO TAKE A STAND AGAINST THE TROJAN HORSE

We must equip ourselves with the knowledge and understanding of our Founding Fathers. We must gain a deeper understanding of the Constitution and American history. This book is a call to action for American patriots, a call to expose the Trojan Horse that sits within our walls and prepare for the looming battle—not a physical battle with weapons but a battle of ideas. Just as we train for war, we must train by reading and learning as much as possible. I'm not encouraging just the reading of books written by conservatives and Republicans, but reading books the progressive Left writes, such as *The 1619 Project*, *White Fragility*, *The Communist Manifesto*, *Socialism: Utopian and Scientific*, and more.

Ancient Chinese general Sun Tzu said, "Know thy enemy and know yourself; in a hundred battles, you will never be defeated." Are we going to allow the progressive Left to take over our country; to tear up our Constitution and throw it in the trash? In an interview on "The View" in March 2022, Elie Mystal, author and justice correspondent for *The Nation*, described the U.S. Constitution as "kind of trash." Sadly, statements like this from the progressive Left are not few but many.

If we sit back and don't allow our voices to be heard, there will come a day when we don't have a voice at all. With the Left's utilization of censorship on social media using Big Tech as a club, we are not far from that being a reality. We must show up to school board meetings, join our Parent-Teacher Associations, and get involved in our local communities. The indoctrination factories that have been created by the Left using our educational system are producing more people who hate America. Our children are being taught to think that institutional racism is still a major problem in the U.S. and to believe the police are hunting down black people in the streets. Joining our local community meetings and having our voices heard will influence community leaders to make shifts in curriculum, policies, and laws. If we don't do this, ANTIFA and Black Lives Matter will increase in number. Rioting will continue, businesses will continue to burn, and crime will continue to increase. More people like Alexandria

Ocasio-Cortez, Bernie Sanders, Ilhan Omar, and Elizabeth Warren will be elected to Congress to push a socialist agenda.

Getting involved with our local communities includes more than what I've listed above. It means getting to know your neighbor regardless of their political stance—Democrat, Republican, Socialist, Communist, or Independent. We used to know our neighbors. We invited them over for dinner, birthday parties, weddings, or just to visit. If we return to getting to know one another and who we truly are, social division can be mended. Knowing your neighbor means treating them like family, and it is family that can be awakened to what is truly going on.

Some patriots might read this and think there is no hope, that America is lost. This book was never intended to make you surrender or give up. It was written to give you ammo to use on the battlefield and to raise awareness of what has been going on for far too long. We should never lose hope in something so great as our country. Troy was once great. Then her citizens made a grave mistake and did not take action to demolish the horse. Some wanted to burn it or throw it off a cliff. They were right; it should have been destroyed. The ideologies of the Left should be destroyed with truth, facts, and wisdom. My hope is that you have gained more truth, facts, and wisdom by reading this book.

There is no doubt that our country has faced some challenges in recent years. But, despite these challenges, America remains strong and resilient. This country was founded on certain values and principles that have always helped us to overcome adversity. Life, liberty, and the pursuit of happiness are more than just words to us; they are the bedrock upon which our country is built. It is these same values that have *always* made America great. Patriotism and love of country have always been strong in America. These values will help us to overcome any obstacles we face.

As we continue to face challenges in the years ahead, we must hold on to what makes America great: our values, our freedoms, and our patriotism.

ACKNOWLEDGMENTS

Writing this book was harder than I thought and more rewarding than I could have ever imagined. None of this would have been possible without my parents, Don and Kim Roberts. They both taught conservative values which helped shape me into the person I am today. I will forever cherish those conversations, discussions, and arguments I had with my father that greatly impacted my way of thinking. You will always be in my heart dad. Thank you to my mother for always supporting me through life and being there for me. I love you more than words can describe.

Furthermore, many people were involved in the making of this book. First, a big thank you to Michael Caryl of Liberty Hill Publishing for accepting my manuscript with open arms. I will never forget our phone conservations about the conservative movement and the future of our great country. It's a privilege to have worked on this book with a true American patriot.

A huge thank you to Dave Wimbish, editor of this book, who had the giant task of bringing this book to life. Your masterful writing is brilliant and truly inspiring. Moreover, I was always thankful for our phone conversations and our discussions about Christianity.

Thank you to Logan Mungo, my representative at Salem, for making the process of publishing this book painless. Your communication and attention to detail are greatly valued.

Thank you to Jason Shingleton, my consultant at Salem, for strategically finding the right editors for this book. If not for your wisdom, I would not have had the pleasure to work with so many great people.

Thank you to the folks at Liberty Hill Publishing that helped make this book a reality. Your focus on publishing books that not only thrust the current state of affairs into the light but publish books that are rooted in the principles of individual liberty is immensely treasured.

Thank you to Paula Lacson, who understood this was a bucket list project. I'm appreciative of your encouragement toward the project and listening to my arguments displayed in this book. Furthermore, thank you for reading my manuscript and helping me improve it every step of the way.

Thank you to my friends, Kyle and Nick, for the various political discussions, philosophical conversations, and various disagreements around the fire pit. Our late-night antics will forever be memorable.

Most of all, thank you to all my listeners, watchers, readers, and social media followers: knowing you are with me in this fight against the progressive left keeps me going. Let's never lose hope in what makes this country great. You are all true American patriots.

Thank you.

NOTES

CHAPTER 1: ANTIFA

1. Paxton, Robert Owen. Essay in *The Anatomy of Fascism*, 200. New York, NY: Knopf, 2004.

2. Ebner, Michael R. "How Fascists Took over Italy with Widespread, Intensely Personal Acts of Political Violence." Slate Magazine. Slate, January 30, 2017. https://slate.com/news-and-politics/2017/01/how-italian-fascists-succeeded-in-taking-over-italy.html.

3. Petersen, J. (1982). Violence in Italian Fascism, 1919–25. In: Mommsen, W.J., Hirschfeld, G. (eds) *Social Protest, Violence and Terror in Nineteenth- and Twentieth-century Europe*. Palgrave Macmillan, London. https://doi.org/10.1007/978-1-349-16941-2_17.

4. Paulas, Rick. "Why Antifa Dresses like Antifa." *New York Times*, November 29, 2017. https://www.nytimes.com/2017/11/29/style/antifa-fashion.html.

5. Euse, Erica. "The Accidental Uniform of the Antifa." I-D, September 27, 2017. https://i-d.vice.com/en_uk/article/pakzk7/the-accidental-uniform-of-the-antifa.

6. Stolberg, Sheryl. Twitter Post. August 13, 2017. https://twitter.com/Sheryl NYT.

7. D'Souza, Dinesh. *Death of a Nation: Plantation Politics and the Making of the Democratic Party* (New York, NY: All Points Books, 2018) Pg. 162.

8. Waters, Maxine. "Rep. Waters on Trump Administration: 'Tell Them They're Not Welcome'." YouTube. *Washington Post*, June 25, 2018. https://www.youtube.com/watch?v=tJCDe7vdFfw.

9. Price, Bob. "Watch: Antifa Attacks Restaurant Patrons in Suburban Vancouver, Washington." Breitbart, October 31, 2020. https://www.breitbart.com/law-and-order/2020/10/31/watch-portland-antifa-invades-vancouver-attacks-restaurant-patrons/.

10. Ibid.

11. Taylor, Sarah. "'Antifa' Issues Veiled Death Threat against Portland Mayor Ted Wheeler in Alarming Video." TheBlaze, April 29, 2021. https://www.theblaze.com/news/antifa-threatens-to-assassinate-portland-mayor-ted-wheeler-in-alarming-video#toggle-gdpr.

CHAPTER TWO: ANTIFA'S FRIENDS IN HIGH PLACES

1. Rodgers, Henry. "Make Them Pay: Michigan Democratic State Rep. Cynthia Jones Threatens Trump Supporters." The Daily Caller. The Daily Caller, December 15, 2020. https://dailycaller.com/2020/12/09/make-them-pay-michigan-democrat-state-rep-threatens-trump-supporters-cynthia-johnson/.

2. Press, Associated. "Rep. Keith Ellison Draws Fire for Tweet about Antifa Handbook and Trump." Chicago Tribune, August 22, 2019. https://www.chicagotribune.com/nation-world/ct-keith-ellison-antifa-handbook-tweet-20180104-story.html.

3. Burns, Katelyn. "Seattle's Newly Police-Free Neighborhood, Explained." Vox. Vox, June 16, 2020. https://www.vox.com/identities/2020/6/16/21292723/chaz-seattle-police-free-neighborhood.

4. Burns, Katelyn. "The Violent End of the Capitol Hill Organized Protest, Explained." Vox. Vox, July 2, 2020. https://www.vox.com/policy-and-politics/2020/7/2/21310109/chop-chaz-cleared-violence-explained.

5. Burns, Katelyn. "Seattle's Newly Police-Free Neighborhood, Explained." Vox. Vox, June 16, 2020. https://www.vox.com/identities/2020/6/16/21292723/chaz-seattle-police-free-neighborhood.

6. CNN's Chris Cuomo: "Please, show me where it says protesters are . . . https://therightscoop.com/cnns-chris-cuomo-please-show-me-where-it-says-protesters-are-supposed-to-be-polite-and-peaceful.

NOTES

7. Wulfsohn, Joseph A. "MSNBC's Ali Velshi Says Situation Not 'Generally Speaking Unruly' While Standing Outside Burning Building." Fox News. FOX News Network, May 29, 2020. https://www.foxnews.com/media/msnbc-anchor-says-minneapolis-carnage-is-mostly-a-protest-as-building-burns-behind-him.

8. CNN Reporter in Minneapolis: I've Never Seen Anything Like This. YouTube. CNN, 2020. https://www.youtube.com/watch?v=KOj8ztqa-gM.

CHAPTER THREE: THE MAINSTREAM MEDIA

1. Hayes, Chris. Twitter Post. December 10, 2020. https://twitter.com/chrislhayes/status/1336823567795822595?s=20&t=S2DvqjtTrkXJz_m1dR9UAw.

2. Gardner, Amy. "Trump Pressured a Georgia Elections Investigator in a Separate Call Legal Experts Say Could Amount to Obstruction." *Washington Post*. WP Company, November 11, 2021. https://www.washingtonpost.com/politics/trump-call-georgia-investigator/2021/01/09/7a55c7fa-51cf-11eb-83e3-322644d82356_story.html.

3. Washington Post panned for massive correction to Trump-Georgia election . . . https://www.foxnews.com/media/washington-post-correction-trump-georgia-votes-election.

4. Trump's Statement on *Washington Post*'s Apology, 'Story Was a Hoax.' https://www.breitbart.com/politics/2021/03/15/ttrumps-statement-on-washington-posts-apology-original-story-was-a-hoax/.

5. Ibid.

6. Gold, Hadas. "3 CNN Staffers Resign over Retracted Scaramucci-Russia Story." POLITICO, June 27, 2017. https://www.politico.com/blogs/on-media/2017/06/26/cnn-resign-russia-scaramucci-239975.

7. Haberman, Maggie. "Trump's Deflections and Denials on Russia Frustrate Even His Allies." *New York Times*, June 25, 2017. https://www.nytimes.com/2017/06/25/us/politics/trumps-deflections-and-denials-on-russia-frustrate-even-his-allies.html.

8. McEnany: Where's Accountability for Media, Dems Who Pushed False Story. Fox News, 2021. https://www.youtube.com/watch?v=bHVA6f2BF1A.

9. Inspector General Debunks Claims Made by Biden, Harris, Left-Wing Media . . . https://www.dailywire.com/news/inspector-general-debunks-claims-made-by-biden-harris-left-wing-media-against-trump.

10. PART 1: CNN Director ADMITS Network Engaged in 'Propaganda' to Remove Trump from Presidency. Project Veritas, 2021. https://www.youtube.com/watch?v=Dv8Zy-JwXr4.

11. Ibid.

12. Kass, John. "Harvard Study: Media Has Been Largely Negative on Trump." chicagotribune.com. *Chicago Tribune*, May 13, 2019. https://www.chicagotribune.com/columns/john-kass/ct-trump-media-coverage-harvard-kass-0521-20170519-column.html.

13. "U.S. Voters Dislike Trump Almost 2–1, Quinnipiac University National Poll Finds; Media Is Important to Democracy, 65% of Voters Say: Quinnipiac University Poll." Quinnipiac University Poll, August 14, 2018. https://poll.qu.edu/Poll-Release-Legacy?releaseid=2561.

14. PART 1: CNN Director ADMITS Network Engaged in 'Propaganda' to Remove Trump from Presidency. Project Veritas, 2021. https://www.youtube.com/watch?v=Dv8Zy-JwXr4.

15. McCaffree, Kevin, and Anondah Saide. "How Informed Are Americans about Race and Policing?" Skeptic Research Center and the Worldview Foundations Research Team, February 20, 2021. https://www.skeptic.com/research-center/reports/Research-Report-CUPES-007.pdf.

16. "Fatal Force: Police Shootings Database." *Washington Post*. WP Company, January 22, 2020. https://www.washingtonpost.com/graphics/investigations/police-shootings-database/.

17. Fondacaro, Nicholas. "CNN's Cuomo Bashes Covington Kids as 'Victims of Their Own Choices'." MRCTV. News Busters, January 23, 2019. https://www.newsbusters.org/blogs/nb/nicholas-fondacaro/2019/01/23/cnns-cuomo-bashes-covington-kids-victims-their-own-choices.

NOTES

CHAPTER FOUR: THE SPECTRE OF RACISM

1. Schweikart, Larry, and Michael Allen. 2019. *A Patriot's History of the United States: From Columbus's Great Discovery to America's Age of Entitlement.* New York, New York: Sentinel, 3.

2. Ibid., 4.

3. Victor Davis Hansen, *Carnage and Culture: Landmark Battles in the Rise of Western Power* (New York: Doubleday, 2001), 195.

4. Schweikart, Larry, and Michael Allen. 2019. *A Patriot's History of the United States: From Columbus's Great Discovery to America's Age of Entitlement.* New York, New York: Sentinel, 8.

5. Ibid., 9.

6. Ibid., 19.

7. D.M.R. Esson, *The Curse of Cromwell: A History of the Ironside Conquest of Ireland 1649-53* (Buckinghamshire, England: Combined Academic Publishers, 2009).

8. Schweikart, Larry, and Michael Allen. 2019. *A Patriot's History of the United States: From Columbus's Great Discovery to America's Age of Entitlement.* New York, New York: Sentinel, 53.

9. Thomas Jefferson, *The Writings of Thomas Jefferson*, Albert Ellery Bergh, editor (Washington, D. C.: Thomas Jefferson Memorial Association, 1903), Vol. I, p. 34.

10. Shapiro, Ben. *How to Destroy America in Three Easy Steps* (New York, NY: Broadside Books, 2021) p. 127.

11. Finkelman, Paul. "The Union Wasn't Worth the Three-Fifths Compromise on Slavery." *New York Times,* February 27, 2013. https://www.nytimes.com/roomfordebate/2013/02/26/the-constitutions-immoral-compromise/the-union-wasnt-worth-the-three-fifths-compromise-on-slavery.

12. Ibid.

CHAPTER FIVE: AMERICA'S FIGHT AGAINST SLAVERY

1. D'Souza, Dinesh. *Death of a Nation: Plantation Politics and the Making of the Democratic Party* (New York, NY: All Points Books, 2018) Pg. 33.

2. Neely, Mark E. Jr. 1982. *The Abraham Lincoln Encyclopedia*. New York: Da Capo Press, Inc.

3. Quoted Online at http://www.bowdoin.edu/~sbodurt2/court/cases/plessy.html.

4. Harlan's Great Dissent — Louis D. Brandeis School of Law Library. https://louisville.edu/law/library/special-collections/the-john-marshall-harlan-collection/harlans-great-dissent/.

5. McKay, Claude. *Home to Harlem*. Boston, MA: Northeastern Univ. Press, 2002.

6. History.com Editors. 2018. "Black History in the United States: A Timeline." HISTORY. A&E Television Networks. November 16, 2018. https://www.history.com/topics/black-history/black-history-milestones.

7. D'Souza, Dinesh. *We the Slave Owners*. Hoover Institution, September 1, 1995. https://www.hoover.org/research/we-slave-owners.

8. Shapiro, Ben. *How to Destroy America in Three Easy Steps* (New York, NY: Broadside Books, 2021) p. 125.

9. Ibid., 127.

10. Ibid.

11. Ibid., 128.

12. Ibid.

13. Jordan, *White over Black*, 325–31, 356–57.

14. Schweikart, Larry, and Michael Allen. 2019. *A Patriot's History of the United States: From Columbus's Great Discovery to America's Age of Entitlement*. New York, New York: Sentinel, 123–24.

15. Ibid., 123.

16. Shapiro, Ben. *How to Destroy America in Three Easy Steps* (New York, NY: Broadside Books, 2021) p. 128–29.

17. D'Souza, Dinesh. *Death of a Nation: Plantation Politics and the Making of the Democratic Party* (New York, NY: All Points Books, 2018) Pg. 45.

18. Ibid., 46.

19. Ibid., 53.

NOTES

20. Tise, Larry E. *Proslavery: A History of the Defense of Slavery in America, 1700-1840*. Athens: University of Georgia Press, 1987.

21. Schneider, Gregory S. "The Birthplace of American Slavery Debated Abolishing It After Nat Turner's Bloody Revolt." *Washington Post*. WP Company, June 1, 2019. https://www.washingtonpost.com/history/2019/06/01/birthplace-american-slavery-debated-abolishing-it-after-nat-turners-bloody-revolt/.

22. Faust, Drew G. "James Henry Hammond and the Old South, Baton Rouge and London," Louisiana State University Press, 1982, pp. 280–81.

23. https://www.law.nyu.edu/sites/default/files/Civil%20Rights%20Act%20of%201866%20and%20Section%201981.pdf.

24. Swain, Carol. "An Inconvenient Truth about an Inconvenient Truth." The Conversation. PragerU, February 20, 2020. https://theconversation.com/an-inconvenient-truth-about-an-inconvenient-truth-81799.

25. Onion, Amanda, Missy Sullivan, and Matt Mullen. "Ku Klux Klan." History.com. A&E Television Networks, October 29, 2009. https://www.history.com/topics/reconstruction/ku-klux-klan.

26. D'Souza, Dinesh. *Death of a Nation: Plantation Politics and the Making of the Democratic Party* (New York, NY: All Points Books, 2018) Pg. 156.

27. "African Americans." Living New Deal, August 20, 2020. https://livingnewdeal.org/waht-was-the-new-deal-inclusion/african-americans-2/.

28. D'Souza, Dinesh. *Death of a Nation: Plantation Politics and the Making of the Democratic Party* (New York, NY: All Points Books, 2018) Pg. 186.

29. Ibid.

30. Ibid., 188.

CHAPTER SIX: THE ANTI-POLICE MOVEMENT

1. Corley, Cheryl. "Massive 1-Year Rise in Homicide Rates Collided with the Pandemic in 2020." NPR. NPR, January 6, 2021. https://www.npr.org/2021/01/06/953254623/massive-1-year-rise-in-homicide-rates-collided-with-the-pandemic-in-2020.

2. Ibid.

3. Kingson, Jennifer A. "Exclusive: $1 Billion-plus Riot Damage Is Most Expensive in Insurance History." Axios, September 16, 2020. https://www.axios.com/2020/09/16/riots-cost-property-damage.

4. Bond, Charlotte Pence. "Former Obama Task Force Member Says Rise in Crime Is 'Fault of the Police'." The Daily Wire, June 21, 2021. https://www.dailywire.com/news/former-obama-task-force-member-says-rise-in-crime-is-fault-of-the-police.

5. Mac Donald, Heather. *The War on Cops: How the New Attack on Law and Order Makes Everyone Less Safe* (New York, NY: Encounter Books, 2017) pg. 1–2.

6. Beckett, Lois, and Amudalat Ajasa. "'Deep Systemic Racism': Will Minneapolis's Police Department Ever Change?" *The Guardian*. Guardian News and Media, April 25, 2021. https://www.theguardian.com/us-news/2021/apr/25/minneapolis-police-race-violence-justice-department-investigation.

7. Boren, Cindy. "A Timeline of Colin Kaepernick's Protests against Police Brutality." *The Seattle Times*. The Seattle Times Company, June 1, 2020. `https://www.seattletimes.com/sports/a-timeline-of-colin-kaepernicks-protests-against-police-brutality/.

8. "Kaepernick Made Prior Statement with Police-as-Pigs Socks." NBC Sports, September 1, 2016. https://www.nbcsports.com/bayarea/49ers/kaepernick-made-prior-statement-police-pigs-socks.

9. Patrick, Robert. "Darren Wilson's Radio Calls Show Fatal Encounter Was Brief." STLtoday.com, July 2, 2019. https://www.stltoday.com/news/multimedia/special/darren-wilson-s-radio-calls-show-fatal-encounter-was-brief/html_79c17aed-0dbe-514d-ba32-bad908056790.html.

10. Department of Justice Report Regarding the Criminal Investigation into The Shooting Death of Michael Brown by Ferguson, Missouri Police Officer Darren Wilson (St. Louis, MO: DOJ, 2015) pg. 29–30.

11. Ibid., 27–28.

12. Ibid., 30.

13. Ibid., 32.

14. Witness: Michael Brown Was 'Shot like an Animal.' YouTube. YouTube, 2014. https://www.youtube.com/watch?v=bpLB4zKKMHo.

NOTES

15. Shapiro, Ben. "Katy Perry, Cher and Macklemore All Lie about Ferguson." YouTube. YouTube, December 2, 2014. https://www.youtube.com/watch?v-O2PYJPPFx9Q.

16. Witness: Michael Brown Was 'Shot like an Animal.' YouTube. YouTube, 2014. https://www.youtube.com/watch?v=bpLB4zKKMH0.

17. Mac Donald, Heather. *The War on Cops: How the New Attack on Law and Order Makes Everyone Less Safe* (New York, NY: Encounter Books, 2017) pg. 22

18. Gerstein, Josh, and Jennifer Epstein. "Obama: U.S. Has Own Racial Tensions." POLITICO, September 24, 2014. https://www.politico.com/story/2014/09/obama-ferguson-un-address-111290.

19. Holder, Eric. "Attorney General Holder Delivers Update on Investigations in Ferguson, Missouri." The United States Department of Justice, August 26, 2015. https://www.justice.gov/opa/speech/attorney-general-holder-delivers-update-investigations-ferguson-missouri.

20. Ibid.

21. Ibid.

22. Ibid.

23. Mac Donald, Heather. *The War on Cops: How the New Attack on Law and Order Makes Everyone Less Safe* (New York, NY: Encounter Books, 2017) Pg. 27--28.

24. Yerak, Becky. "Riot Damage to Ferguson Businesses Could Be Covered with Insurance." *Chicago Tribune*, June 18, 2018. https://www.chicagotribune.com/business/ct-ferguson-business-insurance-1128-biz-20141126-story.html.

25. Ibid.

26. Heath, Brad. "Baltimore Police Stopped Noticing Crime after Freddie Gray's Death. A Wave of Killings Followed." *USA Today*. Gannett Satellite Information Network, July 12, 2018. https://www.usatoday.com/story/news/nation/2018/07/12/baltimore-police-not-noticing-crime-after-freddie-gray-wave-killings-followed/744741002/.

27. Ibid.

28. Ibid.

29. "Crime Rate in Ferguson, Missouri (MO): Murders, Rapes, Robberies, Assaults, Burglaries, Thefts, Auto Thefts, Arson, Law Enforcement Employees, Police Officers, Crime Map." Crime in Ferguson, Missouri (MO): murders, rapes, robberies, assaults, burglaries, thefts, auto thefts, arson, law enforcement employees, police officers, crime map, 2019. https://www.city-data.com/crime/crime-Ferguson-Missouri.html.

30. Owens, Candace. "Candace Owens: The Media Lied to You about George Floyd and BLM." The Daily Wire, April 22, 2021. https://www.dailywire.com/news/candace-owens-the-media-is-lying-to-you-about-george-floyd-and-makhia-bryant?cid=dwnews&mid=e&xid=0.

31. Pelosi, Nancy. Twitter Post. April 20, 2021. https://twitter.com/SpeakerPelosi/status/1384637552133656581?s=20&t=9G-Ea64HekcRi24LCGbeGg.

32. Washington latest. "Keith Ellison: 'We Don't Have Any Evidence' Racism Played Factor in George Floyd's Murder." Washington latest, April 27, 2021. https://washingtonlatest.com/keith-ellison-we-dont-have-any-evidence-racism-played-factor-in-george-floyds-murder/.

33. Schnell, Mychal. "Minnesota AG Explains Why Floyd's Death Not Charged as Hate Crime." *The Hill*, April 26, 2021. https://thehill.com/homenews/state-watch/550211-minnesota-ag-explains-why-floyd-death-not-charged-as-hate-crime/.

34. Lapin, Tamar. "Minnesota AG Keith Ellison Says He 'Felt a Little Bad' for Derek Chauvin." *New York Post*, April 26, 2021. https://nypost.com/2021/04/25/minnesota-ag-says-he-felt-a-little-bad-for-derek-chauvin/.

35. Shiver, Phil. "Minnesota AG Admits There Is No Evidence That Race Was a Factor in George Floyd Killing." TheBlaze, April 26, 2021. https://www.theblaze.com/news/no-evidence-race-george-floyd-killing.

36. Carlson, Tucker. "Tucker Carlson: Everything the Media Didn't Tell You About the Death of George Floyd." Fox News. FOX News Network, March 11, 2021. https://www.foxnews.com/opinion/tucker-carlson-george-floyd-death-what-media-didnt-tell-you.

37. Lemon: Imagine How Inaction Impacts Your Friends of Color. CNN. Cable News Network, 2020. https://www.cnn.com/videos/us/2020/05/28/perspective-race-george-floyd-knee-death-protest-injustice-dialogue-lemon-handoff-ctn-vpx.cnn.

NOTES

38. Owens, Candace. "Candace Owens: The Media Lied to You about George Floyd and BLM." The Daily Wire, April 22, 2021. https://www.dailywire.com/news/candace-owens-the-media-is-lying-to-you-about-george-floyd-and-makhia-bryant?cid=dwnews&mid=e&xid=0.

39. Lee, Jessica. "Background Check: Investigating George Floyd's Criminal Record." Snopes.com, February 24, 2021. https://www.snopes.com/news/2020/06/12/george-floyd-criminal-record/.

40. Singh, Maanvi, and Joan E Greve. "Biden Declares White Supremacists 'Most Lethal Threat' to Us as He Marks Tulsa Race Massacre–as It Happened." *The Guardian.* Guardian News and Media, June 2, 2021. https://www.theguardian.com/us-news/live/2021/jun/01/joe-biden-tulsa-oklahoma-race-massacre-us-politics-live.

41. Stockman, Farah. "'They Have Lost Control': Why Minneapolis Burned." *New York Times,* July 3, 2020. https://www.nytimes.com/2020/07/03/us/minneapolis-government-george-floyd.html.

42. Melugin, Bill. Twitter Post. May 28, 2020. https://twitter.com/BillFOXLA/status/1266125016388628480?s=20&t=jH9dJ5HJc2MsF3PcnulsUA.

43. Starbuck, Robby. Twitter Post. May 28, 2020. https://twitter.com/robbystarbuck/status/1266092746403729410?s=20&t=OmIfO9BYTqjbpCN-FBh_dA.

44. Baker, Brent. Twitter Post. May 30, 2020. https://twitter.com/BrentHBaker/status/1266945397609635840?s=20&t=S8vlwLWQedIxAl8KMGPQhw.

45. Myerson, Jesse A. "Smashy Smashy: When Property Destruction Works." *Rolling Stone,* May 30, 2020. https://www.rollingstone.com/politics/politics-news/ferguson-protest-george-floyd-minneapolis-nine-historical-property-destruction-175763/.

46. Kingson, Jennifer A. "Exclusive: $1 Billion-plus Riot Damage Is Most Expensive in Insurance History." Axios, September 16, 2020. https://www.axios.com/2020/09/16/riots-cost-property-damage.

47. Nilsson, Monica. "Opinion Exchange: Near George Floyd Square: Revolution by Day, Devolution by Night." *Star Tribune,* March 15, 2021. https://www.startribune.com/near-george-floyd-square-revolution-by-day-devolution-by-night/600034699/?refresh=true.

48. Zanotti, Emily. "Residents Trapped by 'George Floyd Autonomous Zone' Beg Minneapolis for Help Following Murder." The Daily Wire. The Daily Wire, March 16, 2021. https://www.dailywire.com/news/residents-trapped-by-george-floyd-autonomous-zone-beg-minneapolis-for-help-following-murder.

49. Chapman, Reg. "Mayor Frey, MPD Chief Arradondo Want to Reopen 38th & Chicago While Honoring George Floyd." WCCO | CBS Minnesota. WCCO | CBS Minnesota, March 11, 2021. https://minnesota.cbslocal.com/2021/03/11/mayor-frey-mpd-chief-arradondo-want-to-reopen-38th-chicago-while-honoring-george-floyd/.

50. Arango, Tim, and Matt Furber. "Where George Floyd Was Killed: Solemn by Day, Violent by Night." *New York Times*, July 29, 2020. https://www.nytimes.com/2020/07/29/us/george-floyd-memorial.html.

51. Ibrahim, Mohamed. "Officer's Trial Could Reopen Intersection Where Floyd Died." *AP NEWS*. Associated Press, March 6, 2021. https://apnews.com/article/trials-coronavirus-pandemic-minneapolis-racial-injustice-derek-chauvin-43e0ec34e2e817a9f2b4d9ae09905390.

52. Wallace, Danielle. "Minneapolis Police Seeks Federal, State Reinforcements after Mass Shooting Kills College Kid before Graduation." FOX News Network, May 24, 2021. https://www.foxnews.com/us/minneapolis-police-federal-state-reinforcements-mass-shooting-officer-shortage.

53. "Workforcesurveyjune2021." Police Executive Research Forum, June 11, 2021. https://www.policeforum.org/workforcesurveyjune2021.

54. Westervelt, Eric. "Cops Say Low Morale and Department Scrutiny Are Driving Them Away from the Job." NPR. NPR, June 24, 2021. https://www.npr.org/2021/06/24/1009578809/cops-say-low-morale-and-department-scrutiny-are-driving-them-away-from-the-job.

55. LizzoBeEating. "Women for Political Change" Instagram, June 10, 2020. https://www.instagram.com/p/CBQwA33gnP7/?utm_source=ig_embed&ig_rid=77722a11-a1d1-41b2-a59c-d9c71965e3a9.

56. Brinkhof, Tim. "Natalie Portman Explains Why She Supports Defunding the Police." We Got This Covered. We Got This Covered, June 15, 2020. https://wegotthiscovered.com/movies/thor-actress-natalie-portman-explains-supports-defunding-police/.

NOTES

57. "White Privilege: Meaning & Definition for UK English." Lexico Dictionaries | English. Lexico Dictionaries. Accessed June 10, 2021. https://www.lexico.com/definition/white_privilege.

58. Arora, Rav. "The Fallacy of White Privilege—and How It's Corroding Society." *New York Post*, July 11, 2020. https://nypost.com/2020/07/11/the-fallacy-of-white-privilege-and-how-its-corroding-society/.

59. Johnson, Jason. "Why Violent Crime Surged after Police across America Retreated." *USA Today*. Gannett Satellite Information Network, April 9, 2021. https://www.usatoday.com/story/opinion/policing/2021/04/09/violent-crime-surged-across-america-after-police-retreated-column/7137565002/.

60. Heffernan, Erin. "St. Louis Homicide Rate in 2020 Highest in 50 Years with 262 Killings." STLtoday.com, April 16, 2021. https://www.stltoday.com/news/local/crime-and-courts/st-louis-homicide-rate-in-2020-highest-in-50-years-with-262-killings/article_b3c323a7-bc38-55bc-812b-08990b0eb289.html.

61. Klepper, David, and Gary Fields. "Killings Spiked in the US and Republicans Blame Calls to 'Defund the Police.' but They Are Also Rising in Cities That Increased Spending on Cops." *Chicago Tribune*, June 10, 2021. https://www.chicagotribune.com/nation-world/ct-aud-nw-crime-spike-police-funding-20210610-graeysr24zapbkvpsbhvlfiakm-story.html.

62. "Work Force Survey." *Police Executive Research Forum*, June 11, 2021. https://www.policeforum.org/workforcesurveyjune2021.

63. Trujillo, Damian. "Police Officers Calling It Quits, Retiring Early at Alarming Rate." NBC Bay Area. NBC Bay Area, June 28, 2021. https://www.nbcbayarea.com/news/local/police-officers-calling-it-quits-retiring-early-at-alarming-rate/2581357/.

64. Allen, Mike. "Cop Crisis: Thousands of Police Officers Have Quit over the Last Year." Axios, June 25, 2021. https://www.axios.com/2021/06/25/police-officers-quitting.

65. Macfarquhar, Neil. "Why Police Have Been Quitting in Droves in the Last Year." *New York Times*, June 24, 2021. https://www.nytimes.com/2021/06/24/us/police-resignations-protests-asheville.html.

66. Patkin, Abby. "'Why Would Any Officer Want to Stay Here': Brookline Police Say Morale Is at a New Low." *Wicked Local*, May 3, 2021. https://

www.wickedlocal.com/story/brookline-tab/2021/04/30/brookline-ma-committee-on-policing-reforms-police-department-officers-morale-all-time-low/7411455002/.

67. Johnson, Ben. "CNN, MSNBC Perplexed Why Portland Police Are Quitting En Masse." The Daily Wire, June 23, 2021. https://www.dailywire.com/news/cnn-msnbc-perplexed-why-portland-police-are-quitting-en-masse.

68. "Defund The Police Movement Backfires." Gop.com. Accessed June 23, 2020. https://gop.com/research/defund-the-police-movement-backfires.

CHAPTER SEVEN: DEBUNKING POLICE RACISM

1. Mac Donald, Heather, "Opinion | the Myth of Systemic Police Racism." The Wall Street Journal. Dow Jones & Company, June 2, 2020. https://www.wsj.com/articles/the-myth-of-systemic-police-racism-11591119883.

2. Mac Donald, Heather. Essay in *The War on Cops: How the New Attack on Law and Order Makes Everyone Less Safe* (New York, NY: Encounter Books, 2017). Pg. 9

3. Tate, Julie, Jennifer Jenkins, Steven Rich, John Muyskens, Kennedy Elliott, Ted Mellnik, and Aaron Williams. "How the *Washington Post* Is Examining Police Shootings in the United States." *Washington Post*. WP Company, July 7, 2016. https://www.washingtonpost.com/national/how-the-washington-post-is-examining-police-shootings-in-the-united-states/2016/07/07/d9c52238-43ad-11e6-8856-f26de2537a9d_story.html.

4. Horowitz, Daniel. "Horowitz: The Rarity of Police Shootings Compared to Black Homicide Victims Is Astonishing." TheBlaze, April 15, 2021. https://www.theblaze.com/op-ed/horowitz-the-rarity-of-police-shootings-compared-to-black-homicide-victims-is-astonishing.

5. Mac Donald, Heather. Essay in *The War on Cops: How the New Attack on Law and Order Makes Everyone Less Safe* (New York, NY: Encounter Books, 2017). Pg. 73.

6. Harrell, Erika, and Elizabeth David. "Statistical Tables–Bureau of Justice Statistics." United States Department of Justice. Office of Justice Programs Bureau of Justice Statistics, December 2020. https://bjs.ojp.gov/content/pub/pdf/cbpp18st.pdf.

NOTES

7. Fagan, Patrick. "The Real Root Causes of Violent Crime: The Breakdown of Marriage, Family, and Community." The Heritage Foundation, March 17, 1995. https://www.heritage.org/crime-and-justice/report/the-real-root-causes-violent-crime-the-breakdown-marriage-family-and.

8. Cynthia C. Harper and Sara S. McLanahan, "Father Absence and Youth Incarceration," *Journal of Research on Adolescence* 14, no. 3 (2004): 369–97.

9. Johnson, David J., Trevor Tress, Nicole Burkel, Carley Taylor, and Joseph Cesario. "Officer Characteristics and Racial Disparities in Fatal Officer-Involved Shootings." *Proceedings of the National Academy of Sciences* 116, no. 32 (July 22, 2019): 15877–82. https://doi.org/10.1073/pnas.1903856116.

10. Mac Donald, Heather. Essay in The War on Cops: How the New Attack on Law and Order Makes Everyone Less Safe (New York, NY: Encounter Books, 2017). Pg. 79.

11. Payne, Jessica T. "Honoring the Fallen: Jacksonville Police Department Holds Police Officers Memorial Ceremony." TylerPaper.com, June 20, 2021. https://tylerpaper.com/news/local/honoring-the-fallen-jacksonville-police-department-holds-police-officers-memorial-ceremony/article_84f8e9cc-b33f-11eb-933e-97c2a9e9caed.html.

12. Mac Donald, Heather. Essay in *The War on Cops: How the New Attack on Law and Order Makes Everyone Less Safe* (New York, NY: Encounter Books, 2017). Pg. 233.

CHAPTER EIGHT: INDOCTRINATION

1. Shields, Jon A., Jonathan Rauch, and Michael P. Zuckert. "The Disappearing Conservative Professor." *National Affairs*, 2018. https://nationalaffairs.com/publications/detail/the-disappearing-conservative-professor.

2. Saad, Lydia. "Socialism as Popular as Capitalism among Young Adults in U.S." Gallup.com. Gallup, November 20, 2021. https://news.gallup.com/poll/268766/socialism-popular-capitalism-among-young-adults.aspx.

3. Nietzel, Michael T. "Low Literacy Levels among U.S. Adults Could Be Costing the Economy $2.2 Trillion a Year." *Forbes Magazine*, September 1, 2021. https://www.forbes.com/sites/michaeltnietzel/2020/09/09/

low-literacy-levels-among-us-adults-could-be-costing-the-economy-22-trillion-a-year/?sh=68be2bd74c90.

4. Adams, John. "Founders Online: From John Adams to John Jebb." National Archives and Records Administration, September 10, 1785. https://founders.archives.gov/documents/Adams/06-17-02-0232.

5. Desnoyer, Brad. "Founding Fathers Agreed: Funding Public Education Is Not a Debate." STLtoday.com, June 7, 2017. https://www.stltoday.com/opinion/columnists/founding-fathers-agreed-funding-public-education-is-not-a-debate/article_f05aa5b0-2fed-5c63-be1a-1b013cf49625.html.

6. Jefferson, Thomas. "Jefferson and the Role of Education in Citizenship." Monticello. Accessed June 2, 2020. https://www.monticello.org/the-art-of-citizenship/the-role-of-education/.

7. "Encyclopedia of Children and Childhood in History and Society." Encyclopedia.com. Encyclopedia.com. Accessed June 2, 2020. https://www.encyclopedia.com/children/encyclopedias-almanacs-transcripts-and-maps/great-depression-and-new-deal.

8. "History–*Brown v. Board of Education*." United States Courts. Accessed June 2, 2020. https://www.uscourts.gov/educational-resources/educational-activities/history-brown-v-board-education-re-enactment.

9. Shapiro, Sarah, and Catherine Brown. "A Look at Civics Education in the United States." American Federation of Teachers, June 7, 2019. https://www.aft.org/ae/summer2018/shapiro_brown.

10. Shapiro, Ben. How to Destroy America in Three Easy Steps (New York, NY: Broadside Books, 2021) p. 176.

11. D'Souza, Dinesh. Essay in *Hillary's America: The Secret History of the Democratic Party*. (Washington, DC: Regnery Publishing, a division of Salem Media Group, 2016) 15–18.

12. "Survey Methodology: How Survey Monkey Gets Its Data." SurveyMonkey. Accessed June 11, 2020. https://www.surveymonkey.com/mp/survey-methodology/.

13. Silverstein, Jake. "Why We Published the 1619 Project." *New York Times*, December 20, 2019. https://www.nytimes.com/interactive/2019/12/20/magazine/1619-intro.html.

NOTES

14. Lincoln, Abraham, Roy P. Basler, Lloyd A. Dunlap, and Marion Dolores Pratt. *The Collected Works of Abraham Lincoln.* New Brunswick, NJ: Rutgers University Press, 1953.

15. "Read Martin Luther King Jr.'s 'I Have a Dream' Speech in Its Entirety." NPR. NPR, January 14, 2022. https://www.npr.org/2010/01/18/122701268/i-have-a-dream-speech-in-its-entirety.

16. Harris, Leslie M. "I Helped Fact-Check the 1619 Project. the Times Ignored Me." POLITICO, 2020. https://www.politico.com/news/magazine/2020/03/06/1619-project-new-york-times-mistake-122248.

17. Prager U: What's Wrong With the 1619 Project?–Vision Launch. https://visionlaunch.com/prager-u-whats-wrong-with-the-1619-project/.

18. Serwer, Adam. "The Fight over the 1619 Project Is Not about the Facts." *The Atlantic.* Atlantic Media Company, December 23, 2019. https://www.theatlantic.com/ideas/archive/2019/12/historians-clash-1619-project/604093/.

19. Zanotti, Emily. "Team USA's Gwen Berry Says She Will Stage Protest If She Medals at Olympics: 'I'll Represent the Oppressed People'." The Daily Wire. The Daily Wire, August 1, 2021. https://www.dailywire.com/news/team-usas-gwen-berry-says-she-will-stage-protest-if-she-medals-at-olympics-ill-represent-the-oppressed-people.

20. Colton, Emma. "Olympic Athlete Raven Saunders Becomes Latest to Inject Politics into Tokyo Games." Fox News. FOX News Network, August 2, 2021. https://www.foxnews.com/sports/tokyo-olympics-political-demonstration-first.

21. Morgan, Joe. "'I Love Representing the U.S.': American Wrestler Gives Patriotic Victory Speech after Winning Gold Medal." The Daily Wire, August 3, 2021. https://www.dailywire.com/news/i-love-representing-the-u-s-american-wrestler-gives-patriotic-victory-speech-after-winning-gold-medal.

22. Fleisher, Lisa. "Americans Are Willing to Take Pay Cuts to Never Go Into the Office Again." Bloomberg.com. Bloomberg, August 3, 2021. https://www.bloomberg.com/news/articles/2021-08-03/return-to-work-americans-willing-to-take-pay-cut-to-never-go-back-to-the-office.

CHAPTER NINE: CRITICAL RACE THEORY

1. "Critical Legal Theory." Legal Information Institute. Legal Information Institute. Accessed June 21, 2020. https://www.law.cornell.edu/wex/critical_legal_theory.

2. Mason, Brad. "A (Relatively) Brief Introduction to Critical Race Theory." Bradly Mason, April 28, 2021. https://alsoacarpenter.com/2021/04/08/a-relatively-brief-introduction-to-critical-race-theory/.

3. George, Janel. "A Lesson on Critical Race Theory." Americanbar.org, Jan. 11, 2021. https://www.americanbar.org/groups/crsj/publications/human_rights_magazine_home/civil-rights-reimagining-policing/a-lesson-on-critical-race-theory/.

4. Shapiro, Ben. "Critical Race Theory Resistance Is Deeply Necessary." The Daily Signal, June 25, 2021. https://www.dailysignal.com/2021/06/24/the-movement-against-critical-race-theory-is-deeply-necessary/.

5. King, Martin Luther. "Martin Luther King I Have a Dream Speech– American Rhetoric." American Rhetoric Top 100 Speeches, August 28, 1963. https://www.americanrhetoric.com/speeches/mlkihaveadream.htm.

6. "What Is Critical Race Theory?" PragerU, 2021. https://www.prageru.com/video/what-is-critical-race-theory.

7. Ben Shapiro and Malcolm Nance on Critical Race Theory | Real Time with Bill Maher (HBO). YouTube. YouTube, 2021. https://www.youtube.com/watch?v=dwgsbZ1MsAE&t=4s.

8. Ben Shapiro Debates Racism & Black Lives Matter. YouTube. YouTube, 2016. https://www.youtube.com/watch?v=Hr3v6jZhI1k&t=2241s.

CHAPTER TEN: DISCRIMINATION AND DISPARITIES

1. Sowell, Thomas. *Discrimination and Disparities.* (New York, NY: Basic Books, 2019) pg. 20–21.

2. Ibid., 21.

3. Ibid., 23.

4. Ibid., 24.

5. Colton, Emma. "Back-To-Back Flash Mob Lootings in San Francisco Area Alarming Experts." Fox News.

November 22, 2021. https://www.foxnews.com/us/repeated-organized-flash-mob-robberies-san-francisco-security-experts.

6. Corrigan, Hope. "Why Is Walgreens Really Closing Stores in San Francisco?" Quartz. Accessed June 2, 2022. https://qz.com/2077384/why-is-walgreens-really-closing-its-stores-in-san-francisco/.

7. Ibid.

8. "Asian American–the Office of Minority Health." 2019. Hhs.gov. 2019. https://minorityhealth.hhs.gov/omh/browse.aspx?lvl=3&lvlid=63.

9. Asante-Muhammad, Dedrick, and Sally Sim. 2020. "Racial Wealth Snapshot: Asian Americans and the Racial Wealth Divide» NCRC." May 14, 2020. https://ncrc.org/racial-wealth-snapshot-asian-americans-and-the-racial-wealth-divide/#_ftn8.

10. Ibid.

11. "Race–Census.gov." U.S. Census Bureau, Population Estimates Program. Accessed July 1, 2020. https://www.census.gov/quickfacts/fact/note/US/RHI525220.

12. Anderson, Monica. "Chapter 1: Statistical Portrait of the U.S. Black Immigrant Population." Pew Research Center's Social & Demographic Trends Project. Pew Research Center, May 30, 2020. https://www.pewresearch.org/social-trends/2015/04/09/chapter-1-statistical-portrait-of-the-u-s-black-immigrant-population/.

13. Ibid.

14. Ibid.

15. Kenton, Will. "What Is Affirmative Action?" Investopedia. Investopedia, November 30, 2021. https://www.investopedia.com/terms/a/affirmative-action.asp.

16. Gersen, Jeannie Suk, Eren Orbey, and Nathan Heller. "The Uncomfortable Truth about Affirmative Action and Asian-Americans." *The New Yorker*, August 10, 2017. https://www.newyorker.com/news/news-desk/the-uncomfortable-truth-about-affirmative-action-and-asian-americans.

17. Mac Donald, Heather. "Affirmative Disaster." *Washington Examiner*, February 11, 2012. https://www.washingtonexaminer.com/weekly-standard/affirmative-disaster.

18. Arcidiacono, Peter, Esteban M Aucejo, and Ken Spenner. "What Happens After Enrollment? an Analysis of the Time Path of Racial Differences in GPA and Major Choice–IZA Journal of Labor Economics." Springer Open. Springer Berlin Heidelberg, October 9, 2012. https://izajole.springeropen.com/articles/10.1186/2193-8997-1-5.

19. Xia, Rosanna. "Cal State Will No Longer Require Placement Exams and Remedial Classes for Freshmen." *Los Angeles Times*, August 4, 2017. https://www.latimes.com/local/lanow/la-me-cal-state-remedial-requirements-20170803-story.html.

20. Anderson, Greta. "Inside Higher Ed." Minority and first-generation SAT scores fall behind, September 24, 2019. https://www.insidehighered.com/admissions/article/2019/09/24/minority-and-first-generation-sat-scores-fall-behind.

21. Griffin, Cynthia E. "More Black Students Pass Exit Exam." *Our Weekly*, October 26, 2021. https://ourweekly.com/news/2014/09/25/more-black-students-pass-exit-exam/.

22. Ibid.

23. Livingston, Gretchen. "Opting out? About 10% of Highly Educated Moms Are Staying at Home." Pew Research Center. Pew Research Center, May 30, 2020. https://www.pewresearch.org/fact-tank/2014/05/07/opting-out-about-10-of-highly-educated-moms-are-staying-at-home/.

24. Gross, Terry. "Soccer Star Megan Rapinoe on Equal Pay, and What the U.S. Flag Means to Her." NPR. NPR, June 23, 2021. https://www.npr.org/2021/06/23/1009403840/soccer-star-megan-rapinoe-on-equal-pay-and-what-the-u-s-flag-means-to-her.

25. Jope, Christian. "NBA VS WNBA: Revenue, Salaries, Attendance, Ratings." World Sports Network, July 17, 2019. https://www.wsn.com/nba/nba-vs-wnba/.

CHAPTER ELEVEN: ABORTION

1. Adams, John. "Founders Online: From John Adams to Massachusetts Militia, 11 October 1798." National Archives and Records Administration. National Archives and Records Administration, October 11, 1798. https://founders.archives.gov/documents/Adams/99-02-02-3102.

NOTES

2. Brenan, Megan. "Religion Considered Important to 72% of Americans." Gallup.com. Gallup, November 20, 2021. https://news.gallup.com/poll/245651/religion-considered-important-americans.aspx.

3. Himes, Norman E. "Medical History of Contraception: Nejm." New England Journal of Medicine, March 15, 1934. https://www.nejm.org/doi/full/10.1056/NEJM193403152101103.

4. "Philosophical, Theological, and Scientific Arguments." Sinauer Associates, 2005. https://www.sinauer.com/media/wysiwyg/samples/BioethicsCh02.pdf.

5. "When Human Life Begins." American College of Pediatricians, 2017. https://acpeds.org/position-statements/when-human-life-begins.

6. "The Carnegie Stages." Contend Projects, February 2, 2018. https://contendprojects.org/the-science/carnegie-stages/.

7. Miriam. "Can You Explain What Pro-Choice Means and pro-Life Means?" Planned Parenthood, October 16, 2019. https://www.plannedparenthood.org/learn/ask-experts/can-you-explain-what-pro-choice-means-and-pro-life-means-im-supposed-to-do-it-for-a-class-thanks.

8. "Women's Rights Movement." National Parks Service. U.S. Department of the Interior, February 26, 2015. https://www.nps.gov/wori/learn/historyculture/womens-rights-movement.htm.

9. Yen, Sophia. "Birth Control throughout History: Facts, Superstitions, and Wives Tales." Pandia Health, April 19, 2022. https://www.pandiahealth.com/resources/birth-control-throughout-history/.

10. McBride, Alex. "The Supreme Court. Expanding Civil Rights. Landmark Cases. *Griswold v. Connecticut* (1965): PBS." The Supreme Court. Expanding Civil Rights. Landmark Cases. *Griswold v. Connecticut* (1965) | PBS. Accessed June 1, 2022. https://www.thirteen.org/wnet/supremecourt/rights/landmark_griswold.html.

11. Vile, John R. *Griswold v. Connecticut*, 2009. https://www.mtsu.edu/first-amendment/article/579/griswold-v-connecticut.

12. Ibid.

13. "Ninth Amendment." Legal Information Institute. Legal Information Institute. Accessed June 1, 2022. https://www.law.cornell.edu/constitution/ninth_amendment.

14. McBride, Alex. "The Supreme Court. Capitalism and Conflict. Landmark Cases. *West Coast Hotel v. Parrish* (1937): PBS." The Supreme Court. Capitalism and Conflict. Landmark Cases. *West Coast Hotel v. Parrish* (1937) | PBS. Accessed June 2, 2022. https://www.thirteen.org/wnet/supremecourt/capitalism/landmark_westcoast.html.

15. Wills, Susan E. "Ten Legal Reasons to Reject Roe." USCCB, 2003. https://www.usccb.org/issues-and-action/human-life-and-dignity/abortion/ten-legal-reasons-to-reject-roe.

16. Cruz, Ted. Essay in *One Vote Away: How a Single Supreme Court Seat Can Change History*, 98–99. Washington, DC: Regnery Publishing, 2020.

17. "Pregnancy Week 5." American Pregnancy Association, December 9, 2021. https://americanpregnancy.org/healthy-pregnancy/week-by-week/5-weeks-pregnant/.

18. Shead, Sam. "Can Two People Have the Same DNA?" BBC Science Focus Magazine. BBC Science Focus Magazine, April 22, 2020. https://www.sciencefocus.com/the-human-body/can-two-people-have-the-same-dna/.

19. Dastagir, Alia E. "Rape and Incest Account for Hardly Any Abortions. so Why Are They Now a Focus?" *USA Today*. Gannett Satellite Information Network, May 24, 2019. https://www.usatoday.com/story/news/nation/2019/05/24/rape-and-incest-account-few-abortions-so-why-all-attention/1211175001/.

INDEX

A
abolitionist societies, 56–57, 75
abortion
    arguments for, debunking, 188–192
    court rulings on, 185–187
    dehumanizing and, 56
    drugs to induce, 182
    history of, 178–182
    overview of, 177–178
    patients seeking, 190–191
    protests against, 46
Abrams, Samuel, 127
academies, private in colonial era, 129
Acosta, Jim, 35
Adam (in Bible), 39–40
Adams, John, 74, 130, 177
Adolescent Well-Being in Cohabiting, Married, and Single-Parent Families (Manning and Lamb), 122–123
adoption, 191
aerospace engineering, 172
affirmative action, 143, 153, 165–169, 170, 194
African American athletes, protests by, 141–142
African American children, killing of, 192
African American President, first, 72
African Americans
    in Armed Forces, 70–71
    arrests, 98, 121–122
    in Congress, 67, 81
    crimes committed by, 122
    criminal justice system treatment of, 119
    defined, 163
    Democratic leanings of, 135, 136
    economic conditions, 70
    education, 79, 81, 130–131, 164, 166–168, 169
    equality and, 49, 50
    high school dropout rate, 168
    household composition of, 164
    household income of, 161, 163
    income disparities among, 163–165
    legal status of, 64
    police killing of, 45–46, 120–121
    police threats, perceived to, 106, 108–109, 114, 195
    political affiliation of, 84–87
    traffic stops, 96–98
African American Vice President, first, 72
Africans, 56, 63
African slaves, 55, 56
altt-right, 12
American Association of University Women, 173
American College of Pediatricians, 181
American colonization, 53
American dream, 139

American education, history
of, 128–136
American exceptionalism, 139
American patriotism, 13, 196
American patriots, values held by, 194
American values, 129–130, 138–139,
194, 196
Andrews, Susan, 17
Annenberg Public Policy Center, 133
anti-American principles, Left
propagation of, 127
Antifa
agenda of, 23
fascism and, 1, 2, 7, 9–10, 12–13,
14, 17, 23
Floyd, G. killing and, 107, 111
foreign policy views of, 24
increasing strength, potential of, 195
Ku Klux Klan compared to, 82
politician opinions concerning,
2, 17–18
riots, activist participation in, 22, 35
tactics of, 11–12, 14–15, 18, 21, 23
vandalism, activist
participation in, 109
writings and publications, 18, 110
Antifa, The Anti-Fascist Handbook
(Bray), 18
anti-government movements, 10
anti-police movement, overview
of, 89–91
anti-slavery movement, 79, 139–140
anti-slavery societies, 56–57, 75
Arcidiacono, Peter, 166–167
Aristotle, 179–180
Aroonsuck, Knute, 117–118
Arradondo, Medaria, 108
Asher, Jeff, 89
Asheville, police attrition in, 117
Asian Americans
discrimination against, 165, 169

education, 165–166, 167, 169
household incomes of, 115,
161–162, 163
Atlantic, 111
Aucejo, Esteban, 166–167
auditors, duties of, 44
Augustine of Hippo, St., 180
Austin, police defunding and crime
increase in, 116
autonomous zones, 15,
18–20, 111–112
Aztecs, 51–52

B

Baby Boomers, 142
The Bald Brad Show, 38
Baltimore, 100–102, 108, 118
Barr, William, 35
The Battle Hymn of the Republic, 65
Behar, Joy, 7
beliefs, standing up for, 10–11
Bell, Derrick, 145, 149
Berry, Gwen, 141
bias in media, 25–26, 38
Biden, Joe
abortion stance, 191–192
Antifa, relationship with, 24
Antifa, views on, 7, 17–18, 21
on danger to African Americans,
106, 108
Floyd, G. killing,
commentary on, 106
on Lafayette Park protester
dispersal, 36
media coverage of, 33, 42–43
swearing in of, 23
"big switch," false narrative of, 135–136
Bilbo, Theodor, 83
Bill of Rights, 129, 184, 185, 186, 189
biological differences by gender, 174
birth control, 178, 183–184, 185

INDEX

Birth Control Federation of America, 183
birth-control movement, 183
birth control pills, first, 183
Birth of a Nation (film), 70, 82
Black, Hugo, 83
Black Hebrew Israelites, 46
black immigrants, 163–164
Black Lives Matter
    Brown, M. killing, response to, 95, 96
    creation of, 119
    Floyd, G. killing, response to, 107
    increasing strength, potential of, 195
    minorities, action impact on, 112
    nuclear family *versus*, 125
    riots, activist participation in, 22, 35
    supporters of, 15, 192
Blackmun, Harry A., 186, 187
blacks, Muslim trade for, 55
Blackshirts, 8–9, 10, 12–13, 14
Blaze Media, 38
blended learning, 137
"bloc tactic" (term), 10
Boston Latin School, 129
Boston Tea Party, 110
Bray, Mark, 18
Brennan, Justice, 187
British Empire, 139–140
Brookline Police Department, 117
Brooks, Rayshard, 121
Brosnan, Devin, 121
Browder v. Goys case, 71
Brown, Michael, killing of, 91–93
    arguments for, 121
    court rulings and findings concerning, 95–96
    police defunding campaign following, 102
    presidential statements following, 119
    public reaction to, 108
    riots following, 99
    witness statements concerning, 94–95
Brown v. Board of Education, 71, 132, 149
Bureau of Labor Statistics, 170, 171
Burmese Americans, 162
Burnett, Erin, 36
Burns, Katelyn, 18–19
Butler, Pierce, 60
Buxton, C. Lee, 183

C

Calhoun, John C., 80–81
California, high school exit exam waived in, 168
campuses, limiting speech on, 143
Capital Hill Autonomous Zone (CHAZ), 18–20
Capital Hill Organized Protest (CHOP), 19–20
capitalism, 2, 128
career choices, gender differences in, 172
Carlson, Tucker home, attack on, 17
Carnegie Foundation, 127
Carnegie Stages of Human Embryonic Development, 181
Caruso, Phil, 160
Catholic Church, 180, 191–192
Catholic Covington High School, 46–47
censorship on social media, 195
Central-American black immigrants, 164
centralized government role in fascism, 6
Charlottesville, Va. protest, 2017, 12
Chase, Chevy, 168–169
Chauvin, Derek, 104, 105, 106

Chavis, John, 130
chemical engineering, 172
Chester, Charlie, 41, 42, 43, 48
Chicago, 89, 99, 116
child, cost of caring for, 190
childhood education in colonial era, 129
children in intact families, 122
children of color, alleged oppression of, 141
children of single parents, 122
China role in COVID-19 spread, 31, 52
Chinese Americans, 162
Chinese Exclusion Acts, 1840s, 150
Chisholm, Shirley, 71–72
Christian doctrines, 180
church, education role of, 129–130
cities, growth of, 131
citizenship, birthright, 66
civics education, 129–130, 132–133
civil rights, 67–72
Civil Rights Act, 1866, 81
Civil Rights Act, 1964, 67, 71
Civil Rights Act, 1965, 71
Civil Rights movement, 69–72, 86, 132
Civil War, 65–66
Civil Works Administration, 132
The Clansman (Dixon), 70
climate change, 43
CNN
    agenda of, 43
    on Antifa, 21
    bias of, 25
    conservative media in contrast to, 38
    lawsuits against, 47–48
    leftist trust in, 44
    propaganda pushed by, 41, 42
    Russian investment fund covered by, 33–34
    violence covered by, 22
Coffee, Linda, 186
cognitive constructivism, 131
collective guilt, 153
college education, 130
color-blindness, legal equality based on, 147
Columbus, Christopher, 51, 52
common core standards, 168
Common Core State Standards Initiative, 133–134
The Communist Manifesto, 195
communist socialist country, America as quasi-, 143
communities
    involvement in local, 195, 196
    police defunding impact on, 115–116
communities of color, 125
company financial documents, auditing and review of, 44
computer science, 172
Comstock Laws, 183
conception, life beginning at, 181, 182, 188
conception as divine process, 180
concepts, understanding, 131
conservative exodus from leftist states, 118
conservative news outlets, 25, 35–36, 38, 44, 112–113
conservative professors, decline of, 127
conspiracy theorists, conservatives labeled as, 44
conspiracy theory, 120
Constitution
    abortion and, 178, 187
    American values embodied in, 129, 194
    importance of understanding, 195
    marital privacy and, 183
    for moral and religious people, 177

INDEX

rights and liberties
    guaranteed by, 186
    slavery and, 60, 64
    threats to, 194
constructivism, 131, 137
contraceptives, 178, 183–184, 185
Cooper, Anderson, 36
Cortes, Hernando, 51
Cortez, Darrell, 117
cost of living as income factor, 162–163
cotton gin, 78
countries' cultures and institutions, other, price of ignorance about, 154
COVID-19
    deaths from, 52
    epidemic, 137
    lockdowns during, 89, 160–161
    media coverage of, 30–31, 45
    racism and, 52
COVID fatigue, 43
Crenshaw, Kimberlé, 146
crime
    in autonomous zones, 20
    family breakdown as factor in, 122–123
    racial breakdown of, 98
    rise in, 89–90, 101–102, 116, 118, 195
Critical Legal Studies (CLS), 145–146, 155
Critical Race Theory (CRT), 145–156
critical thinking, 127
Cromwell, Oliver, 54
culture as income factor, 162, 163–164
culture war, 91
Cunningham, Brittany Packnett, 89–90
Cuomo, Chris, 21, 47, 106

D

The Daily Wire, 38
Dale, Daniel, 36
David (biblical king), 55
Death of a Nation (D'Souza), 13, 64, 77
decision making, 158–159, 164–165
Declaration of Independence
    African Americans and, 49, 64
    American values embodied in, 138–139, 194
    slavery and, 57–60, 66, 74, 76–77
    true intention behind, 140
Delgado, Richard, 146–147, 149
democracy, 4, 133
Democratic Party
    abortion policy, 189, 191–192
    African American public office holders in, 81
    African Americans in, 84–87
    civil rights legislation and, 86
    on following science, 189
    history of, 135–136
    inner cities dominated by, 87
    Ku Klux Klan and, 66, 81–82
    media relationship with, 33
    racism and, 50, 78, 80, 81–84
    radical left *versus*, 23
    slavery and, 65, 79, 80–81, 87
    South dominated by, 130
Democratic Party headquarters, Ore., vandalism at, 23
Democrats on race, 67, 69, 107
demonstrations, 89
development as divine process, 180
Dewey, John, 131–132, 137
discrimination, 150, 157–161, 164–165
Discrimination and Disparities (Sowell), 157
disparity(ies)
    causes and factors behind, 155, 169
    and discrimination, 150, 157
    in income, 161–165
    laws propagating, 145–146

leftist efforts to eliminate, 143, 151, 153, 165–169, 170, 194
The Diversity Delusion (Mac Donald), 166
diversity in education, 143, 165, 166
diversity quota, 165
Dixiecrats, 82
Dixon, Thomas, 70
DNA, 190
domestic terror groups, 2, 82
Douglas, William O., 183–184, 186
Douglass, Frederick, 77, 138
Dred Scott v. Sandford, 63, 64, 81
D'Souza, Dinesh, 13, 64, 77, 87, 135–136
Du Bois, W.E.B., 69–70
due process clause, 185, 186
Duke University, 166
Durkan, Jenny, 18, 20

E

education
    diversity in, 143, 165, 166
    history of, 128–136
    inequities in, 138
    leftist influence on, 142
    opportunities, increasing, 165
    shift in philosophy of, 130
    technology impact on, 137
educational system bureaucracy, 132
Eisenhower, Dwight, 71
Eisenstadt v. Baird, 185
election debates, 2020, 17
election fraud claims, investigation of, 31–33
Ellison, Jeremiah, 109
Ellison, Keith, 17, 18, 105–106
Ely, Hart, 187
Emancipation Proclamation, 65–66
embryo, development of, 181

The Emerging Democrat Majority (Teixeira), 152
enemy of the people, media accused of being, 29–30
English language arts, 133
ensoulment, 179–180, 181
entertainment, hierarchy of, 174
entry level course prerequisites, reducing, 167
equality ("all men are created equal")
    as American creed, 194
    Civil Rights movement and, 70
    Civil War, 65
    equal rights under law, 78
    Founding Fathers understanding of, 49, 63, 73–74, 77
    leftist omission of, 139
    Lincoln, A. understanding of, 77
    Native American treatment *versus*, 62
    realization of ideal, 71–72
equal protection clause, 68
Euse, Erica, 11
Eve (in Bible), 39–40
Every Student Succeeds Act, 133
exploration, age of, 50–53

F

fact from fiction, discerning, 2
factory model of schooling, 131
Fair Housing Act, 71
"fake news," 29, 31, 33–34, 38, 45
false doctrines, 1–2, 10
false gospel, dangers of, 1–2
false narratives
    "big switch," 135–136
    of black lives under siege, 106
    Ferguson, Missouri shooting, 93, 94
    of police racism, 96, 100, 109, 119
    1619 Project as, 142
    U.S. history teaching based on, 138

INDEX

false truths, 2
families, rebuilding, 125
family, education role of, 128–129
family, media as part of national, 30
family breakdown, 122–123
family structure role in crime prevention, 124–125
fascism
    contemporary, 9–10
    history of, 3–6, 7–9
    nature and tactics, 2, 7–8, 12–13, 14, 17, 23
    opposition, alleged to, 1
fascist, identifying, 24
fatherless families, 123
fathers, abandonment by, 122
"favors the historically privileged," 145, 146
Federal Emergency Relief Administration, 132
federal property, 37
felony crimes, downgrading of, 160
Ferguson, Missouri
    black drivers in, 97
    crime increase in, 102
    police shooting in, 91–96, 99, 108
    riots in, 110
Ferguson Commission, 90
Ferguson Police Department, 96–97, 98
fetus, development of, 188
Fifteenth Amendment, 67
Fifth Amendment, 184
Filipino Americans, 162
First Amendment, 21–22, 184
First World War, 5
Floyd, George, killing of, 102–105
    aftermath of, 35, 111
    crime increase following, 112–113, 116
    Floyd background, 107–108

    media presentation of, 119
    narrative concerning, 108–109
    police defunding in wake of, 114, 116
    property damage following, 89, 110
    public opinion concerning, 106
Foner, Eric, 81–82
forbidden fruit, lie told about, 39–40
Forrest, Nathan Bedford, 152
Forrester, Kevin, 101
Forrest Gump (movie), 152, 154
Founding Fathers
    crowning achievement, 78
    Judeo-Christian beliefs upheld by, 194
    knowledge and understanding, equipping ourselves with, 195
    race, views on, 49, 73–74
    as slaveholders, 63, 75
    slavery, views on, 57, 77
Fourteenth Amendment
    Democrats opposed to, 67
    overview of, 66
    right to privacy, connection to, 184, 185, 186
    segregation challenged via, 71
    test of, 68
Fourth Amendment, 184
four-year college, preparedness for, 168
Fox News, 25, 35–36, 44, 112–113
Fox News fallacy, 152
Frank, Thomas, 34
Franklin, Benjamin, 74
Franklin, John Hope, 73
Freedman's Bureau, 130–131
freedom, fragility of, 194
freedoms, America's greatness stemming from, 196
free speech, xi
"The Free State of George Floyd," 111

G

garden of Eden, 39–40
Gates, Henry Louis, 74
gender, seeing through lens of, 134–135
gender wage gap, 170–175
Gen Z, 142
George Floyd #JusticeinPolicing Act, 105
George Floyd Square (autonomous zone), 111–112
Georgetown University, 172
global warming, 43
Goldberg, Arthur, 184–185
Gordon, Hymie, 188
Gotanda, Neil, 146
government, communities of color independence from, 125
government, education in function of, 129–130, 132–133
GPA, racial differences in, 166
graduation rates, measures to increase, 133–134, 167–168
Gray, Freddie, 100, 101
Great Britain, slavery, role in, 57, 74
Great Depression, 132, 136
"Great Society," 85
Greece, ancient, ix–xi
Greek societies, abortion in, 179
Griffith, D.W., 70, 82
Griswold, Estelle, 183
Griswold v. Connecticut, 183, 185, 186
Gross, Terry, 173, 174
group, seeing people as members off, 161
guns, restricting, 194
Gutierrez, Gabe, 117–118
Guttmacher Institute, 190

H

Hammond, James Henry, 80
"Hands up, don't shoot" narrative, 94, 95, 108
Hannah-Jones, Nikole, 137–138, 139–140, 141, 146
hard left, 12
Harlan, John M. (1833-1911), 68–69
Harlan, John Marshal, II (1899-1971), 185
Harlem, 70
Harris, Kamala, 36, 72
Harris, Leslie, 139
Harris, Lex, 34
Harvard University, 165, 166
Hayes, Chris, 30–31
Health, Brad, 101–102
Hebrews (Bible), 11
Henry, Patrick, 79
Heritage Foundation, 122
Higginbotham, A. Leon, 85
high-crime areas, developer avoidance of, 159
higher education, Left stronghold on, 127–128
high school dropout rate, 168
high school exit exams, 167–168
Hillary's America (D'Souza), 135–136
Himes, Norman, 178, 179
hiring decisions, 158–159
Hispanic students, 167
Hitler, Adolf, 6, 13, 70
Holder, Eric, 95, 96, 97–98, 105
Home to Harlem (McKay), 70
homicides, rise in, 89, 90
Hoover Dam, 168–169
hours worked, gender disparity in, 172
household, size and composition of, 162
household incomes, 115, 161–165
humanities major, switch to, 166
humanity, failure to recognize other's, 56

INDEX

human life, abortions terminating, 181
human sacrifices, 51–52
human soul, types of, 179–180
hybrid learning, 137

I

"I Have a Dream" speech, 139
immigrant children, 14
immigrants, household composition of, 163–164
immigrant women, pregnancies among, 182–183
immigration, media coverage of, 45
incest, pregnancy due to, 190
income inequality, 138, 161, 162, 163
inconvenience argument for abortion, 190, 191, 192
indentured servitude *versus* slavery, 54
independence *versus* slavery, 76–78
Indian Americans (Asian), 115, 162
Indian Removal Act, 61–62
Indians (term), 52
Indigenous People March, 46
individual choices
    as academic achievement factor, 169
    as income factor, 163–165, 175
individualism, judgment based on, 158
individuals, seeing people as, 161
indoctrination
    America hating spawned by, 195
    in Critical Race Theory, 155, 156
    overview of, 127–128
    revisionist history and, 136
    schools as tools of, 143
    with wrong values and creeds, 194
inequality in resources and opportunities, 170
inequality *versus* inequity, 155
infanticide, 178
inner cities, Democratic domination of, 87

innocent child, death of, 190, 191
innocent human being, no right to kill, 189
in-person instruction, 137
Inside the White House (Kessler), 85
institutionalized racism, 146, 195
"instrument of oppression," 146
intact families, 122, 125
intellectual soul, 179, 180
intermarriage, white-Native American, 54
Ivy League colleges, 129, 166

J

Jackson, Andrew, 61, 79
James, LeBron, 108
James Forte (American colony), 53–54
Japanese Americans, 115, 162
Jefferson, Thomas
    as Declaration of Independence author, 57
    education policy, 130
    on equality (all men created equal), 62, 73, 76
    new territory acquired by, 60–61
    as slaveholder, 63
    slavery, views on, 57, 75, 76
Jenkins, Daryle Lamont, 11
Jerome, St., 180
Jesus, resurrection of, reports concerning, 26–28
Jewish doctrines, 180
Jewish priests, 28
Jim Crow laws, 71, 78
Johnson, Dorion, 92, 93–94
Johnson, Lyndon B., 84, 85
Jones, Cynthia, 17, 18
Judeo-Christian ideals and beliefs, 194
Justice Department, 94, 95
juvenile crime, 122–123

K

Kaepernick, Colin, 90–91
Kennedy, Anthony, 166, 187
Kennedy, John F., 85
Kessler, Ronald, 85
King, Martin Luther, 71, 139, 147
King, Rodney, 111
Kirk, Charlie, 13
Kueng, J. Alexander, 103
Ku Klux Klan
    establishment of, 66, 81–82
    film depiction of, 154
    members of, 83
    political party of, 78, 136
    revival of, 70
    teaching about, 152
Ku Klux Klan Act, 1871, 82

L

labor, demand for, 56
Lafayette Park, protesters cleared out of, 35–37
Lamb, Kathleen A., 122–123
law enforcement
    black treatment at hands of, 105–106
    disparity within, 115
    police defunding impact on, 115–116
    systemic racism, alleged of, 119
laws, equal protection of, 66
Lazarus, Edward, 187
lecturing, direct instruction through, 131
Left ideology
    combating, 196
    destructive nature of, 23, 193–194
    media outlets influenced by, 28
leftist areas and states, conservative exodus from, 118
leftist narrative, historic reality versus, 55
leftist news media, misinformation spread by, 40
leftist propaganda machine, 41–43
leftward shift, education gaps contributing to, 133
legal system origin, slavery role in, 138
Lemon, Don, 21, 106, 110
Lichtblau, Eric, 34
life, beginning of, 179, 181, 182, 188
lifestyle choices as gender wage gap factor, 171–172
Lincoln, Abraham
    on American ideals, 138–139
    collage of, 73
    Emancipation Proclamation issued by, 65–66
    equality (all men created equal), understanding of, 77
    house divided, commentary on, 64–65
    political party of, 136
Lindsay, James, 148
literary rate, 129
Lizzo, 113
local communities, involvement in, 195, 196
looting, 100–101, 109, 110
Los Angeles
    homicides in, 89
    police defunding and crime increase in, 116
    police funding restoration in, 118
    protests in, 110
    riots in, 99, 111
Louder With Crowder (podcast series), 38
Louisiana Purchase, 61, 63
Louisville, 116
low-income areas, crime in, 102

low-income car owners, 97
lynchings, 82, 136

M

Mac Donald, Heather, 97, 98, 166
Maher, Bill, 149, 152, 153
mail-in ballots, examination of, 31–32
mainstream media (MSM)
    agenda of, 37–38, 43, 48
    Biden, J. as portrayed by, 42–43
    blame shifted by, 34
    conspiracy theorist labeling by, 44
    Floyd, G. as portrayed by, 104–105, 106, 119
    on following science, 189
    law enforcement racism claimed by, 120
    leftist bias of, 20–21, 25–26, 33, 141
    narratives crafted by, 47
    news spun by, 40
    propaganda pushed by, 41, 48
    responsibility of, 28
    themes chosen by, 45
majors, choice of, 166–167
Mann, Horace, 131
Manning, Wendy, 122–123
marital privacy, right to, 183, 184–185
Marques, Miguel, 22
Marshall, Thurgood, 85
Martin, Steven, 124–125
mass shootings, 45
mathematics
    Critical Race Theory in, 155–156
    deficiencies in, 134
    hybrid and blended learning applied to, 137
    knowledge expected in, 133
    major, pay yielded by, 172
    performance in, 167
    study resources, 170
Mathew-Roth, Micheline, 188
Matsuda, Mari, 146
Matthew 28, 26–27
mayor of Portland, 14–15
McCorvey, Norma, 186
McKay, Claude, 70
media
    accusations against, 29–30
    Antifa covered by, 18–21
    indoctrination by, 48
    information from, importance of researching, 45, 48
    sources, handling of, 32, 33–37
    See also mainstream media (MSM)
Medical History of Contraception (Himes), 178
Melugin, Bill, 110
Mensah-Stock, Tamyra, 142
men's sports, 173–175
menstrual cycle, 179
mental gymnastics, 185, 186
meritocracy, 151
metaphorical plantation, 85, 86, 87, 125
Mexican American War, 63
Middlebury College, 130
Milwaukee, 116
Minneapolis
    crime in, 111–113
    police force, 90, 112–113, 114, 117
    police killing in, 102–111
minorities
    Black Lives Matter impact on, 112
    communities, police defunding impact on, 118
    disparities, leftist efforts to eliminate, 165–169
    SAT exam scores, 167
    whites' earnings compared to certain groups, 115
minority status, 147
miscarriages, inducing, 179

misdemeanors, felony crimes reduced to, 160
Missouri Compromise, 63
moral and religious roots, return to, 178
Morris, Governor of Pa., 59–60
mother's life, danger to, 186
MSNBC, 22, 30–31, 44
Mudede, Charles, 155
multiple generations under one roof, 162
murder, abortion as, 180
Mussolini, Benito, 3–6, 8, 9, 13
"my body, my choice" (term), 189
Mystal, Elie, 195

N

NAACP, 70
Nance, Malcolm, 149, 150–155
National Committee on Federal Legislation for Birth Control, 183
nationalism, 13
National Lampoon's Vegas Vacation (movie), 168–169
National Socialism (concept), 6
National Woman's Rights Convention, Worcester, Mass., 1850, 182
Native Americans
  diseases and epidemics among, 52–53
  displacement of, 61–62
  European contact with, 51, 53–54
  killing among, 62
  killing of, 52
  media coverage of, 46–47
Nazism, 13
NBA, 174–175
neighbors, getting to know, 196
New Deal, 83, 84, 132
news media sector, 38
New World, slavery in, 60

New York City
  crime in, 98
  homicides in, 89, 116
  police attrition in, 117
New York Times, 34–35
Ngô, Andy, 14
Ninth Amendment, 184, 185
No Child Left Behind Act, 133
non-white people, slavery among, 54
Northwest Ordinance, 79
no-true-Scotsman fallacy, 153
nuclear family, 125
nutritive soul, 179

O

Oakland, police funding restoration in, 118
OAN, 44
Obama, Barack
  America "remaking" as goal of, 13
  Brown, M. shooting, commentary on, 94, 95
  education policy, 133
  as first African American President, 72
  immigrant children in cages under, 14
  law enforcement policy of, 90
  on laws and racism, 119
Ocasio-Cortez, Alexandria, 195–196
Olympian athletes, 141–142
Omar, Ilhan, 195–196
opinions, silencing differing, 143
opponents of fascist state, violence against, 7–9
oppressed, demonstrations of solidarity with, 141
oppressed *versus* oppressor, 153
Owens, Candace, 13–14

INDEX

P

parents, student guidance by, 169, 170
Parker, Robert, 85
Parks, Rosa, 71
partial truths, 38–40
patriarchy, world built on, 171
patriotism, 13, 134–135, 196
Paul (apostle), 1–2, 10, 75
Paulas, Rick, 10
Paxton, Robert, 7
The Peculiar Institutions (Stampp), 86–87
Pelly, Scott, 105
Pelosi, Nancy, 105, 191–192
people of color
    differing opinions of, 141–142
    education, 129
    police targeting of, 91
    rights lacking for, 141
A People's History of the United States (Zinn), 134
personal responsibility and racial disparities, 155
Petersen, Jens, 9
petroleum engineering, 172
pharmaceutical science, 172
Phillips, Nathan, 46–47
Phillips, Stephanie, 146
Pincus, Gregory, 183
Pius IX, 180
Planned Parenthood, 182, 183
plantation owners, 79, 81
Plessy, Homer, 67–68
Plessy v. Ferguson, 67–69
police
    abolishing, calls for, 102, 113, 115
    attacks on, 15
    attrition, 117–118
    brutality, claims of, 18, 45, 90–91, 100
    defunding, calls for, 91, 102, 108, 113–118, 125
    fascism and, 9
    killings by, 119–120, 123–124
    post-traumatic stress and departures among, 112–113
    racism, alleged of, 96–98, 100, 101–102, 104, 105–106, 108, 109, 119, 120
Police Executive Research Forum (PERF), 113, 117
political representation, slaves counted for, 58–59
Portland, 116
Portland, mayor of, 14–15
Portman, Natalie, 114, 115
Portugal, 50, 53
Portuguese, role in slave trade, 49
posterity, American ideas passed down to, 138–139
pregnancy, 188, 190, 191
presidents, media coverage of, 41–42, 45
Preston, Dean, 160
Price, Bob, 14
primitive societies, 178
Princeton University, 165–166
privacy, right of, 184, 185, 186, 187, 189
private schools, 130
privilege, 114–115, 150, 161, 162
pro-abortion arguments, debunking, 188–192
pro-abortionists, description of, 182
production, state control over, 6
profession, specialties within, 172
Progressive Movement, 131
progressives, ideas targeted to American youth, 134
Project Veritas, 41, 42
pro-life movement, 182

propaganda (defined), 41
property damage and destruction
    Brown, M. killing followed by, 99
    Democrats as target of, 23
    federal, 37
    Floyd, G. killing followed by, 111
    Gray, F. killing followed by, 100
    intention to commit, 11
    Left attitude concerning, 100
property theft, downgrading of, 160
Proposition 47, 159–160
Psalms, 55
public education, 130
public health, inequities in, 138
public opinion, media impact on, 45
public schools, 130, 131, 132
public university, first, 130

R

race
    competence to speak about, 147
    fixating on, 153
    Founding Father views on, 49, 73–74
    identity defined through, 155
    lens of, seeing through, 134–135, 158
    social construction of, 146
    university admission and, 165–169, 170
    wage gap, 170
racial caste system, 146
racial disparities, 145–146, 151, 153, 155, 165–169
racism
    American institutions as extensions of, 145
    competence to speak about, 147
    in Critical Race Theory, 147–148
    decline of, 86, 135
    Democratic Party and, 50, 78, 80, 81–84, 136
    economic disparities as evidence of, 155
    individual choice *versus*, 164–165
    Left perception of, 49–50, 73, 114–115
    modern outgrowth of, 141
    progress against, 72–73
    United States origin, role in, 137–138
    white inability to understand, 147
racists, Antifa attacks on accused, 12, 13–14
"Rally Against Hate" event, Berkeley, Calif., 12
rape, 190
Rapinoe, Megan, 173–174
Rayburn, Sam, 83
Reagan, Ronald, 194
reality, changing perception of, 38
Real Time with Bill Maher (TV talk show), 149–155
Reconstruction, 67, 130–131
Reid, Joy, 35–36
Reilly, Wilfred, 140
religion, 129, 177–178
reparations, 18, 65, 81
Republican Party
    abortion policy, 192
    African American exodus from, 84
    amendments passed by, 66–67
    civil rights legislation and, 86
    Democratic switch to, 135–136
    education policy, 130–131
    media relationship with, 33
    racism and, 50, 78, 136
    slavery and, 65, 81
    in South, 135–136
    white supremacy, record on, 78

INDEX

Republican presidents, media attacks on, 29
retail theft, 159–161
Revels, Hiram Rhodes, 67
Revolutionary War, 140
"right of privacy," 184
rights, chiseling away at, 194
"right to choose," 189
riots
    Antifa activist participation in, 22, 35
    Brown, M. killing followed by, 91, 95, 102
    continuing, potential of, 195
    cost of, 99–100
    Floyd, G. killing followed by, 109–110
    Gray, F. killing followed by, 100
    increase in, 89
    Left attitude concerning, 100
    media coverage of, 109–111
robot, human-like, 56
Rock, John, 183
Roe, Jane, 186
Roe v. Wade, 178, 182–187, 189, 192
Rogers, Katie, 36
Rolfe, Garrett, 121
Rolling Stone, 110
Romans (Bible), 75
Roman societies, abortion in, 179
Rome, ancient, 3
Ronaldo, Cristiano, 174
Roosevelt, Franklin D., 42, 82–84, 132
Roosevelt, Theodore, 69
Russian collusion, 45
Russian hacking attacks, alleged, 34–35
Russian investment fund, 33–34
Rybak, R. T., 90

S

Saad, Lydia, 128
Sanders, Bernie, 195–196
Sandmann, Nicholas, 46, 47–48
San Francisco, 116, 159–161
Sanger, Margaret, 182–183
San Jose Police Department, 117
Satan, 39, 40
SAT scores, 166, 167
Saunders, Raven, 141
Scalp Act, 1749, 150, 154
Scaramucci, Anthony, 34
school board meetings, attending, 195
schooling, learning good habits for, 169
schools as indoctrination tools, 143
schools measuring progress of, 133
science, following, 189
scientific facts, lack of agreement on, 182
Scott, Brandon, 118
Scott, William, 160
Seattle, 21, 116, 117
Seattle Police Department, 19–20
Seattle Police Department East Precinct, 18
Second World War, 70–71
security measures, business payment for, 159, 160–161
segregation, 82, 132, 136, 149, 194
Select Board's Committee on Policing Reforms, 117
self-induced abortions, 182
semi-automatic guns, 194
Senate Intelligence Committee, 33–34
sensitive soul, 179–180
separate but equal doctrine, 68–69, 132
sex, abstaining from, 191
Shapiro, Ben, 146–147, 149–155
silphium, 179
sin, 75

single-parent families, 122–123
The 1619 Project
    CRT compared to, 145
    dangers posed by, 142
    overview of, 49, 137–141
    systemic racism view pushed by, 143
    writings and publications, 49, 137, 146, 195
slavery
    among Native Americans, 62
    attitudes concerning, 56–57, 73–76, 79–81, 87
    counter-measures, 75–76
    court rulings on, 63–64
    Democratic Party and, 78
    denial of, 152
    early history of, 50, 54–55
    economic impact of, 140
    end of, 65–66, 78
    independence *versus*, 57–60, 66, 74, 76–78
    Left fixation on, 49
    and Native American displacement, 61
    opposition to, 139–140
    technology boosting, 78–79
    United States and other countries compared, 55
    United States origin, role in, 137–138
slaves, education prohibited for, 79
Smith, John (James Forte colony leader), 53–54
social constructivism, 131
social interactions, 131, 147–148
socialism, 3, 4–6, 128, 195–196
socialist country, America as, 143
social media, censorship on, 195
social sciences major, switch to, 166
society, importance of contributing to, 129–130

soldiers, ban against quartering, 185
soul, human body gaining, 179
Souls of Black Folk (Du Bois), 69
South
    education in, 130–131
    political parties in, 135–136
Sowell, Thomas, 140, 157, 158
Spain, role in exploration of Americas, 51, 52, 53
speech, limiting on campuses, 143
Spenner, Ken, 166–167
sports, wage gap in, 173–175
Stampp, Kenneth, 86–87
standardized test scores, 133
Starbuck, Robby, 110
state role in fascism, 6–7
statistics, real *versus* media-influenced perceptions of, 45–46
stay-at-home mothers, 171–172
Stefancic, Jean, 146–147, 149
STEM (science, technology, engineering, math) major, 166–167
Stewart, Oscar Lee, Jr., 111
St. John's Episcopal Church, Trump photo op at, 35–37
St. Louis, 116
Stolberg, Sheryl Gay, 12
Stone, Geoffrey, 187
student admission rates, college and university, 165–166
student progress, measuring, 133
subjects, gaps in grasp of basic, 133, 134
Sun Tzu, 195
Supreme Court
    abortion, rulings on, 178, 182, 185–187, 189
    affirmative action rulings, 166
    appointments to, 83, 85
    civil rights, rulings affecting, 67–69, 71

contraceptives, rulings concerning, 183–184, 185
survival, judgment based on, 158
systemic discrimination, 157
systemic racism, alleged
    Critical Race Theory and, 148
    income disparity cited as proof of, 163
    in law enforcement, 90–91, 96, 98, 101, 106, 119, 120
    Left views questioned, 49–50, 65, 79
    1619 Project role in teaching, 143

T

Taney, Roger, 63, 64
Task Force for Twenty-First Century Policing, 90
teaching, pushing back against wrong, 142–143
"teach to the test," 133
technology in education, 137
Tecumseh (Shawnee chief), 61
Teixeira, Ruy, 152
Tenochtitlan (*later* Mexico City), 51
testing standards, lowering, 151
Third Amendment, 185
Thirteenth Amendment, 66
Thomas Aquinas, St., 180
three-fifths compromise, 57
tobacco, 54
Tokyo Olympics, 2021, 141–142
traffic stops, racial breakdown of, 96–97
Trail of Tears, 62
Trojan War, ix–x, 193
Truman, Harry S., 71
Trump, Donald
    administration officials, harassment of, 14
    Antifa, views concerning, 2, 18
    COVID-19, handling of, 30, 31
    election, 2020, comments and actions regarding, 31–33
    at election debates, 17
    media, relationship with, 28–29, 30, 31–33, 35–37
    news coverage of, 41–42, 45
    as patriot, 13
    photo ops, 35–37
    supporters pf, 12, 17, 46–47
    twitter posts, 45
    "witch hunt" term used by, 96
truth from lies, discerning, 2
Twilight, Alexander Lucius, 130
Type Ib decision making, 159
Type Ib discrimination, 159
Type I discrimination, 157–158, 159, 160
Type II discrimination, 157, 159, 160, 161, 164, 165
tyrants, prosperity breeding, 138–139

U

unborn babies
    development of, 188, 190
    humanity, failure to recognize, 56, 188–189
    status of, 179
unconscious racism, 147, 148
United States
    destructive ideologies threatening, 193–194
    economy, slavery impact on, 140
    expansion, 61, 63
    family, comparison to, 29–30
    imperialism, alleged of, 24
    independence, 76–78
    leftist perception of, 42–43
    overarching story of, 72–76
    strength and resilience of, 196
United States history
    Critical Race Theory and, 148

importance of understanding, 195
Left rewriting of, 134–135, 145
progressive revisionist, 136
The 1619 Project, 49, 137–141
and structure, evil as media theme, 45
universal right to choose, fallacy of, 189
university, first public, 130
University of Texas at Austin, 166
unreasonable searches and seizures, 185
unwanted pregnancy, 182–183
U.S.-born blacks. *See* African Americans
U.S. Census Bureau, 171

V

vandalism, 23, 109
Velshi, Ali, 22, 109
victims of violence, public attitude toward, 7–8
violence, 20, 138
    fascist-inspired, 9
    leftist, 11, 14–15, 21, 22
voting rights, 71, 142
Voting Rights Act, 1965, 67, 71

W

Wade, Henry, 186
wage gap, 170–175
Walgreens, 159–161
Walsh, Robert, 79–80
Walton, Frances, 31
The War on Cops (Mac Donald), 97
Warren, Earl, 132
Warren, Elizabeth, 195–196
Washington, Booker T., 69–70
Washington, D.C., 116
Washington, George, 74–75
Washington Post, 31–33, 47–48, 119–120
Washington Post database, 46
Waters, Maxine, 14, 17
Watkins, Michael, 168
Weddington, Sarah, 186
welfare state, 84–85
West Coast Hotel v. Parrish, 185
What Is Critical Race Theory? (video), 147–148
Wheeler, Ted, 116
White, Byron, 185, 187
White, Timothy, 167
white men, dying for freedom, 65–67
white-over-color supremacy, system of, 147
white privilege, 114–115, 150, 161
whites
    incomes, 115, 161
    racism of, 148
    SAT scores, 167
white supremacists, 12
white supremacy
    American institutions rooted in, 145, 146, 148
    cost of removing, 147
    Democratic Party and, 50, 67, 78
    historic conditions, 73
    income disparity and, 161
    meritocracy as outgrowth of, 151
    terrorism from, 108
Whiting, Shawn, 20
Whitney, Eli, 78
Why Antifa Dresses Like Antifa (Paulas), 10
Wilson, Darren, 92, 93, 95
Wilson, James, 57
Wineburg, Sam, 134
WNBA, 174–175
womb, movement in, 181
women
    education, 129
    right to choose, 189

in sports, 173–175
women's rights movement, 182–183
words, twisting, 25, 40, 55
working from home, 142
workplace opportunities, increasing, 165
Works Progress Administration (WPA), 84
World Trade Organization protests, 1990s, 10
Wray, Chris, 17

Y

Yale, Eli, 140
Yale University, 140, 165
Yerak, Becky, 99–100
Yiannopoulus, Milo, 12
young adults, views of, 128
young people, leftward shift in, 133
YouTube, 137

Z

Zack, David, 117
Zinn, Howard, 134, 135, 141
"zone of privacy," 184, 187, 189
Zoom, 137

ABOUT THE AUTHOR

Bradley Roberts was born and raised in the United States of America—specifically, in California—where the effects of liberal policies and the polar divide between the political left and right sparked his interest in history and current affairs. He became serious about his Christian faith as a teenager, and the Bible continues to inform his values. He enjoys engaging with the public through his YouTube channel *The Bald Brad Show*, and his social media accounts.

CPSIA information can be obtained
at www.ICGtesting.com
Printed in the USA
BVHW042324100323
660178BV00003B/731